LIFE-SPAN AND CHANGE IN A
GERONTOLOGICAL PERSPECTIVE

LIFE-SPAN AND CHANGE IN A GERONTOLOGICAL PERSPECTIVE

EDITED BY

Joep M. A. Munnichs

Department of Social Gerontology
Psychological Laboratory
Catholic University
Nijmegen, The Netherlands

Paul Mussen

Department of Psychology
and
Institute of Human Development
University of California, Berkeley

Erhard Olbrich

Institute for Psychology
University of Erlangen–Nuremberg
Erlangen, Federal Republic of Germany

Peter G. Coleman

Department of Social Work Studies
University of Southampton
Southampton, England

1985

ACADEMIC PRESS, INC.

Harcourt Brace Jovanovich, Publishers

Orlando   San Diego   New York   Austin
London   Montreal   Sydney   Tokyo   Toronto

Quotations on p.247 are reprinted by permission of Macmillan Publishing Company, from *The symphonies of Sibelius* by Simon Parmet, originally published by Cassell and Co. Ltd.

ACADEMIC PRESS, INC.
Orlando, Florida 32887

United Kingdom Edition published by
ACADEMIC PRESS INC. (LONDON) LTD.
24–28 Oval Road, London NW1 7DX

LIBRARY OF CONGRESS CATALOGING IN PUBLICATION DATA

Main entry under title:

Life-span and change in a gerontological perspective.

Papers from a July 1981 symposium organized by Hans
Thomae of the Psychologisches Institut, University of
Bonn, and the Dept. of Social Gerontology of the
Psychological Laboratory of the Catholic University,
Nijmegen.
      Includes index.
      1. Aged—Psychology—Congresses.   2. Developmental
psychology—Congresses.   I. Munnichs, J.   II. Mussen,
Paul Henry.   III. Olbrich, Erhard.   IV. Thomae,
Hans, Date   .   V. Katholieke Universiteit Nijmegen.
Psychological Laboratory. Dept. of Social Gerontology.
BF724.8.L54   1985   155.67   85-1410

ISBN 0-12-510260-7 (alk. paper)
ISBN 0-12-510261-5 (paperback)

PRINTED IN THE UNITED STATES OF AMERICA

86 87 88   9 8 7 6 5 4 3 2 1

CONTENTS

I
INTRODUCTION

II
EMPIRICAL STUDIES
A. Trait-Oriented Studies

B.   Process-Centered Studies

6 PERCEIVED UNCHANGEABILITY OF LIFE AND SOME BIOGRAPHICAL
   CORRELATES

HERMANN-JOSEF FISSENI

7 COPING AND DEVELOPMENT IN THE LATER YEARS: A
   PROCESS-ORIENTED APPROACH TO PERSONALITY AND DEVELOPMENT

ERHARD OLBRICH

III
SOCIAL, INTERGENERATIONAL, AND
THEORETICAL STUDIES

8 THE DEVELOPMENT OF ADULT DEVELOPMENT: RECOLLECTIONS AND
   REFLECTIONS

HENRY S. MAAS

CONTRIBUTORS

Numbers in parentheses indicate the pages on which the authors' contributions begin.

BENGTSON, VERN L. (257), Andrus Gerontology Center, University of Southern California, Los Angeles, California 90007

CHIRIBOGA, DAVID (177), Department of Psychiatry, University of California, San Francisco, California 94143

COLEMAN, PETER G. (239), Department of Social Work Studies, University of Southampton, Southampton S09 5NH, England

FISKE, MARJORIE (177), Department of Psychiatry, University of California, San Francisco, California 94143

FISSENI, HERMANN-JOSEF (103), Department of Psychology, University of Bonn, 5300 Bonn, Federal Republic of Germany

FOOKEN, INSA (77), Department of Psychology, University of Bonn, 5300 Bonn, Federal Republic of Germany

HAAN, NORMA (17), Institute of Human Development, University of California, Berkeley, California 94720

KUYPERS, JOSEPH (257), School of Social Work, University of Manitoba, Winnipeg, Manitoba R3T 2N2, Canada

MAAS, HENRY S. (161), University of British Columbia, Vancouver, British Columbia V6T 1W5, Canada

McCULLOCH, ANDREW W. (239), Department of Social Work Studies, University of Southampton, Southampton S09 5NH, England

MUNNICHS, JOEP M. A. (3), Department of Social Gerontology, Psychological Laboratory, Catholic University, 6500 HE Nijmegen, The Netherlands

MUSSEN, PAUL (45), Department of Psychology and Institute of Human Development, University of California, Berkeley, California 94720

OLBRICH, ERHARD (3, 133), Institute for Psychology, University of Erlangen-Nuremberg, 8520 Erlangen, Federal Republic of Germany

RUDINGER, GEORG (63), Department of Psychology, University of Bonn, 5300 Bonn, Federal Republic of Germany

STAPLEY, JANICE (211), Department of Psychology, Rutgers University, New Brunswick, New Jersey 08903

TROLL, LILLIAN E. (211), Department of Psychology, Rutgers University, New Brunswick, New Jersey 08903

FOREWORD

The Nijmegen conference on "Life-Span and Change in Gerontological Perspective" was one of the pre-conferences for the XIIth International Congress of Gerontology (Hamburg, 1981). Due to the efforts of the organizers of this conference and editors of this volume, this publication includes a very valuable critical evaluation of different methodological and theoretical approaches to the study of behavioral development in a life-span perspective. It demonstrates that 50 years after the first edition of Charlotte Bühler's "Der menschliche Lebenslauf als psychologisches Problem" there exists a rather broad range of information on consistencies and changes in behavior during the years beyond adolescence.

Even in comparison with the studies available two decades ago, the present state of life-span development is impressive not only with regard to quantity but also due to a high degree of methodological sophistication. What is becoming evident, also, is the decisive role of the Berkeley Longitudinal Studies for the recent development of life-span developmental psychology. Therefore I may be permitted to quote one of the founders and leaders of these studies, Harold E. Jones. In a paper on "Problems of method in longitudinal research" prepared for *Vita Humana* (later *Human Development*), a journal which he helped to launch, Jones (1958) wrote:

> It is clear that longitudinal research requires a certain doggedness which cannot quickly reflect popular turns of interest. It encounters the status–hazard of being sometimes in vogue and sometimes out of step. It may be both too far ahead and too far behind the contemporary preoccupation. If we recognize this as one of our calculated risks, it need not disturb us nor deflect us from what we have set out to do. Moreover, it has often been noted that when an area in psychology achieves high prestige it is already beginning to decay. (p. 96)

If we replace the word *longitudinal* by *life-span*, Jones may help us in assessing the status of our art. Is Life-Span Developmental Psychology still before the point of its highest prestige, or do signs of decay already show up? Considering the high standard of the chapters of this book, I am confident that the climax in the "prestige" of the life-span approach is still ahead of us. So there is time left to obtain that sort of doggedness Jones suggested as a coping device in times of lower prestige.

HANS THOMAE
University of Bonn
Federal Republic of Germany

ACKNOWLEDGMENTS

This book addresses the need for more-integrated knowledge in the field of gerontological and life-span psychology. It is an outgrowth of a symposium held in Nijmegen in July 1981, attended by psychogerontologists and developmentalists with experience in longitudinal research. The symposium was organized jointly by the Department of Social Gerontology, Psychological Laboratory, Catholic University, Nijmegen, The Netherlands, and Professor Hans Thomae, Psychological Institute, University of Bonn, Federal Republic of Germany. We thank Professor Thomae, and Nan Stevens and Cees Knipscheer (University of Nijmegen) for their support and help.

For the financial support of this symposium our thanks are due to the German Volkswagen Foundation, to the Dutch Society of Gerontology and the Dutch Institute of Gerontology, to the Dutch Ministry of Education and Sciences, and to the Faculty of Social Sciences, especially the Psychological Laboratory, of the University of Nijmegen. The final editorial work was completed in Wassenaar during the first editor's stay at the Netherlands Institute of Advanced Study in the Humanities and Social Sciences.

We would like to thank our colleague Carolien Smits for her grammatical help and Patricia Van Ooyen, deft as ever, for her secretarial support. We thank the editors and staff at Academic Press for their patience and kind support.

I

INTRODUCTION

1

LIFE-SPAN AND CHANGE IN A GERONTOLOGICAL PERSPECTIVE

by Joep M. A. Munnichs and Erhard Olbrich

INTRODUCTION

The increasing psychological knowledge about different periods of the life-span raises the question of concept integration. The original view of the first developmentalists was not only oriented to youth or childhood; it led off with a life-span concept. Once started with empirical research, however, the work itself asked for a reduction: a concentration on single periods or phases of the life-span. A second reason for this early theoretical splitting of the life-span was that the concept of development was not being applied to the processes of change that can be observed in adulthood and old age. As a consequence child psychology and gerontology developed separately. The first major change in this tendency occurred when gerontologists asked for the antecedents of the behaviour of the subjects they studied. Developmentalists and gerontologists became aware of the fact that they were studying the same subject at different points of the life-span. At that time the young developmentalists took up the thoughts of the first pathfinders in Europe (Bühler, 1933; Quetelet, 1835;) and in the United States (Hall, 1922; Hollingworth, 1927) to develop new concepts of development and the life-span (cf. Baltes & Goulet, 1970). The growing body of knowledge about different periods of the life-span was the basic condition for this book.

The major impetus for this work was a dialogue, sometimes a confrontation, between psychologists doing longitudinal research in the fields of development and ageing. Their different categories had much in common. The major questions, were, What are the consequences of the findings in ageing people for our knowledge about development in younger years? and, How will, for example, a specific personality-organisation in youth predict, at least partly, the behaviour of adults or old people? In this book some of the most important longitudinal studies will be highlighted in a life-span perspective. The gerontological perspective has its importance. But data on old age gain descriptive and explanatory value when interpreted within a frame of information about the whole biography. As a true developmentalist following a life-span psychology, one has no alternative but to adhere to this kind of interpretation.

TYPES OF STUDIES

The structure of the book is determined, on the one hand, by the nature of the studies conducted until now and, on the other hand, by the theory contained (whether implicitly or not) in the approaches of the life-span researchers. First, we focus on those categories of studies that are represented here.

In general, three types of interest in gerontological research can be distinguished:

1. The first type of study is represented most clearly by the longitudinal investigations of the Institute of Human Development at Berkeley. This research has followed subjects from their youth, keeping track of them over their entire adulthood. And now, as their subjects have grown older, these studies turn into gerontological investigations. The advantage of this research is that the researchers can make use of the knowledge of the biographies of their ageing subjects.

2. The second type of study is best described by the Bonn Longitudinal Study on Aging. This research followed the members of two cohorts in their sixties or seventies, from 1965 to 1981. The investigation describes and explains development in a relatively late period of life. Since intervals between measurement points were relatively short, the study allows an assessment of the process of ageing. The life-span orientation of these researchers is shown by their knowledge that a person's biography, even before he enters old age, contains most of the differentiating conditions explaining the various "patterns of ageing."

3. The third group of studies is characterised, on the one hand, by its comparisons of gerontological data with data gathered in earlier phases of life. Such comparisons can be based on repeated measurements of the same sample, as is true for the Midtown Study (cf. Srole, 1980). We call these studies follow-up studies. On the other hand, studies with intergenerational comparisons also belong to this category: data

from younger and/or middle aged and/or older individuals, tested at the same point in time, are correlated to each other. A feature of these types of studies is that they had either large intervals between their successive observations or large age differences between sample studies. Interpretations of a developmental process are therefore dubious. The concrete interests of researchers who have conducted studies of this type have prompted them to interpret information on the directly observable differences, rather than on processes that would have to be inferred.

We will come back to the types of studies described when we go into more detail on this book's contributions.

Figure 1.1 shows the different types of studies. The shaded parts indicate when the observations took place. This figure illustrates two aspects: first, if these three types are telescoped into each other, longitudinal information appears to exist on all stages of the life-span. Hence, the two-pointed arrow in the left, showing that results from Type 3 studies can provide data, ideas, and suggestions to Type 2 investigators.

Second, Figure 1.1 shows that life-span data not only can be studied from youth through middle age to old age, but that the reverse sequence is possible too (e.g., what do the data from the Bonn study suggest with respect to studies of middle-aged subjects?) This way numerous ques-

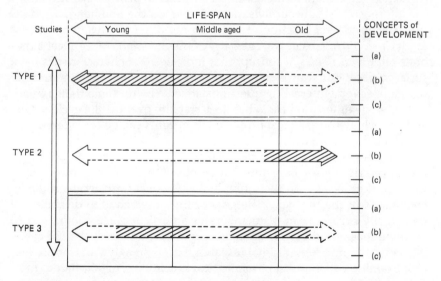

FIGURE 1.1 Types of studies, concepts of development, and time/period of measurement. Shaded portions are time(s) of measurement.

tions can be asked. Such a scheme illustrates the potential fruitfulness of a convocation of researchers interested in life-span research, regardless of the period of life in which they are particularly interested.

APPROACHES IN LIFE-SPAN RESEARCH

In life-span research we can identify three different approaches: the trait-centered, the process-centered, and the intergenerational, diachronic-centered approach. A short description of each follows.

1. Trait-centered approach. The earliest longitudinal research was concerned with the issue of stability versus instability of various characteristics or traits of an organism or personality. Most prevalent was research on intelligence and, to a lesser degree, on personality traits. The first category of research was especially stimulated by the rapid development of intelligence tests. Originally it was not well founded. In the case of personality traits, research was based on the theory of temperament and characterology, the implicit assumption being that only differences in level (quantitative differences) would appear. The traits, or the more or less crystallised constructs, are assumed to have a rather high degree of generality (i.e., situational invariance) and universality (i.e., they are assumed to exist in many individuals). Behaviour allows the inference and conceptualisation of traits on the one hand, whereas it is conceived as a function of traits on the other (Cattell, 1973; Costa & McCrae, 1976; Costa, McCrae, & Arenberg, 1980). More recent theories refer to *attributes*, a concept that indicates that characteristics have social implications. Reviewing the results of trait-centered longitudinal research, several interesting questions arise: Why do some traits remain stable, while others do not? What does stability over the life cycle mean? and, Which methodological problems or insights can be considered outcomes of this approach?

2. Process-centered approach. The longitudinal research based on this approach shows two different trends. On the one hand there is research that focuses on the individual's personality structure at different phases of the life-cycle; the goal of this research is to describe the personality organisation of members of a particular age cohort and to examine these for evidence of stability and change across the life-cycle. A second trend in longitudinal research, based on a dynamic approach, is to examine variations in psychological functioning in adulthood (middle age or old age) and to identify early-life antecedents of the variations that are found. Most investigators are concerned with identifying those

factors within the individual and his surrounding environment, leading to the development of "healthy functioning" in adulthood; a few other researchers choose to study pathology. However, the primary focus is on the aspects of people's lives relating to adaptability and emotional health, such as coping ability or the capacity for intimacy. The general feature of this approach stresses the interactions between personality and situational factors. It emphasises the process in rather short time-intervals. It allows a process-oriented view of personality: personality is formed in encounters between situational demands and a person's perceptual appraisal and response to these demands. Viewed this way, personality is "becoming". Development can then be conceptualised as a process of interactions occurring repeatedly over time in similar form ("crystallisation") or in sequences of differing interactions.

Both trends of research mentioned above are based on a dynamic approach and raise questions worthy of examination. Is there evidence that supports a particular model of development over the life-span (for example, a stage-sequential model)? What are the consequences of a particular conception of adaptability or psychological health for the interpretation of the results of a study? Do pathways into healthy psychological functioning (or pathology) in later life differ for men and women? Is there evidence that certain experiences in adulthood serve to compensate for negative experiences in childhood or adolescence?

3. Intergenerational–diachronic approach. This view takes into account interactions between preceding and subsequent processes or person and environment interactions. Subsequent processes, taking place at a later stage in a biography, will still interact with those having occurred at an earlier point in time. In this description we also conceptualize the concept *intergenerational* as an intrabiographical feature of the individual personality. On the other level, *intergenerational* means a concept to describe the interrelationships between representatives of different generations. This field of research is also included within this approach.

Therefore, not only intraindividual–diachronic themes and questions are important, but also intergenerational ones (e.g., the impact on ageing of social psychological and sociological factors and processes in the kinship system.

The breadth of this conceptualisation has to be stressed: neither subject factors nor situation factors, nor interactions of both, explain behaviour in all its variability, but rather explain episodically interacting subject–situation encounters in their diachronic interaction. Thus, behaviour is viewed as a function of subject factors that gain variability along both a range of situations and a range of points in time.

CLASSIFICATION OF CONTRIBUTIONS

This differentiation of three approaches is very helpful in character-
ising individual contributions. Knowledge of the range of each particular study has facilitated better understanding, especially since some
contributions can be ordered into different categories.

In addition to these two dimensions of classification (type of study;
conceptualisation of development), we can distinguish contributions as
characterised by research reports, reviews and discussions of sets of
data, and theoretical models of discussions of development (see Figure
1.1). An overview of individual contributions, ordered according to these
three dimensions (and to the content of this book), is given in Table 1.1.

This table shows a clear correlation between the age of the research
and the concept of development. Frequently, the concept of development is not well defined. Most of the contributors to this book describe
the results of their own research.

DISCUSSION AND TENTATIVE CONCLUSIONS

This book on "Life-Span and Change in a Gerontological Perspective" shows that the number of molar variables has increased rather
than decreased during the past decades. While the trait-centered approach was feasible, thanks to a strongly reduced object (i.e., few intraindividual aspects of the person), the process-oriented approach
already assumed an agent, that is, the individual steering the process
or undergoing it.

TABLE 1.1

CLASSIFICATION OF CONTRIBUTIONS

Author	Type of study	Concept of development	Kind of report
Haan	1	a, b	I
Mussen	1	a	I
Rudinger	2	a	I
Fooken	2	b, a	I
Fisseni	2	b, c	I
Olbrich	2	b, c	II, III
Maas	3	b, c	II
Fiske/Chiriboga	3	b, c	II
Trol et al.	3	a, c	II
Coleman/McCulloch	2	b, c	II, III
Bengtson/Kuypers	3	b, c	III

Thus molar variables exist, such as heredity (the biological component), social context (including a social–cultural component), nonhuman environment (the ecological component) and, last but not least, an individual's life-span (the biographical component) (Thomae, 1983). Recognition of each of these factors' importance does not simplify research. Another important conclusion, although not new, is that, in a life-span orientation, the emphasis on development in all periods of life requires a conceptual connection between the antecedent and the consequent processes. During adulthood and ageing however, these processes are personality rather than developmental processes, because personality plays the central role in them.

A third issue is the possible integration of the various conceptualisations. Can trait-centered and process-orientation approaches be combined? Here we would like to refer to the concepts of "continuity and discontinuity" or "stability and change." First of all, within continuity minor changes may exist (see Haan, Chapter 2, this volume). *Stability* also means "the same within certain limits." *Discontinuity* or *change* evokes differences between two different points in time. For the moment, a solution has been found in favour of the view that both phenomena—continuity and discontinuity—can occur at the same time. The question then is, How will these two concepts relate to one another? Usually the more or less stable personality will adapt to change by coping in a positive way. In this context we can also apply the concept of *crisis*, recently well defined by Erikson (1978): "Crisis does not necessarily connote a threat of catastrophe but rather a turning point, a crucial period of increased vulnerability and heightened potential" (p. 5). This "vulnerability" will evoke present, old, or new coping strategies. "Heightened potential" refers to new strategies or possible transcendence of one's own limitations.

Another problem is how to conceptualise stability. Let us stick to the concept of trait. A *trait* can be defined as a process that is relatively crystallised over time and relatively general over situations. In other words, a trait appears to be a "coagulated process" having a rather broad generality.

Another concept is coping (and coping strategy and coping style). We can define *coping* as an episodic process in which a person deals with demands that cannot be smoothly mastered with the help of his habitualised programs of reaction. When coping, the person has to utilize additional resources, either personal or social in nature. Coping can lead a person to change or develop his behavioral programs. In other words, it may lead to an adaptive modification of a person's strategies or programs in the use of resources.

The crystallisation of coping processes ensues when a person repeatedly encounters situational demands of an identical or similar kind and when coping stands the test. Coping programs are likely to become fluid in situations that are experienced as challenging, stressful, or threatening in a new way. Such situations are critical life events; periods of transition; and situations requiring adaptability of the individual and situations and subsequent modifications of strategy action, or reaction. This picture of the life-span behavior frequently leads to an emphasis on the plasticity of a person in adulthood and old age. Plasticity is not only found in cognitive functions, it is also observed in affective and motivational proceses. It was found to exist in old age as a prerequisite for a person's expansion of his programs of action and reaction.

The congeniality of these views with Hans Thomae's dynamic theory of personality is recognized. In 1951 Thomae had already emphasized that anything fluid can become crystallised (i.e., can become part of the hardware program). He also elaborated that crystallised structures can become fluid again. These views are neither acknowledged sufficiently nor empirically supported to a sufficient degree. A process-oriented development in psychology, which also considers episodic and diachronic interactions, is at present best realised in research that analyses coping processes as well as developmental processes. A combination of coping research in personality psychology and developmental psychology is considered to be a promising field of work.

It is felt that developmental research in adulthood and old age, (and in other stages) can provide not only new insights into processes specific to the later periods of the life span, but also new theoretical conceptualisations of development and its determinants during the whole life-span.

REFERENCES

Baltes, P. B., & Goulet, L. R. Status and issues of a life span developmental psychology. In L. R. Goulet & P. B. Baltes (Eds.), *Life span developmental psychology: Research and theory*. New York: Academic Press, 1970.

Bühler, Ch. *Der menschliche Lebenslauf als psychologisches Problem*. Leipzig: Hirzel, 1933.

Cattell, R. B. *Personality and mood by questionnaire*. San Francisco: Jossey–Bass, 1973.

Costa, P. T., & McCrae, R. R. Age differences in personality structure. A cluster analysis approach. *Journal of Gerontology*, 1976, *31*, 564–570.

Costa, P. T., & McCrae, R. R. Still stable after all these years: Personality as a key to some issues in aging. In P. B. Baltes & O. G. Brim, Jr. (Eds.), *Life-span development and behavior (Vol. 2)*. New York: Academic Press, 1980.

Costa, P. T., McCrae, R. R., & Arenberg, D. Enduring dispositions in adult males. *Journal of Personality and Social Psychology*, 1980, *38*(5), 793–800.

Erikson, E. H. Reflections on Dr. Borg's life cycle. In E. H. Erikson (Ed.), *Adulthood*. New York: Norton, 1978.

Hall, G. S. *Senescence: The last half of life*. New York: Appleton, 1922.

Hollingworth, H. L. *Mental growth and decline: A survey of developmental psychology*. New York: Appleton, 1927.

Quetelet, A. *Sur l'homme et le développement de ses facultés*. Paris: Bachlier, 1835.

Srole, L. The Midtown Manhattan Longitudinal Study versus "The Mental Paradise Lost" doctrine. *Archives of General Psychiatry*, 1980, *37*, 209–221.

Thomae, H. *Persönlichkeit, eine dynamische Interpretation*. Bonn: Bouvier, 1951.

Thomae, H. *Alternsstile und Altersschicksale, ein Beitrag zur differentiellen Gerontologie*. Bern: Huber, 1983.

II

EMPIRICAL STUDIES

A

TRAIT-ORIENTED STUDIES

INTRODUCTION

The studies gathered and presented under this heading may be characterised by the fact that they were based, at least initially, on the trait model rather than on a process-oriented model of personality. As mentioned before, there is a connection between the age of longitudinal studies and the theory used implicitly. In that sense scientific research is the child of its age. The advantages of a not over-profiled theoretical approach are evident when we compare the two studies that came forth from the investigations of the Institute of Human Development (i.e., those by Norma Haan & Paul Mussen). While the latter is an almost classic example of an analysis at trait level, or of factors based on it, the personality factors with which Haan tries to analyse her data produce completely different results. It is even debatable whether Haan's structuring of data fits into a trait-oriented study because of the emphasis with which she refers to the environment in her discussion, saying: "People respond in different ways to different episodes."

In the third study of this section Rudinger discusses the Bonn data on intelligence of the elderly. Had similar intelligence data been presented by Berkeley, a more detailed comparison would have produced some interesting suppositions for those Californian respondents who are still only heading toward old age.

The results that Rudinger presents impress by their stability. Intelligence as a construct does not change over the years under observation. Change does, however, appear in Haan's results, which show differences from early adolescence to middle adulthood with respect to "open/closed to self."

Haan describes this as "Janus-faced observation," explaining it in a way that might partly take account of the stability of Rudingers intelligence data at an older age: "organisations of people's personalities shift from time to time and when stability is maintained, cognitive invest-

15

ment is often a predominant theme.'' This is irrespective of the selection of subjects in Bonn that is found as a result of the survival effect. Even though there is no talk of complete life styles, Haan's conclusion on the appearing heterogeneity is of great importance; especially if this would mean that the observed heterogeneity remains stable or increases over time.

The question of where these diverging personality organisations will lead to immediately rises. The next question is whether this result could be connected with Friedman and Rosenman's (1959) A and B typology.

Apart from this one wonders if heterogenity should be expected in other aspects of old age. This would reinforce the hypothesis that individualisation increases with age.

Finally, the question, What do these contributions say about the general problems of gerontology and life-span psychology? The contributions also suggest methodological problems. How can data be gathered with greatest reliability and furthermore analysed with greatest objectivity? It is not only here that the researcher manifests himself. What is he after? The research should be sensitive to this too. The role of his own personality (in a broad sense) cannot be precluded. The careful way in which the Berkeley and Bonn studies have been conducted are to be recommended. This appears to be feasible only where the disinterested searching of the true reality is permitted.

J. M.

REFERENCE

Friedman, M., & Rosenman, R. Association of a specific overt behavior pattern with blood and cardiovascular findings. *Journal of the American Medical Association*, 1959, *21*, 1286–1295.

2

COMMON PERSONALITY DIMENSIONS OR COMMON ORGANIZATIONS ACROSS THE LIFE-SPAN?

Norma Haan

INTRODUCTION

The need of life-span research to describe and explain trends in human personality across many years may eventually produce a consensus about the fundamental definition of personality. The task of life-span investigation itself highlights our present confusions about personality. To encompass the life-span, a conceptualization of personality—whether dynamic, trait, social or intergenerational—will have to be relatively abstract and general because the concrete and ever-changing details of individual lives and situations need to be transcended at the same time that the movement of life itself must be captured. The basic question of life-span research is in itself a dynamic one: What stays the same about people, and what changes across the life-span and why? In this essay I offer empirical findings that suggest which qualities and organizations of personality stay the same and which change. I also offer several programmatic suggestions for discovering why.

In earlier work (Haan, 1976; Haan & Day, 1974), I made an attempt to address this question. My colleagues and I used four categories for classifying the Q-sort items that were used to describe the personalities of the longitudinal study members of the Institute of Human Development from early adolescence to middle adulthood. These four categories were information processing, interpersonal reactions, socialization, and self-presentation. This classification was one of convenience simply based on the items at hand. It was not one of conceptual elegance. However, seemingly convincing results were obtained: According to our criteria, the socialization and self-preservation items registered the greatest stability across the 35 years (46 and 39%, respectively), whereas those representing styles of information processing changed the most (4% consistent, compared to 35% changing), and almost all the interpersonal items were classified as unstable. The main implications were that basic reactions to society's expectations and forms of self-presentation endure and do not especially accommodate to life experiences. Understandably, styles of information processing did change, along with increasing ability and experience, from the early teens to the middle years. Interpersonal reactions seemed to change because they were a function of the hospitality or threat of immediate life contexts. The stability of the self-presentation items is especially interesting. Evidently people generally think of themselves as much the same person across the years, and this finding may explain why cross-time correlations for personality inventory scales generally have greater stability (see, e.g., Brooks, 1982) than do correlations between observations made at different points in time by outside observers.

In any event, whether or not these particular results truly inform us about which aspects of personality change or stay the same, they remind us of the synchronies and dysynchronies of living. People require a modicum of certainty about who they are, but they need flexibility in order to interact dialectically with their life-event experiences and others' expectancies.

Until the consensually validated definition of personality is achieved, we may benefit from modest, empirical descriptions such as the one I now present. A statistically derived framework that fitted four different sets of observations across the life-span was generated in the two studies I describe. These measures were for the Institute of Human Development's study members from their early adolescence through the middle years. The first study had the conventional focus on the development of variables across time. The second study was concerned with the organization of these variables within persons at different points in time.

Although these dimensions were common to all periods studied, they probably do not all represent the ultimate life-span themes. To reduce the some 90 variables to manageable proportions, a three-way, principal-component factor analysis (PARAFAC) was used to yield a unified model of people and variables over occasions (Harshman & Berenbaum, 1976). Finally, a substantial portion, but not the entire life-span, is bracketed in these two studies—from 12 to approximately 40 years for the Guidance Study (GS) participants and from 12 to 47 years for the Oakland Growth Study (OGS).

For readers to evaluate the results, the psychological implications of Q-measures must be taken into account, as well as the gains, sacrifices, and biases that the PARAFAC methodology imposes on the actualities of development over years. Whether personality measures made at different ages are scaled equivalently is a particularly thorny problem in long-term studies of personality. The same score for a personality variable may not be equivalent for child and adult nor may the adult's characteristic be a transformed version of the child's. If age-graded stages of personality were known to exist, they could constitute one kind of age-related measurement that would permit descriptive statements of ordinality—"psychologically younger or older than." But without verification of the truth of stage sequences, measurement of personality or maturation in personality across age periods has no clear or absolute mooring. Recognizing this problem, the staff of the Institute of Human Development turned some years ago to measuring personality within the ipsative framework of the Q-sort (Block in collaboration with Haan, 1971). This form of scaling involves ranking attributes as they seemed to be ordered within individuals (rather than attempting to measure personality as absolute quantities that vary between people). A different score for a characteristic that is ipsatively measured at two time periods represents a change in the salience of this characteristic within a person's personality organization. Each person is his own frame of reference. No claim is made, overtly or covertly, that absolute measures of differences in personality are measured, an idea that is probably an illusion. Thus the Q-sort provides a modest mooring for measurement and gives information only about the relative importance of different characteristics within personality organizations.

Another feature of Q-sort measurement that affects results is its forced distribution. Approximately 40% of the items of the Q-sort used (Block, 1961) represent "healthy" qualities and another 40% pathological qualities. Because our study members are generally well-functioning persons, most pathological items have low values and "healthy" items, high values. This phenomenon produces positive correlations within the pathological set and healthy set of items but negative correlations between the two sets. Therefore, the general level of intercorrelation among items in our samples is not only higher but also more patterned than if a sample represented the full range of psychological well-being in the population. As a secondary result of this interaction between the item pool and the sample, the various factors identified by PARAFAC probably suggest that more bipolarity exists between pathology and adequacy than is probably true for the population at large.

In using PARAFAC one predetermines the number of factors to be derived and then proceeds to a single, simultaneous solution for this number for several samples (here four) across several time periods (here also four). PARAFAC solutions are based on the assumption that a factor can be meaningfully understood as a linear combination of certain original variables. Although this assumption is the practical basis of much research, it probably does not always represent the personality of real people.

If important personality variations occur within only one time period, they will not be included in PARAFAC's solution, which includes all time periods. As a consequence, the total variance that PARAFAC accounts for is less than investigators are used to considering (here approximately 65%). This restriction does not sacrifice too much information, for life-span research is still in an elementary state; even an incomplete empirically based description has its worth. Also, period-specific variances may reflect temporary reactions instead of historically relevant change. However, period-specific variance could have later important effects on qualitatively different common dimensions, but PARAFAC cannot reveal this possibility. The purpose here is to identify and describe common *developmental* themes with the gain that neither a child-centric nor adult-centric model of development (Baltes & Schaie, 1973) determines the results. All time periods have equal opportunity to affect the general solution.

The substantive implications of these methodological features are several. Persons are assumed to possess certain constellations of characteristics (the factors) across time periods. These constellations are expected to have greater or lesser importance in the overall personality organizations of persons, because the original context of measurement is an ipsative one. Therefore, a theory of personality that describes development as a qualitative transformation of variables evident early in life (e.g., as concrete cognitive operations are reworked and incorporated into formal operations in Piaget's theory) cannot be directly represented by this methodology. In other words, PARAFAC finds and capitalizes on the sameness of constellations across time periods. Change is observed as the variances and mean levels of the factor scores fluctuate.

Finally, the factorial solution used here is orthogonal: a decision of methodological convenience that is consistent with the idea that personality is composed of independent faculties or dimensions. This effect runs counter to the supposition that people's personalities are unitary in nature, a view I actually hold.

No factor-analytic procedure, including PARAFAC, can generate a developmental model if the pool of input variables is not relevant to development. The items of the California Q-sort (Block, 1961) and its adolescent-relevant version (Block in collaboration with Haan, 1971) have the merit of being easily understood because they represent attributes that psychologists commonly use to describe people. However, this Q-sort does not include all qualities that may be important in describing the life-span from adolescence to the middle years. For instance, some tender, noninstrumental characteristics, such as empahty and depression, are not well represented.

Also lacking are structural-developmental variables, such as the personality manifestations of concrete or hypothetical-deductive thinking or interpersonal reciprocity, which are undoubtedly critical in developmental study. With these caveats and elaborations stated, I can now turn to the two studies. Both were done with the same data.

METHOD

PARTICIPANTS

Four different subsamples (total $N = 136$) with Q-sort descriptions for all four time periods—early and late adolescence and young and middle adulthood—are used: OGS females ($N = 41$) and males ($N = 37$); GS females ($N = 32$); and males ($N = 26$).

To minimize capitalizing on chance, I consider a finding meaningful only if it is replicated in at least two of the four samples with significance levels of .05 or better. This is a stringent requirement because members of all long-term longitudinal samples have vastly different life experiences that should interactively generate concurrent and long-term personality differences. Furthermore, a 7-year age difference separates OGS and GS, and the four subsamples have always had other striking, personal-demographic differences. These variations among samples and the requirement of replication should ensure the reliability of results.

Compared to the other samples, the OGS females had significantly less education and more divorces; they achieved the lowest IQ scores in the recent Wechsler Adult Intelligence Scale (WAIS) testing and were generally more politically conservative. The GS females were better educated, had higher IQs, were infrequently divorced, and were most frequently politically liberal. The OGS males showed marked upward socioeconomic mobility, had the highest adult socioeconomic status (SES) and IQs at the last follow-up (approximately age 50), and were politically conservative. The GS males had the most education and came from the most advantaged homes, but they themselves were actually downwardly mobile in SES (if they were to move, some had no direction to go but down).

Finally, we cannot assume that these subsamples are representative of their age groups or locale, although demographically they were not markedly different from the original samples, first recruited in about 1930.

DATA

The main data were derived from the California Q-sort (Block, 1961), which has 90 items with equivalent meanings for all four time periods. Only 86 items were actually used, however, because four items had insufficient reliability (r's $< .45$). The data basis for all time periods was extensive clinical material: Interviews at adulthood were used but various anecdotal records, projective tests, and test scores for the two adolescent periods. Details of the complex methods to ensure reliability (which ranged for items from .62 to .71) have been repeatedly reported in the literature (see, e.g., Eichorn, Clausen, Haan, Honzik, & Mussen, 1982; Haan & Day, 1974). The PARAFAC procedures produced an orthogonal solution that fitted nonnormalized covariance matrices for the samples at each time period and provided six factor scores for each person at each time period. These are the base scores used in all analyses.

RESULTS

DESCRIPTION OF FACTORS

Table 2.1 shows the distinctive constellations of items (factor loadings at least 1.5 standard deviations from the mean) that give each factor its flavor. The names are shorthand labels that do not fully represent all facets of each dimension. Slashes in the titles indicate bipolar factors (i.e., both extremes define clear constellations). The negative end does not always precisely represent the opposite version of the positive end.

Factor 1, called *Cognitively Invested*, is positively defined by a pattern of items that indicates ease and skill in dealing with intellectual matters, deliberate reflectiveness, and, concomitantly, interest in personal achievement. Together, the items define a dimension that represents, on the high end, successful adaptation, achievement, and use of abilities; whereas the low end includes various defenses that probably hinder adaptation, achievement, and efficient use of abilities.

Factor 2, called *Emotionally Under/Overcontrolled*, is defined at the positive end by items that represent a pressured, dramatic, and aggressive

TABLE 2.1

DISTINCTIVE ITEM LOADINGS OF COMMON DIMENSIONS (1½ STANDARD DEVIATIONS FROM THE $\overline{X}$)

High positive loadings		High negative loadings	
FACTOR 1: Cognitively Invested			
Values intellectual matters	2.6	Self-defensive	1.9
Ambitious	2.1	Undercontrolled	1.8
Verbally fluent	2.0	Withdraws when frustrated	1.7
Wide interests	1.6	Uncomfortable with uncertainty	1.6
Productive	1.6	Pushes limits	1.5
Introspective	1.6		
Philosphically concerned	1.6		
Appears intelligent	1.6		
Dependable	1.5		
FACTOR 2: Emotionally Under/Overcontrolled			
Self-dramatizing	2.1	Calm	2.4
Talkative	1.9	Emotionally Bland	2.1
Undercontrolled	1.7	Overcontrolled	1.9
Pushes limits	1.5	Dependable	1.8
Assertive	1.5	Sympathetic	1.6
Rebellious	1.5	Submissive	1.5
Unpredictable	1.5		
FACTOR 3: Open/Closed to Self			
Insightful	2.5	Conventional	2.5
Introspective	2.3	Uncomfortable with uncertainty	2.3
Thinks unconventionally	1.8	Repressive	2.1
Rebellious	1.7	Fastidious	1.5
Interesting	1.7	Power-oriented	1.5
FACTOR 4: Nurturant/Hostile			
Giving	2.1	Aloof	2.4
Sympathetic	2.0	Negativistic	2.0
Warm	1.9	Rebellious	1.8
Gregarious	1.7	Condescending	1.8
Arouses liking	1.7	Distrustful	1.7
Cheerful	1.6	Skeptical	1.7
Protective	1.5	Deceitful	1.6
Dependable	1.5	Pushes limits	1.5
FACTOR 5: Under/Overcontrolled, Heterosexual			
Interested in the opposite sex	2.1	Overcontrolled	2.5
Undercontrolled	1.9	Aloof	1.8
Eroticizes situations	1.8	Dependable	1.7
Talkative	1.8	Ruminative	1.6
Gregarious	1.7	Fearful	1.6
Self-indulgent	1.7	Values intellectual matters	1.5
Self-dramatizing	1.6		

(Continued)

TABLE 2.1 (*Continued*)

High positive loadings		High negative loadings	
FACTOR 6: Self-Confident			
Assertive	2.2	Fearful	2.0
Satisfied with self	2.1	Self-defensive	1.9
Poised	2.0	Withdraws when frustrated	1.8
Values independence	1.8	Feels victimized	1.8
Productive	1.5	Brittle ego defenses	1.7
		Feels life lacks meaning	1.7
		Reluctant to act	1.5
		Ruminative	1.5

approach to interpersonal exchanges (self-dramatizing, talkative, undercontrolled, pushes limits, assertive, rebellious, and unpredictable) and, at the negative end, by a calm, dependable, and sympathetic approach which is, nevertheless, clearly restricted (emotionally bland ["flattened affect"], overcontrolled, and submissive). Thus, neither approach is an effective means of handling conflict. The two commonly observed ways that people react when they are stressed—fight or flight— seem to be represented. Because this dimension is clearly bipolar, indications of both extremes are included in the title.

Factor 3 is also bipolar. Called *Open/Closed to Self*, it is positively defined by a pattern of items that suggests an openness to one's own thoughts and experiences along with an easy self-expressiveness. In contrast, the pattern of negatively weighted items suggests need for certainty and reliance on external, conventional standards coupled with a striking lack of self-awareness. This dimension reflects the self-reflexive or metacognitive ways that persons deal with their own psychological beings, whether as objects of interest and resource or, warily and defensively, as unpredictable entities that need external limitation.

Factor 4, called *Nurturant/Hostile*, is positively defined by a constellation of items that features consideration, warmth, and responsiveness to other people; whereas the negatively weighted items indicate hostility, suspiciousness, and distance from others.

Factor 5, called *Under/Overcontrolled, Heterosexual*, is positively defined by items that again suggest undercontrol, like Factor 2, but here the impulsiveness is sexualized, gregarious, and self-indulgent instead of aggressive and rule-violating. The low items for Factor 5 define an obsessive–compulsive constellation that includes affective vulnerability, compensatory investment in thinking, and asexuality.

Factor 6, called *Self-Confident*, is positively defined by a pattern of items that indicates great effectiveness in interpersonal relations, and, concomitantly, self-confidence. In sharp contrast, the negative items suggest a sense of self as vulnerable.

In summary, the various factors seem to reflect several known aspects of personality: *Cognitively Invested*, an effective or ineffective use of cognitive abilities; *Emotionally Under/Overcontrolled*, reacting to stress by attacking or withdrawing; *Open/Closed To Self*, views of the self as self-guided or as regulated by external rules and standards; *Nurturant/ Hostile*, relating to other persons, generously and openly or hostilely and closed; *Under/Overcontrolled, Heterosexual*, openly expressing the self in heterosexual relations or guarding against interpersonal involvements; and *Self-Confident*, regarding one's self in social contexts as competent or vulnerable.

I will describe the fate of these dimensions in two ways, first as variables (their stability, developmental trends, and convergence-divergence within samples) and second, as they are organized within persons at different time periods. Because I have already reported the details of the first study (see Eichorn, et al., 1982), the developmental description of the variables will be abbreviated.

STABILITIES OF THE COMMON DIMENSIONS ACROSS DIFFERENT AGES

The correlations of the factor scores between time periods for the members of the four samples are shown in Table 2.2. The total number of significant correlations, irrespective of time interval, serves as a rough indication of the extent of overall stability: 63 (66%) were significant at the .05 level or better.

Larger numbers of significant correlations occur for the shorter intervals than the longer ones: of the 63 significant correlations, 35% are for the two adjacent adolescent periods; 32% for the adult interval of approximately 10 years; 19% from late adolescent to young adult years, a matter of 12 years for GS and 19 for OGS; and 14% for the entire span of 28 and 35 years for the GS and OGS, respectively. Whether these findings indicate that the dimensions are impressively or mildly stable over time probably depends on one's theoretical bent. To me, the implication is that people change, but slowly, while maintaining some continuity. The adolescent to adult period seems to be the time of greatest discontinuity. The evidence does not suggest—even when these dimensions were corrected for imperfect reliabilities in separate analyses—that the personalities of these study members were immutable.

TABLE 2.2

Correlations between Time Periods for the Common Dimensions

	OGS				GS			
	14-17	17-37	37-47	14-47	14-17	17-30	30-40	14-40
Women								
Cognitively Invested	.70[a]	.54[a]	.66[a]	.49[b]	.52[b]	.42[c]	.38[c]	.03
Emotionally Under/Overcontrolled	.58[a]	.30	.44[b]	.48[b]	.72[a]	.54[b]	.45[b]	.30
Open/Closed to Self	.43[b]	.39[c]	.49[b]	.37[c]	.75[a]	.57[a]	.62[a]	.46[b]
Nurturant/Hostile	.57[a]	.49[b]	.48[b]	.13	.54[b]	.27	.40[c]	.20
Under/Overcontrolled, Heterosexual	.64[a]	.46[b]	.69[a]	.42[c]	.54[b]	.62[a]	.19	.11
Self-Confident	.48[b]	.44[b]	.65[a]	.30	.54[b]	.36[c]	.38[c]	.41[c]
Men								
Cognitively Invested	.63[a]	.58[a]	.78[a]	.62[a]	.73[a]	.40[c]	.59[b]	.34
Emotionally Under/Overcontrolled	.52[a]	.26	.56[a]	.32[c]	.67[a]	.21	.53[b]	.36
Open/Closed to Self	.30	−.08	.37[c]	.16	.35	.36	.45[c]	−.06
Nurturant/Hostile	.55[a]	.30	.29	.16	.65[a]	.24	.16	.37
Under/Overcontrolled Heterosexual	.65[a]	.21	.33[c]	.03	.62[a]	.29	.21	−.05
Self-Confident	.61[a]	.24	.43[b]	.01	.66[a]	.27	.50[b]	.57[b]

[a] $p \leq .001$.
[b] $p \leq .01$.
[c] $p \leq .05$.
[d] $p \leq .10$.

Although the two study groups have approximately the same degree and pattern of stabilities, differences between the sexes are noteworthy: women are markedly more stable than men between late adolescence and young adulthood (83% of their correlations are significant compared to 16% for the males). Males were also less predictable than women over the entire span studied (25% of their correlations were significant compared to 50%).

The different dimensions vary in stability: 87% of the correlations for Cognitively Invested are significant and 80% for Self-Confident. Other dimensions do not show this degree of stability: 69% for Emotionally Under/Overcontrolled; 62% for Open/Closed to Self; 56% for Under/Overcontrolled, Heterosexual; and 44% for Nurturant/Hostile. Altogether then, the dimensions that are most directly concerned with the self are more stable—Cognitively Invested, Self-Confident, and Open/Closed to Self (the latter, particularly for women). Dimensions that more directly reflect the quality of the participants' interpersonal-relations—Nurturant/Hostile and Under/Overcontrolled, Heterosexual—are less stable. The participants' standings on these interpersonal dimensions were probably effected, at various times, by actual changes in their interpersonal relationships that result from such life events as death, divorce, illness, birth, work success and failure. The importance of assessing interactive influence in subsequent study cannot be underestimated.

ANALYSES OF THE EFFECTS OF TIME, SEX, AND SAMPLE

To assess the factor score's developmental trends within the context of sex and sample, multivariate analyses of variance were done separately for each factor score. Orthogonal polynomial decomposition was used so that no assumptions about the homogeneity of covariance were necessary (Bock, 1975; McCall & Appelbaum, 1973). The modal chronological ages for each sample at each time period defined the points in time. The analysis of greatest interest was for the developmental trends as changes in mean levels of each dimension across time, with sex and sample controlled. Additional analyses were for (1) sample differences as cohort or original sampling contrasts, with sex and time controlled; (2) sex differences for each dimension, with sample and time controlled; and (3) interactions between sex, sample, or time for each dimension (No three-way interactions were significant; 5 of the 18 two-way interactions were significant. Here I discuss only the most significant one ($p < .001$). Please note again that the ipsative framework of Q-sort mea-

surement means that the results below represent differences or changes
in the importance of a dimension within individuals.

Main Effects for Sample and Sex Differences

No significant differences between the GS and OGS samples were
found (see Table 2.3). However, three strong sex differences emerged.
Irrespective of time and sample, the females were strikingly higher for
Nurturant/Hostile and Under/Overcontrolled, Heterosexual; but considerably lower for Self-Confident. Plots of the means for the factor
scores for each sample and time (see Figure 2.1) show that these differences generally held for all time periods. Interpretively, these differences suggest that the women, more than the men, extended themselves
toward others, nurturantly and sexually; but these behaviors appear not
to have been personally rewarding because the women also lacked self-
confidence.

Developmental Trends

Analysis of the developmental trends produced less expected results.
All dimensions but Emotionally Under/Overcontrolled showed strong
and significant developmental trends with sex and sample controlled.

Cognitively Invested generally rose for all four samples from modal
age 14 to the middle years. Apparently intellectuality and achievement
interests came to occupy an increasingly important role in the participants' personalities from adolescence to the middle years. Marked gains
occurred during adolescence and adulthood, but little change occurred
between adolescence and adulthood. The reasons for these two different
periods of strong gain are undoubtedly different. The adolescent's bur-
geoning cognitive ability probably accounts for the early gain. However,
the increased reflectiveness and deliberation during adulthood may follow resolutions of questions concerning career, marriage, and parenthood. In a word, middle-aged adults become "wise" and cognitively
competent.

Emotionally Under/Overcontrolled is interesting. Despite its substantial variance at four time periods, its developmental trend is not significant. Consequently, this nondevelopmental dimension may be reactive
to adventitious personal situations which are bound to occur in the lives
of 136 persons from time to time. Fight of flight approaches are ways
that people of any age can react to stress. The dimension's modest stability across time suggests that people respond in different ways to different episodes. For example, overreactive, emotional boys may become

TABLE 2.3

MULTIVARIATE ANALYSES OF VARIANCE FOR EFFECTS OF SEX, SAMPLE, AND TIME PERIODS

	F ratios					
	Main effects			Interactions		
	Sex	Sample	Time	Sex × sample	Time × sex	Time × sample
Cognitively Invested	.19	1.75	15.92[a]	.00	1.54	1.26
Emotionally Under/Overcontrolled	1.14	1.11	1.28	3.78[c]	1.70	1.01
Open/Closed to Self	.40	.02	17.07[a,e]	.08	6.92[a]	2.99[c]
Nurturant/Hostile	16.12[a]	3.57	5.69[a]	.00	1.46	4.46[b]
Under/Overcontrolled, Heterosexual	15.54[a]	.00	10.21[a]	3.26	4.80[b]	1.58
Self-Confident	7.22[b]	.04	4.91[b]	.32	1.13	.55

Three-way F ratios are not shown; none were significant.

[a] $p \leq .001$.
[b] $p \leq .01$.
[c] $p \leq .05$.
[d] $p \leq .10$.
[e] Significant at $p < .0001$.

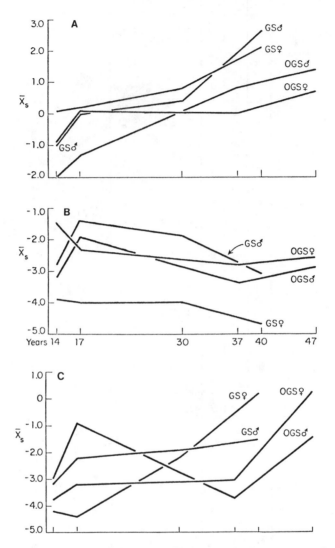

FIGURE 2.1 Average scores on personality dimensions for four time periods: A, Cog-
nitively Invested (Factor 1); B, Emotionally Under/Overcontrolled (Factor 2); C,
Open/Closed to Self (Factor 3); D, Nurturant/Hostile (Factor 4); E, Under/Overcontrolled
Heterosexual (Factor 5); F, Self-Confident (Factor 6).

stoic men. The nonsystematic shifts on this dimension are consistent
with Haan's (1977) finding that people's preferences in defensive processes are less stable over time than their preferences in coping processes.

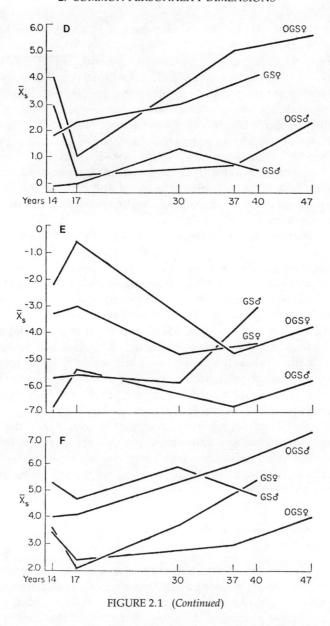

FIGURE 2.1 (*Continued*)

Open/Closed to Self has the strongest developmental trend. Its curves are complex, but the basic movement of all samples is toward greater openness. A highly significant two-way interaction between time and sex occurred. During adolescence, both male samples were more open than the females, but by the middle years they had become less open than the females.

Nurturant/Hostile has a significant time trend, but of smaller magnitude. The highly significant sex difference indicating that women were consistently more nurturant is clearly seen in Figure 4. Nevertheless, after comparatively low scores at late adolescence, typically a time of great self-preoccupation, the long-term movement for all samples is toward greater nurturance. The general substance of the findings for Nurturant/Hostile is consistent with those for Cognitively Invested and Open/Closed to Self. With increasing maturity, these study members became not only more cognitively invested and open to their own personal experience, but also better able and more willing to interact with others generously and dependably.

Under/Overcontrolled, Heterosexual has a substantial time trend with similarly shaped curves for all samples. The mean scores increase to high levels—especially for females—at late adolescence, decrease at the first adult follow-up, and then increase moderately by the middle years. Clearly the late adolescent peak is compatible with our understanding of the adolescent's sexual interest and activity. However, the resurgence of this dimension at the middle years reveals renewed sexual and self-expressiveness at a time in life when such a trend is not usually anticipated. Whether this is a phenomenon of liberation, compulsion, nostalgia, or compensation is not certain. But in view of the participants' increased cognitive investment, awareness of self, and nurturance, their sexual expressiveness seems likely to reflect liberation.

Finally, Self-Confident generally increases over time, despite the moderately significant sex differences that indicate that men were more self-confident at late adolescence but then steadily improved, as did the OGS males throughout the middle years. Only the GS males' relatively flat curve is exceptional.

TRENDS TOWARD SAMPLE HETEROGENEITY OR HOMOGENEITY

Time-related trends toward greater homogeneity or heterogeneity within each sample represent another aspect of development. When a sample becomes more heterogeneous than it was before, I hypothesize that a transitional phase is generally underway and that individual persons' initial reactions are experimentally diverse. When a sample becomes more homogeneous, I infer that the age group has generally accommodated to common social experiences with similar solutions. The method used to test these convergences and divergences was *t* tests of the factor scores' variances between time periods (McNemar, 1969). I do not show these results in a table. Because multiple *t* tests were done, the stringent requirement that results for two samples be significant at the .01 level or better was instituted. By this criteria two dimensions have noteworthy convergences and divergences: Open/Closed to Self and Under/Overcontrolled, Heterosexual.

Both samples of females became more heterogeneous with respect to Open/Closed to Self from early to late adolescence. All samples became more heterogeneous with respect to Open/Closed to Self from early adolescence to middle adulthood. The social-psychological transitions of adolescence were evidently diversely handled by females. Some may have used the experience to achieve greater liberation and more differentiated understandings of themselves, whereas others may have conservatively foreclosed on their new experiences and possibilities. Successively salubrious or deleterious experiences in dealing with stress across the life-span may be the reason that the samples bifurcated. This finding may reflect the Janus-faced observation of common sense: people become increasingly liberated as they age; people become increasing closed and rigid as they age. Again this divergence needs further study, particularly as these people continue to age.

Members of three samples—OGS men and women and GS women—converged between late adolescence and adulthood on the dimension Under/Overcontrolled, Heterosexual, and the same three samples also converged over the entire period of study. Therefore the adolescents' new opportunities for sexual self-expressiveness—legitimated by society's expectancies and empowered by their own biological maturations—although initially experienced and reacted to in diverse ways, generally drew common solutions by early adulthood and continued to do so through middle adulthood.

In sum, these people became more individualized in their openness to psychological experience over time but more alike in their sexual self-expressiveness.

SUMMARIZATION OF DEVELOPMENTAL FINDINGS
FOR EACH DIMENSION

An account of the dimension Cognitively Invested can be simply given: across the life-span it was generally stable; but its importance in the hierarchies of the participants' personality attributes increased while its within-sample heterogeneity remained constant. Therefore Cognitively Invested seems to be an important, omnipresent dimension of development that increasingly plays a more important role in personality organization over the life-span.

Emotionally Under/Overcontrolled was stable within the adolescent and adult periods but not between these periods. No changes (gains or losses) were registered; variability within samples did not change; and no sex differences were found. Although this dimension accounted for a sizable variance at each time period, it was not developmentally relevant. It probably represents reactions to idiosyncratic life events and, if so, must be taken into account to understand the effects of stress on life-span observations and to control error variance that masks developmental trends.

Open/Closed to Self was stable for women for all intervals and for men during adulthood. It increased its importance in the members' personality organization throughout the entire span studied, but, nevertheless, the samples had significantly bifurcated by the middle years. In a subsequent follow-up, it will be important to evaluate whether this trend continues. The clear sex difference in the extent of stability indicates that females are more likely to adopt a basic position of being open or closed to themselves by early adolescence, and then maintain this orientation over the years. In contrast, the men did not adopt a stable orientation toward themselves until the adult years. Men's openness may be more situationally responsive and inconsistent with career achievement.

Nurturant/Hostile was stable for all samples during adolescence and for women during adulthood. Scores generally increased after a temporary decrease during late adolescence; sample variations remained relatively constant across time. Males and females were sharply distinguished, with the women being considerably more nurturant than the men.

Under/Overcontrolled, Heterosexual was stable for all samples during the short adolescent interval. Scores for this dimension changed in complex ways—the curves had high points at late adolescence and middle age, but samples generally became more homogeneous over the entire time. This dimension was more important in females' than males' personality organizations. Apparently different persons chose one or another of these routes during their adolescence, but the samples generally moved developmentally toward more temperate, homogeneous solutions by the later years.

Finally, Self-Confident was generally stable only within the adolescent and adult periods; as a developmental dimension it registered moderate gains across the years. Samples maintained approximately equal variations within themselves across time, and men were generally more confident than women.

RELATIONSHIPS OF THE BASIC DIMENSIONS TO SOCIOECONOMIC STATUS AND MOBILITY

The relationships of these dimensions to both concurrent and achieved SES were considered. If the correlations between factor scores and concurrent SES at the various time periods were high, it could not be said that the dimensions represent common developmental trends. Instead, their levels and trends would reflect the advantages or disadvantages of the participants' socioeconomic circumstances. I will not report these results in detail. None of the dimensions had systematic relations with the adolescent or adult measures of socioeconomic status, with the exception of Cognitively Invested. At adolescence this dimension had strong and positive correlations with concurrent SES, and this association increased in magnitude with each successive time period.

Because these analyses indicate that socioeconomic advantage was generally not a major determinant of the levels nor the developmental paths of these dimensions, we may regard five of these dimensions, with the exception of Cognitively Invested, as being class general.

ORGANIZATIONS OF PERSONALITY ACROSS THE LIFE-SPAN

Another way of studying personality over the life-span that more closely models the life progression of individual persons as it actually occurs is to determine the persistence or change in personality organization across time. Consider the following line of reasoning: Persons could be characterized throughout their life as possessing an attribute to a marked degree, but at certain times the quality may have different intrapsychic meanings and social impacts, depending on its context. For example, socially sensitive persons may seem empathic and warm when their context or life situation is nonproblematic and comfortable, but seem suspicious and over-reactive when they are stressed. Given the variety of normative and adventitious life stresses at various times in people's lives, different organizations may serve to accommodate different situations or different life circumstances at different points in time.

To uncover the organizations that the study members used at each of four time periods, I performed 16 "person" clusters (4 time periods × 4 samples); each included all six PARAFAC scores. These 16 cluster solutions each produced 4 clusters so that 64 personality organizations were identified with each having cluster scores for the six PARAFAC variables. These sets of 64 scores were then treated *as if* they represented 64 persons and were resubmitted to a second-order person clustering, which produced five main *supraordinate* clusters, each, again, having cluster scores on the six PARAFAC dimensions. The intercorrelations among these five clusters ranged from −.20 to −.25, with a median of .05. The contents of the clusters are shown in Table 2.4. Their names are based on the two most salient scores, whether high or low, and a hyphen is included to indicate positive linkage between two factor dimensions. On the basis of their membership in the first-order cluster, study members were assigned at each time period to the appropriate supraordinate cluster. Most participants clearly belonged at each time period to only one supraordinate cluster. A few participants (about 8%) had *mixed* assignments; that is, they belonged to two clusters. However, at middle adulthood, 20% were of mixed type, but 17 out of these 20 were women whose membership was split between Self-Confident–Cognitively Invested and Nurturant/Cognitively Invested. The implication is that cognitive investment in women is not invariably associated with self-confidence but is instead tempered by nurturance. The percentage of persons belonging to these organizations at the four time periods, with males and females separated is shown in the top of Figure 2.2. Because a few study members had high negative loadings on the main clusters, three additional clusters (and the mixed group) are also shown at the bottom of Figure 2.2. These included (1) Closed to Self–Not–Cognitively Invested, (2) Undercontrolled–Heterosexual, (3) Nurturant–Cognitively Invested.

The most striking general thrust shown by Figure 2.2 is that some organizations appear only at certain times in life and/or for only one sex. Open to Self-Cognitively Invested does not appear until adulthood. It is, therefore, a life achievement. Undercontrolled-Heterosexual occurs for only a few females and then only at late adolescence. In addition, Nurturant–Cognitively Invested is a purely female organization. In less dramatic contrast, males are more likely to be assigned to Self-Confident–Cognitively Invested at all time periods. The organization of a sizable portion of the females at late adolescence is Closed to Self-Emotionally Overcontrolled. Finally, the organization of a small group of males at earlier periods is Hostile-Not Cognitively Invested.

The previously described analysis of variables produced consistent findings—for instance, the males' significantly higher scores for Self-Confident, and the females' for Nurturant/Hostile and Open/Undercontrolled, Heterosexual. But the first analyses did not pinpoint these variables as especially characterizing particular subgroups at par-

TABLE 2.4

THE SUPRAORDINATE CLUSTERS WITH INDICATIONS OF THEIR SUBSTANTIVE MEANINGS

Cluster	Cluster score
A: Self-Confident, Cognitively Invested	
Cognitively Invested	63
Closed to Self	59
Hostile/Nurturant	52
Emotional Under/Overcontrol	50
Under/Overcontrolled, Heterosexual	44
Lacks Self-confidence	32
B: Overcontrolled, Heterosexual Closed to Self	
Closed to Self	60
Emotional Under/Overcontrol	58
Lacks Self-Confidence	56
Hostile/Nurturant	51
Cognitively Invested	45
Under/Overcontrolled, Heterosexual	30
C: Closed to Self Emotionally Overcontrolled	
Closed to Self	65
Lacks Self-Confidence	57
Cognitively Invested	55
Not Nurturant	44
Under/Overcontrolled, Heterosexual	44
Emotional Under/Overcontrol	35
D: Hostile, Not Cognitively Invested	
Hostile/Nurturant	70
Closed to Self	54
Lacks Self-Confidence	51
Under/Overcontrolled, Heterosexual	45
Emotional Under/Overcontrol	42
Cognitively Invested	40
E: Open to Self, Cognitively Invested	
Cognitively Invested	64
Lacks Self-Confidence	59
Hostile/Nurturant	54
Under/Overcontrolled, Heterosexual	45
Emotional Under/Overcontrol	42
Closed to Self	35

ticular points in time. Being analyses of the mean differences of repeated measures, they could not directly reflect the variations that occurred within particular subgroups at different time periods.

Close examination of Figure 2.2 also indicates that people apparently accommodate to passing life situations by periodically reorganizing their personalities. It suggests that very few people could have been members

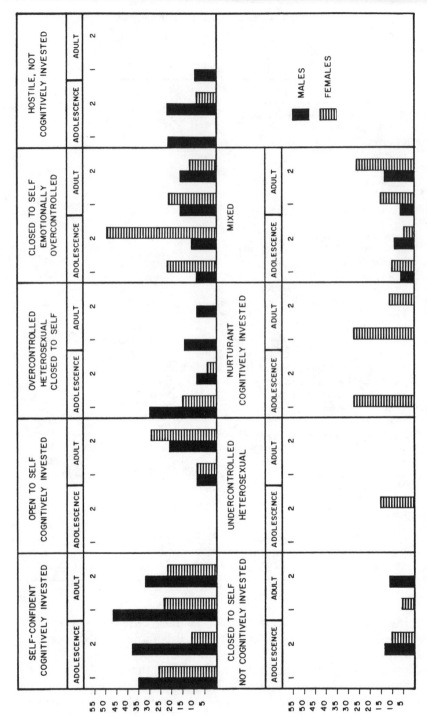

FIGURE 2.2 Percentage of males and females assigned to different personality organizations at each time period.

of the same organizational grouping for all time periods. This possibility runs counter to the theoretical assumption underlying an earlier work (Block in collaboration with Haan, 1971). The methodology employed then also resulted in organizations, which were called *typologies*. However, the source data were for only the early adolescence and early adulthood periods combined. In other words, that particular methodology tended to identify people who maintained the same organization in early adolescence as they did at early adulthood.

In the present analyses, the incidence of participants who used the same organization for all four time periods was only 9%; 9 of the 12 persons were males, 7 of whom were seen as Self-Confident–Cognitively Invested at all periods. When the criterion was relaxed in a count of the number of persons using the same organization for three periods instead of four, the incidence of stability rose to 35%. Again, proportionately more males were included—14 more who qualified as Self-Confident–Cognitively Invested and 6 women who qualified as Nurturant–Cognitively Invested. Unlike the men, all these females were not classified in this organization at the same point in time (late adolescence). Other additions to the number of persons using the same organization for three points in time were nine women and four men identified as Closed to Self–Emotionally Overcontrolled.

The main implication is that organizations of people's personalities shift from time to time, and when stability is maintained, cognitive investment is often a predominant theme. Examination of the possibility that organizations changed in certain sequences did not uncover such trends.

We may learn more by inquiring whether persons of certain previous organizations had certain outcomes at middle adulthood. This question was addressed by counting the number of shifts in organizational membership made by each person within three groups from one time period to the next: first for those who were identified at middle adulthood as Self-Confident–Cognitively Invested and those identified as Open to Self–Cognitively Invested. (Only three groups had sufficiently large membership to make these analyses worthwhile.) Comparison between these two groups controls for cognitive investment but compares the course of development for these two groups of adults who have reached effective but different states of personality at middle adulthood—either Self-Confident or Open to Self. A chi-square test of the distribution of shifts in organizational memberships (from 0 to a possible 3) showed a highly significant difference ($x^2 = 21.5$, $p < .001$), with the Open to Self group shifting the organization of their personalities much more frequently than the Self-Confident group ($x^2 = 2.6$ compared to 1.7). This difference suggests that being open to one's self at middle age requires earlier experimentation with one's self and perhaps exposure to a variety of experiences. I hypothesize (1) that the members of the Open to Self-Cognitively Invested group had experienced greater prior life stress than the Self-Confident–Cognitively Invested group and (2) that their previous experiences and their style of adapting may eventually make it possible for them to accommodate to aging with less difficulty.

Comparing these two groups with the apparently troubled Closed to Self–Emotionally Overcontrolled group showed that this latter organization is also very stable. Their number of shifts in personality organization was not significantly different than the Self-Confident group, they did shift significantly less than did the Open to Self group ($\chi^2 = 16.46$, $p < .001$). Therefore, middle-aged people of one kind of effective middle adulthood organization and one kind of ineffective organization had histories of greater stability, but middle-aged persons whose effective organization was typified by their openness to self had a history of change.

DISCUSSION

Basic Personality

At the beginning of this essay I suggested that analysis of data spanning 35 years might help us discover the fundamental aspects of personality that develop over the life-span. These results probably do not accomplish that end, although they seem to indicate that cognitive investment, uses of self as a psychological and sexual being, being confident, and having caring or hostile relations with others are developmental. These findings depart only slightly from common sense formulations of development. Although the first study of variables described these systematic developments, the analyses of organizations clearly showed that various subgroups take unsystematic "side trips" at different points in time. I do not think we will understand these side trips, nor will we uncover the general developmental course, until we have adequate decriptions of how people assimilate and accommodate to the inevitable events of the life course and to the adventitious experiences that typify most lives. These studies were limited, because the life experiences of these people at various points in time—which surely represented a vast and differentiating array—was only inferred rather than known and analyzed.

As the results for the study of variables now stand, they seem to portray the general way that the active and interactive self progressively changes its functions from adolescence to the adult years: increasingly relying on the efficacy of cognitive accommodations, progressively utilizing the self's own reactions as pertinent and valuable information, and attending more to the needs of others and growing in confidence that the self is a satisfactory being. This positively linear expression of the effects of living on personality is qualified, however, in three ways: (1) Direct sexual expressiveness reached its peak in adolescence for the women, then receded and later reappeared, less saliently and undoubtedly in some transformed way, at the middle years. The highly ambitious OGS men and the often-divorced GS men also showed some recrudescence in their sexual interest at the middle years after being remarkably uninterested in sex, compared to the women, at adolescence. (2) The fight–flight dimension, Emotionally Under/Overcontrolled, accounted for a sufficient amount of and variance the PARAFAC method identified it as common for the four time periods; but further analysis showed that it was not developmental, a finding that is instructive for life-span research. Its presence at all times, unimpressive stability, lack of developmental meaning, and substantive representation of two general ways to deal with stress remind up that the "subjects" of life-span research do not live laboratory-controlled lives. Consequently, their adventitious—not developmentally expected—experiences will cloud our understanding of developmental curves. (3) Across time, the self-reflective dimension, Open/Closed to Self, became an efficient means of sorting members of all four samples into two categories: those who became progressively more open and those who became progressively more closed to their own inner experience. Two hypotheses are suggested: that different concatenations of both life course and adventitious events accounted for this bifurcation, and that this trend will become even more striking and meaningful as these people engage the unbidden, irrevocable, and therefore stressful, experience of becoming aged.

The variables used in these analyses represent a potpourri of personality contents. Their organization by PARAFAC into personality dimensions produced sectors of meaningful organizations that represent the participants' cognitive and social (Nurturant/Hostile) orientations, styles of sexual expressiveness, and self-reflexiveness (Open/Closed; Confident/Fearful). Plainly there is nothing very surprising about these age-common factors. That the trends for these variables generally moved toward a standard of high effectiveness by the middle years is interesting. For a better understanding of these life-span results to be achieved, measures of life experiences must be brought into the account. If people are regarded as centers of cognizant transaction, then some mark on their personalities must be left from the ways they processed their experience with life course events, adventitious events, and the particular circumstances of both these kinds of events. In other words, I am suggesting that life-span research can hardly proceed without better understandings of life stress and facilitation.

The analyses of personality organizations produced three quite different subgroups that can be characterized as successful. All included cognitive investment as a salient characteristic, but this commitment is flavored differently in each case—with self-confidence, nurturance, or openness to self. This pattern of findings in itself indicates the error of basing definitions of mental health on one index.

Five subgroups of ineffective organization were also identified: two involved constructions that typified subgroups especially during adolescence—for males, Overcontrolled, Heterosexual–Closed to Self, and for females, Closed to Self–Emotionally Overcontrolled. Two organizations involved an inflated "acting-out": Hostile–Not Cognitively Invested, especially for males at earlier periods, and Undercontrolled, Heterosexual for females at late adolescence. The fifth ineffective organization is Closed to Self–Not Cognitively Invested, which was neither period nor sex specific. These groups could not have been identified without the organizational analyses, and their very existence leads to the question of why these people took these temporary side trips. The explanation may be provided by the investigation of people's adventitious experiences. Please note that the course of people's life-span experiences is not the same as their early or late experiences; both these are included along with those events experienced in transit from early to later life.

INVESTIGATORS' PRECONCEPTIONS AND LIFE-SPAN DESCRIPTION

Different ways of viewing subjects and, in consequence, different designs and procedures of data collection, determine results. Important differences exist between retrospective interview data or personality inventories on the one hand, and the procedures used at the Institute of Human Development on the other. The Q-sorts are a formalization of clinicians' observations, and evaluations of the participants' processes of self-presentations and self-reporting; they are not self-reports per se. Participants' self-reports and descriptions are taken into account, but clinical judges do not translate self-reports directly and naively into item scores. Subjects' readiness to deceive themselves, their willingness to cooperate and be led by investigators' questions means that their self-descriptions, presently or retrospectively constructed, cannot be taken at face value.

Moreover, the Q-sorts for each time period were independent of all other periods, so neither the clinicians' preconceptions about development nor the participants' retrospective opinions about the drama of their own life course could determine the nature of the results. No clinician evaluated the same study member at two different time periods nor did they have access to information about the study members' past histories and evaluations. Had the clinicians wished to characterize the life-span in a certain way, they could not have achieved this goal. So far, I argue, we have no more direct way of capturing the complexity of personalities than Q-sorting and no better way of describing life change and stability in personality than independent observations at each time period. The dynamic convolutions of human functioning can only be reasonably captured by equally complex human minds.

Nevertheless, the present research does not address the most fundamental question of development (i.e., the dialectical interplay between self-conservation and the person's interest in changing in reaction to his new assimilations of the meanings of life events and his subsequent accommodations).

SUGGESTIONS FOR STUDYING PERSONALITY ACROSS THE LIFE-SPAN

1. The fundamental variables have to be more abstract than the ones used here, and they have to be age-impartial, that is, potentially observable at all ages.

2. Methods of reducing and analyzing these observations should also be age-impartial.

3. Adults as well as children can be expected to undergo impressive changes as they interact with the progression of their lives, so life events need to be brought into the account.

4. Self-reports probably do not provide a reliable base for building a general developmental theory, given each person's understandable interest in his own life drama and the irreducible and inevitable stresses and strains of all lives.

5. Developmental changes need to be "found" empirically between independent, time-separated observations; our personal biases about how development should proceed make it too hazardous to attempt to measure change directly, especially retrospectively.

6. Judging by the present study, life-span variables that are either

patho-centric or child-centric do not yield sufficient understanding of the accruing strengths that seem to typify development from early adolescence to the middle years.

7. Cross-time analyses of both variables and people provide different kinds of information and allow different kinds of questions to be addressed.

REFERENCES

Baltes, P. B., & Schaie, K. W. (Eds.). *Life-span developmental psychology: Personality and socialization*. New York: Academic Press, 1973.

Block, J. *The Q-sort method in personality assessment and psychiatric research*. Springfield, IL: Thomas, 1961.

Block, J., in collaboration with Haan, N. *Lives through time*. Berkeley, CA: Bancroft Books, 1971.

Bock, R. *Multivariate statistical methods in behavioral research*. New York: McGraw-Hill, 1975.

Brooks, J. Social maturity in middle age and its developmental antecedents. In D. H. Eichorn, J. A. Clausen, N. Haan, M. P. Honzik, & P. Mussen (Eds.), *Present and past in middle life*. New York: Academic Press, 1982.

Eichorn, D. H., Clausen, J. A., Haan, N., Honzik, M. P., & Mussen, P. (Eds.). *Present and past in middle life*. New York: Academic Press, 1982.

Haan, N., & Day, D. Change and sameness in personality development: Adolescence to adulthood. *International Journal of Aging and Human Development*, 1974, 5, 11–39.

Haan, N. " . . . Change and sameness . . . " reconsidered. *International Journal of Aging and Human Development*, 1976, 7, 59–65.

Haan, N. *Coping and defending: Processes of self-environment organization*. New York: Academic Press, 1977.

Harshman, R., & Berenbaum, S. *PARAFAC–CANDECOMP three-way factor analysis of longitudinal data: Theory and empirical examples*. Paper presented at the annual meeting of the Psychometric Society, Murray Hill, NJ, April 1976.

McCall, R., & Appelbaum, M. Bias in the analysis of repeated-measure designs: Some alternative approaches. *Child Development*, 1973, 44, 401–415.

McNemar, Q. *Psychological statistics* (4th ed). New York: Wiley, 1969.

3

EARLY ADULT ANTECEDENTS OF LIFE SATISFACTION AT AGE 70*

Paul Mussen

INTRODUCTION

As interest in adaptation to aging has increased, more attention is being paid to the concept of life satisfaction and to factors underlying satisfaction or dissatisfaction (see, e.g., Edwards & Klemmack, 1973; Neugarten, Havighurst, & Tobin, 1961; Palmore & Kivett, 1977; Palmore & Luikert, 1972; Spreitzer & Snyder, 1974). With few exceptions (e.g., Palmore & Kivett, 1977), the relevant research has been cross-sectional, focusing primarily on contemporaneous social and health variables associated with life satisfaction in the later years. The findings of a number of studies are consistent in indicating that, among older individuals, current good health and secure socioeconomic standing as well as relatively high levels of sexual and social activity are associated with stronger feelings of satisfaction (Palmore & Kivett, 1977; Palmore & Luikert, 1972; Spreitzer & Snyder, 1974). For example, among mothers of participants in the Guidance and Berkeley Growth studies, those who at about 70 were anxious and *disengaging*—who had lost interest in social activity and were distant from others—scored low in life satisfaction, whereas group-oriented women received higher ratings on life satisfaction (Maas & Kuypers, 1974).

To understand the development of degrees of life satisfaction in the later years, we need more information about its earlier antecedents. Can we identify personal attributes of young persons that are predictive of

*This research was supported by Grant HD 03617 from the U.S. Public Health Service. Requests for reprints should be addressed to the first author at: University of California, Institute of Human Development, 1203 Tolman Hall, Berkeley, CA, 94720.

later life satisfaction? This question is, of course, closely related to a major issue in the psychology of personality—the issue of whether or not personal characteristics tend to persist over long periods of time. We (Mussen, Eichorn, Honzik, Bieber, & Meredith, 1980), as well as others (see Moss & Susman, 1980), have reported evidence for such consistency over time. Therefore, we hypothesize that individuals who are happy, emotionally stable, and of high ego strength as young adults are more likely to be contented and well adjusted during their later years.

A test of this hypothesis requires longitudinal data on a broad spectrum of social, personality, and cognitive characteristics. Fortunately, data pertinent to the issue are available in the archives of the Guidance Study (GS), one of three long-term longitudinal studies conducted at the Institute of Human Development at the University of California, Berkeley. In 1930 and 1931, parents of the members of the GS were interviewed and rated on a variety of social, personal, interpersonal, and family characteristics (Macfarlane, 1938). About 40 years later, when the surviving parents were about 70, they were interviewed and rated again. In addition, at the later time, each parent was assigned a Life Satisfaction Rating (LSR) (Neugarten, Havighurst, & Tobin, 1961). Hence, we can examine the extent to which satisfaction in later life can be predicted from such characteristics in early adulthood. The results of these analyses are presented here.

METHODS

EARLY ADULT ASSESSMENTS

When the participants in the Guidance Study were 21 months old, their parents were interviewed about their child, marriage, and family. The mothers were, on the average, 30 years old; the fathers' average age was 33.5. Two interviews were conducted with each parent. The first was done in the home by one of the two psychiatric social workers, who interviewed the parents about the child and made observations of parent–child relationships. Shortly thereafter, Jean Macfarlane, Director of the GS and a highly sensitive clinician, held intensive interviews about their marital and family relationships with each parent separately in her office at the Institute.

Two kinds of evaluation of the parents were made independently by each interviewer. The first consisted of rating scales of 21 mothers' characteristics (fathers were not rated on these variables at this time). Each scale had 7 points and included descriptions at the extreme and midpoints. For example, a rating of 1 for energy output was described as "tremendous output of energy, overactive;" the midpoint (rating of 4) was described as "average;" and a rating of 7 was described as "extremely sluggish." All 21 of these characteristics were rated for mothers of the Guidance subgroup, and 12 of them were rated for mothers of the carefully matched Control group.

Interrater correlations from these ratings are a more stringent test of agreement than are conventional reliability correlations, because the raters based their judgments on observations in different situations. Therefore we used .40, rather than a higher intercorrelation, as the "cut-off" for ratings to be omitted because of low reliability. On this basis, three characteristics—tendency to criticize, tendency to criticize child, and interest in child (all of which particularly reflect the difference in situation and interview topics)—were dropped from our analyses. The measures of the 18 characteristics we retained were derived by averaging the two independent ratings. These characteristics and their interrater correlations are listed in the second and third columns of Table 3.1.[1]

In addition, our previous study included a Stationary Factor Analysis (SFA) of the 21 maternal characteristics rated for the 53 mothers of the Guidance subgroup. This longitudinal factor analysis identified three factors present both at age 30 and 70, two factors unique to age 30, and three factors unique to age 70. To increase the power of our present analyses, we included the 28 control mothers interviewed and rated at both 30 and 70. Because they were rated on only 12 of the 21 characteristics, factor scores for the total group of 81 mothers could not be computed. However, in Table 3.1 the characteristics are grouped as nearly as possible according to the factor structure revealed by the SFA. The factors on which the characteristics load are indicated by roman numerals; a minus sign preceding the numeral indicates a negative loading. Several variables had substantial loadings on more than one factor. Where the primary loading was on one factor and a lesser, but substantial, loading occurred on another factor, the secondary loading is listed in parentheses. If the loadings were of almost equal magnitude, they are listed in order of magnitude but without parentheses.

[1]The correlations presented in these tables have not been corrected for attenuation, that is, for unreliability of the measures, because the reliability coefficients reported were calculated by correlating independent ratings made on very different bases (see text). This method probably yielded lower reliability correlations than would have been obtained in the usual way, that is, if both raters based their scores on the same set of observations. Using these reduced reliability coefficients in correcting for attenuation would undoubtedly lead to an overestimation of the true correlations between the early ratings and LSR at age 70.

TABLE 3.1

CORRELATIONS BETWEEN LIFE SATISFACTION RATINGS AT 70
AND MOTHERS' CHARACTERISTICS AT 30

Factor membership	Characteristics at 30[a]	Interrater correlation at 30	Correlation with life satisfaction at 70	Partial correlations (SES partialled out)
V, (I)	Use of Language	.74	.28**	.05
V, (I)	Intellligence	.68	.33**	.13
I, V, III	Speed of Mental Processes[b]	.46	.21	.10
I	Mental Alertness	.57	.45***	.40***
I	Accuracy in Thinking[b]	.63	.15	
I	Open-Mindedness[b]	.63	.11	
I, IV	Frankness in Discussion[b]	.61	.04	
−II	Worrisomeness	.47	−.22*	−.24*
II	Satisfaction with Lot[b]	.60	.30*	.34*
II	Self-Esteem[b]	.43	.22	.22
II	Freshness (not fatigued)[b]	.50	.34*	.31*
II, III	Cheerfulness	.59	.39***	.46***
III	Excitabililty	.55	.02	
III	Energy Output[b]	.52	.05	
−III	Self-Assurance, Poise	.53	.31**	.32**
III	Restlessness	.52	.02	
III, IV	Talkativeness	.63	.15	
IV	Personal Appearance	.58	.23*	.07

[a]1 = low; 7 = high.
[b]Rated for Guidance subgroup only, so $n = 53$; n for all other r's = 81.

*$p < .05$.
**$p < .01$.
***$p < .001$.

A second type of assessment, the Early Family Ratings, was also made independently from the early adult interviews by Macfarlane and the psychiatric social workers. Those ratings were done only for mothers and fathers of the Guidance subgroup. They were 5-point ratings, with descriptions of all points of the scale. The final ratings on each of the 63 items listed in Table 3.2 are essentially conference ratings or weighted averages. "On the whole, Macfarlane's rating was given a heavier weighting on the marital situation, which her interviews covered, but

TABLE 3.2

CORRELATIONS BETWEEN EARLY FAMILY RATINGS (1930)[a] AND MOTHERS'
AND FATHERS' LIFE SATISFACTION AT 70

Early family ratings[a]	Mother		Father
	r_{12} ($n = 53$)	$r_{12}{}^b$ ($n = 53$)	r_{13} ($n = 25$)
Health			
Health of mother	.36**	.32*	.48**
Health of father	.08		.37*
Physical stamina of mother	.11		.39*
Physical stamina of father	.00		.44*
Nervous stability of mother	.07		.58**
Nervous stability of father	−.02		.40*
Nervous stability of parents	.03		.60**
Concern about health: mother	−.12		.35*
Concern about health: father	.31*	.24*	−.33*
Education			
Mothers' concern about education	.05		−.21
Fathers' concern about education	.06		−.24
Similarity of educational values	.06		.02
Income and occupation			
Adequacy of income	.43***	.30*	.15
Agreement on expenditures	.20	.24*	.25
Shared management of income	.26*	.15	.03
Satisfaction with fathers' occupation: mother	.22	.04	.26
Satisfaction with fathers' occupation: father	.06		.47**
Mother's adjustment to her work	.22	.21	.21
Amount of help in housework	.19	−.11	−.28
Home, leisure time, and recreation			
Pride in home: mother	.06		.16
Pride in home: father	−.06		.12
Amount of leisure time: mother	.34**	.23*	.10
Amount of leisure time: father	.21*	.11	.06
Similarity of recreational interests	.22*	.29*	.19
Adequacy of play facilities in the home	.30*	.18	.08
Family compatibility			
Marital adjustment	.27*	.31*	.32
Close bond: mother to father	.03		−.03
Close bond: mother to child	−.01		.10
Close bond: father to mother	.27*	.26*	.04
Close bond: father to child	−.18	−.07	−.13
Friendliness of mother to father	.36**	.40***	.33**
Friendliness of mother to child	.18*	.26*	.28
Friendliness of father to mother	.27*	.36*	.16
Friendliness of father to child	−.14		−.03
Expressive of affection: mother	.03		−.11

(Continued)

TABLE 3.2 (*Continued*)

Early family ratings[a]	Mother r_{12} ($n = 53$)	Mother $r_{12}{}^b$ ($n = 53$)	Father r_{13} ($n = 25$)
Expressive of affection: father	−.04		−.11
Sexual adjustment	.19	.24*	.32
Favors having more children: mother	.01		−.05
Favors having more children: father	.02		.17
Parental characteristics			
Irritability of mother	−.11		−.38*
Irritability of father	−.14		.12
Energy level of mother	.05		−.14
Energy level of father	.08		.54**
Tense or worrisome: mother	−.18	−.21	−.48
Tense or worrisome: father	.10		−.20
Withdraws from conflict: mother	.01		−.11
Withdraws from conflict: father	.25*	.18	−.22
Social adjustment of mother	.17	.05	.04
Social adjustment of father	−.05		.21
Self-confidence of mother	.32**	.33**	.44*
Self-confidence of father	−.10		.47**
Sense of privacy (versus sharing): mother	.05		.25
Sense of privacy (versus sharing): father	.14		−.08
Mother even tempered	.14		−.54**
Father even tempered	.01		.19
Areas of parental conflict			
Conflict with relatives	−.11		−.56**
Conflict over cultural standards	−.40**	−.41**	−.14
Conflict over religion	−.19	.19	−.13
Conflict over recreation: mother	−.32**	−.39**	−.34*
Conflict over recreation: father	−.08		−.27
Conflict over size and management of income	−.17	−.22	−.42*
Conflict over standards of neatness	−.10		.36*
Conflict over discipline of children	−.26*	−.35**	.00

[a]For ease of presentation and interpretation all family variables in the correlations were rated the same way: from 1 = low to 5 = high. For example, high scores in agreement or conflict indicate strong agreement or great conflict between Mother and Father; high ratings in stamina mean the individual had great endurance. This rating system necessitated reversing the original direction of some of the scales.
[b]Partial correlations—SES partialled out.
 *$p < .05$.
 **$p < .01$.
 ***$p < .001$.

[the other raters'] ratings were given a heavier weighting on parent–child relationships since they had more opportunity to observe these relationships" (Macfarlane, 1938, p. 110).

Even casual inspection of Table 3.2 suggests that not all of these 63 variables are independent. Therefore, a principal component analysis of the covariance matrix of these early family ratings was performed. In addition, a Tryon cluster analysis (Tryon, 1955) was available in the GS archive. The clusters and components are listed in Tables 3.3 and 3.4, respectively.

The socioeconomic status (SES) of the GS families was assessed periodically. For example, when the participants were about 1 month old, a social economist conducted detailed socioeconomic interviews with the parents in their homes and observed and rated the dwelling and neighborhood; subsequent SES data was obtained from interviews with the parents, either at the Institute or in the home. Because SES may be expected to influence life satisfaction, correlations were computed between LSR and SES, as indexed by Warner ratings (Warner, Meeker, & Eels, 1949): a composite score based upon occupation, source of income, dwelling, and neighborhood. SES could then be partialled out of correlations between LSR and mothers' characteristics or early family ratings when necessary.

LATER ASSESSMENTS

Between 38 and 40 years after the first ratings were completed—that is, between 1968 and 1970—many of the surviving parents were inten-

TABLE 3.3

CORRELATIONS BETWEEN LIFE SATISFACTION AT 70 AND TRYON CLUSTER SCORES BASED ON THE EARLY FAMILY RATINGS

Cluster	Mother	Father
Marital adjustment	.30*	.33*
Job satisfaction	.29*	.39*
Tendency to withdraw: father	.08	−.06
Tendency to withdraw: mother	−.06	.14
Placid mother	.14	.54**
Strength: father	.06	.53**
Parental conflict with child	.04	−.08
Even-tempered: father	.01	.19

*$p < .05$.
**$p < .01$.

TABLE 3.4

CORRELATIONS OF LIFE SATISFACTION RATINGS AT 70 WITH SCORES
ON PRINCIPAL COMPONENTS DERIVED FROM EARLY FAMILY RATINGS

Component	Mother	Father
I. Good marital adjustment; close, friendly relationship between the parents; good sex adjustment; little conflict over recreation and disclipine of children	+.22	−.08
II. Mother emotionally stable, not tense or worrisome, expresses affection	.09	.70***
III. Both parents satisfied with father's occupation, adequate income, and leisure time for mother	.37**	.24
IV. Father emotionally stable, not worrisome or tense, with good physical stamina	−.15	.43*
V. Father expresses affection, is a private person, withdraws from conflict	−.05	.22
Multiple R	.47	.90

*$p < .05$.
**$p < .01$.
***$p < .001$.

sively interviewed in their homes. Included were 53 mothers and 25 fathers of the Guidance subgroup and 28 mothers of the Control subgroup. At that time, the mothers were, on the average, 69 years old, and the fathers were 72. The interviewers had not known these parents previously and had no information about them or about how they were rated 40 years earlier.

After the interviews were completed, the interviewers followed standard instructions in rating each participant on the five characteristics that together comprise the widely used global LSRs of Neugarten, et al., (1961): zest versus apathy, resolution and fortitude, congruence between desired and achieved goals, self-concepts (from "feels at his best" to "feels worthless"), and mood tone (ranging from "happy, optimistic attitudes and mood" to "pessimistic," "complaining" and "bitter feelings").

Another staff member, also a trained clinician, read the interview protocols carefully, and from this basis, also made the LSR for each elderly parent using the same instructions. The uncorrected correlations between the two independent global LSRs, that is, the interrater reliabilities, were .73 for the mothers and .72 for the fathers. The LSRs that constitute the dependent variable in this study are the averages of the composited global ratings assigned by the interviewer and the second rater.

RESULTS

MOTHERS' COGNITIVE AND
PERSONALITY–SOCIAL CHARACTERISTICS

Correlations between the 21 characteristics on which mothers were rated at about age 30 and LSRs approximately 40 years later are listed in the fourth column of Table 3.1. Nine of the 18 correlations, corrected neither for attenuation nor for association with SES, are significant at the .05 level or better. Despite the general hypothesis stated in our introduction (i.e., that "individuals who are happy, emotionally stable, and of high ego strength as young adults are more likely to be contented and well-adjusted during their later years"), we have used the more conservative two-tail test for all correlations reported in this essay, because we did not make separate predictions for each variable examined.

As would be expected from the literature, SES is moderately and significantly correlated with the ratings of Intelligence and Use of Language but is less closely associated with the other three ratings of cognitive functioning. Of the 13 personality–social variables, only Personal Appearance is significantly correlated with SES; all other correlations with SES are negligible, the majority being of the order of ±.04. For mothers, SES, as indexed by the Warner ratings, is also significantly correlated with LSR (.35, $p < .01$). This correlation is reduced to .18 (not significant) if the rating of Intelligence is partialled out.

The last column of Table 3.1 presents the partial correlations (SES partialled out) for the mothers' characteristics at age 30 that have significant first-order correlations with LSR at 70. With this correction, 6 of the 18 characteristics at 30 remain significantly predictive of LSR at 70. Mothers who scored high on LSR at 70 had in early adulthood been Mentally Alert ("keenly responsive" rather than "remote, detached") and Cheerful, Satisfied with their lot. They had Self-Assurance, Poise and did not appear Fatigued, Self-Conscious or anxious (high scores on *Worrisome* indicate a constant undertone of anxiety and low scores, no worries or being light-hearted in spite of cause for worry). As can be seen in Table 3.1, four of these six significant predictors load on Factor II derived from the stationary factor analysis (SFA) of mothers' characteristics (see brief description above and Mussen, et al., 1980), namely, Worrisome (negatively loaded), Satisfaction with Lot (the two primary definers of Factor II), and *Cheerful, Freshness* (not fatigued). The fifth significant predictor, *Self-Assurance, Poise* was negatively loaded on Factor III, which reflected tempo and temperament (primarily defined by Excitability and Energy Output and secondarily by Self-Assurance, Talkativeness, and Restlessness). Mentally Alert, the sixth significant predictor, is primarily identified with Factor I, which seemed in the SFA to represent cognitive style (the highest loadings were, in order, for Open-Mindedness, Accuracy in Thinking, and Frankness in Discussion), and secondarily with Factor V, an intelligence factor (the highest loadings were for Use of Language and Intelligence).

In the present analysis the combination of these six characteristics presents a picture of a satisfied woman at 70 as one who had in her early 30s a positive, buoyant, and responsive attitude toward life. The fact that Intelligence and SES are significant predictors of LSR at 70 only in combination (neither is significant with the other partialled out) indicates that if a woman had both superior intelligence and economic advantages at 30 she was more likely to be satisfied with life in her later years.

EARLY FAMILY RATINGS ON MOTHERS AND FATHERS

Unlike the finding for mothers, men's LSR at 70 were not significantly correlated with Warner ratings of SES ($r = -.17$). This sex difference in association of LSR and SES is supported by a similar contrast for the correlations of LSR at 70 and Adequacy of Income at 30 (see Table 3.2). This correlation is .15 (not significant) for men, but for women the correlation is .30 ($p < .05$) when Warner SES is partialled out. Hence, partial correlations were computed only for mothers' Early Family Ratings for which the first-order correlation with LSR was significant or approached significance ($p < .10$). Because the correlations of SES with most of these ratings for mothers are low, the level and significance of the associations with LSR changes very little (see columns 2 and 3 of Table 3.2).

Individual Variables

Of the 63 ratings in early adulthood, 32 are significantly correlated with LSR at 70, 25 variables show significant first-order correlations for fathers, and 16 have significant partial correlations for mothers. Relatively few of the significant correlates are common to both sexes.

A number of the fathers' own characteristics at about 30, as well as characteristics of their wives and marital situations are predictive factors. Men rated high on life-satisfaction at 70 were, in their early 30s, likely to be described as healthy but not preoccupied with their health, of good physical stamina, emotionally stable, energetic, self-confident, satisfied with their jobs, and as having a strong sense of privacy. Their wives tended to be healthy, concerned about their health, self-confident, even-tempered, and not tense or worrisome. They and their spouses had little conflict with relatives or over standards of neatness, the size and management of the family income, or the mother's recreation.

In contrast to the findings for men, few of the women's own characteristics at 30 or those of their husbands are predictive of the mothers' LSR at 70. Rather, most of the significant correlates for women are aspects of the home and marital situation. As for the men, good health and self-confidence in early adulthood are associated with higher LSR at 70. The husband's concern about health is also a significant predictor for women, but in the opposite direction from the association in men. That is, the husband's lack of preoccupation with his health in early adulthood is significantly predictive with his later life satisfaction, whereas the later life satisfaction of the wife is significantly associated with her husband's concern about his health. Each spouse's concern for their own health at 30 is a significant predictor of the other spouse's LSR at 70.

Thirteen of the 16 significant predictors for women describe their experiences and behavior within the family context at 30: adequacy of income; amount of leisure time; sexual adjustment; marital adjustment (adjustment to each other); the friendliness (as opposed to hostility) of the mother toward her husband and child; the friendliness of the husband toward the wife; the closeness of his bond to her (whether friendly or hostile); and agreement of the spouses on expenditures, recreational interests and recreation for the mother, cultural standards, and discipline of the children. Of these 13 items only the friendliness of the wife toward the husband and lack of conflict over the wife's recreation are also significant predictors for men. However, for several variables the correlations for fathers are of about the same magnitude as those for mothers but are not significant, probably because of the smaller size of the male sample. These possibly shared varibles include sexual and marital adjustment, friendliness of mother to child, agreement on expenditures, and, perhaps, similarity of recreational interests.

Tyron Cluster Scores

The interpretation that aspects of Marital Adjustment are important predictors for both men and women is supported by the significant and

approximately equal correlations of this cluster score in early adulthood
with LSR at 70 (see Table 3.3). This cluster includes sexual adjustment,
adjustment to each other, friendliness of mother to father and friendliness of father to mother. The other cluster score that is significantly correlated with LSR at 70 for both sexes is *Job Satisfaction*, which includes
adequacy of income as well as each spouse's satisfaction with the father's job. The correlations for these individual variables, cited above, suggest that the three variables are differently weighted for men and
women.

As would be expected from the sex difference in the pattern of correlations between individual variables at early adulthood and LSR at 70,
two other clusters reflecting personal characteristics of the mother and
father are highly significant predictors for men but not for women. The
cluster labelled *Placid Mother* includes the mother's emotional stability,
concern about her health, and tenseness (the last two variables are negatively weighted). All three are variables for which the individual correlations are also significantly predictive for fathers but not for mothers.
Included in the cluster labelled Strength-Father are his health, physical
stamina, and energy level. Again, all three variables are significant individual predictors of later LSR for men, but only health is a significant
correlate for women.

Principal Components Analysis

As noted in the Methods section, a principal component analysis of
the covariance matrix of the Early Family Ratings was performed to reduce the 63 variables to a smaller number of underlying dimensions.
The first two components correlated significantly ($p < .05$) with LSR at
70 for the mothers, while components 1, 4, and 5 correlated significantly
($p < .01$) with LSR at 70 for the fathers. Because the next three components extracted were not significantly correlated with LSR for either
sex, the first five components (accounting for 52% of the total variance)
were rotated by a varimax rotation to obtain a clearer picture of the associations between LSR at 70 and the set of family ratings at 30. Table
3.4 presents the results.

Of the five rotated components, two are significantly correlated with
LSR at 70 for men, and a third is a significant correlate for women. As
in the Tyron cluster analysis and our interpretation of the individual
variables, characteristics of the wife at 30, as well as the father's own
early adult characteristics, emerge as significantly predictive components for men. The variables defining these components are also similar
to those involved in the clusters—the wife's emotional stability, lack of

tension, and her expression of affection toward the husband; and the father's own emotional stability, physical stamina and, lack of tension.

Again, components reflecting their own or their husbands' characteristics were not predictive for women. Instead, the only significant correlate of LSR at 70 for women is a component reflecting, at age 30, both parents' satisfaction with the father's occupation, amount of their leisure time, and adequacy of their income. Among the individual variables, as well as in the cluster analysis, job satisfaction was also a significant predictor for men. Component III, which includes job satisfaction for men, is positively correlated with LSR at 70 for fathers ($r = .24$), but the correlation does not reach significance, perhaps because the other variables represented in this component are not significant individual predictors for men and/or because a higher level of correlation is required for significance in the small male sample.

In the cluster analysis, Marital Adjustment in early adulthood is a significant predictor of LSR at 70 for both sexes. Before rotation, Component I (Marital Adjustment) was also significantly correlated with LSR for both men and women. However, after the forcing produced by rotation, this component approaches significance only for women ($p < .08$). Aspects of marital adjustment for males seem to have been absorbed by the wives' characteristics that would be expected to contribute to marital adjustment (e.g., emotional stability and her expression of affection toward the husband).

The multiple Rs for the components demonstrate what may also be inferred from the sex difference in the number and level of correlations between components and LSR, namely, that life satisfaction at 70 is better predicted from the variables included in the Early Family Ratings for men than for women. The multiple R is .90 for men and .47 for women, a difference that is significant at the .05 level, conservatively estimated. Of particular interest is the fact that a major proportion of the unusually high multiple R for men is accounted for by the strong association between men's LSR at 70 and their wives' personalities at 30.

DISCUSSION

In the main, the correlations of cluster and component scores derived from the Early Family Ratings with LSR at about 70 are consistent with the pattern of correlations for the individual variables. The differences, like those between the correlations for clusters and components, are mainly in emphasis. As would be expected from the differences in statistical methodologies, the Tryon cluster scores and the individual variables yield highly similar results, whereas rotation forces the components in a way that sharpens the results for the strongest predictors but, in the process, reduces the variance associated with the marital adjustment component, especially for men.

As judged from correlations with the Early Family Ratings, particularly after reduction to a limited number of dimensions through cluster or component analysis, men's satisfaction in later life is most powerfully predicted by a group of their own and their wives' traits reflecting a relaxed, emotionally stable personality that is supported, at least for the men themselves, by good physical condition. Women's later life satisfaction, on the other hand, seems, on the basis of the Early Family Ratings, to be more strongly influenced by qualities of the early marital relationship and other life circumstances (such as adequate income and leisure time), than by their own or their husbands' traits.

To conclude, however, that the early marital relationship is of no long-term consequence to men, and that women's personal characteristics when young adults have no important bearing on their later adjustment, would be an overstatement. We have already noted that a marital adjustment cluster, as well as a number of individual variables reflecting aspects of marital compatibility, are significant for men and that the principal component anaylsis produced a marital adjustment cluster significant for both sexes, but it was reduced to insignificance by rotation. Further, the wives' characteristics that are predictive for men are ones that make for a comfortable interpersonal relationship—emotional stability, lack of tension, and expression of affection for the husband.

As shown by our first analysis, based on ratings done at 30 only for mothers, a group of women's traits at 30 are predictive of their life satisfaction at 70. These ratings indicate that women who at 30 were mentally alert, cheerful, satisfied with their lot, self-confident, and neither worrisome nor fatigued were at 70 more likely to rate high on life satisfaction. Self-confidence in women from the Early Family Ratings is also significantly predictive of LSR at 70, and the level of the correlation with LSR for Worrisome is almost identical in the two sets of ratings for mothers but is not significant in the second analysis because the sample is smaller (Guidance subgroup only). The other four Mothers' Characteristics that are significant predictors of LSR for women are not represented in the Early Family Ratings.

For both sexes, then, certain of their own traits at 30 are predictive of later life satisfaction, although most of these characteristics are not the same for fathers and mothers. A buoyant, positive, responsive attitude toward life is predictive for women and good emotional and physical health for men.

Good physical condition should also not be dismissed as a predictor for women. Good health was a significant individual predictor among the Early Family Ratings for women, and not being worn out or fatigued at 30 was a significant predictor among the characteristics rated only for mothers. The inference of the long-term importance of health for both sexes is underscored by a quite different sort of analysis (Maas & Kuypers, 1974) for a larger group that included not only the GS parents in our sample but also parents of members of the Berkeley Growth Study, who are of the same birth cohort as the GS parents. Mothers and fathers were separately grouped into two sorts of typologies: one based upon their life styles at age 70 and the other upon Q-sort descriptions of their personalities. Both sets of data were derived from interviews with the parents at 70, but the codings for life style and personality were done independently by different sets of raters. "In all four of the mothers' personality Q-groups, health measures showed up with significant associations," and "Regarding life styles, "negative" health strongly differentiated both the disabled–disengaging mothers and the unwell–disengaged fathers from the other parents" (Maas & Kuypers, 1974, p. 207). Further, "health problems in old age" were "clearly foreshadowed in the early-adult years."

Also relevant to the interpretation of our results are two other major conclusions from the Maas and Kuypers study. First, continuities in personality from early adulthood to about age 70 were "more apparent for mothers than fathers, and most apparent for those mothers whose aging personality Q-groups evidence symptoms of low adaptive capacities" (p. 203) and tend toward anxiety, depression, self-doubt, interpersonal conflict, and ego disorganization. Note that in our component analysis the correlation of the fathers' own characteristics at about 30 with his later LSR is .43. Several of the traits rated under Mothers' Characteristics at 30 have significant correlations of about this magnitude with LSR, and several other traits have lower but significant correlations. We have not attempted to compare multiple Rs from one set of ratings with multiple Rs from the other set, but our results certainly are not inconsistent with better prediction of later life characteristics from early adult ones for women than for men.

More importantly, Maas and Kuypers' other major finding suggests a reason why the context of the home in early adulthood (e.g., marital relationship, income) is a more influential predictor of later life satisfaction for women than men. After examining a number of both contemporaneous and antecedent (early adult) correlates of life style and personality at 70, Maas and Kuypers concluded that

Contexts such as marital and economic status, as well as context measures of network, space, and time, are more frequently associated with mothers' than with the fathers' life styles. Such findings suggest that the women's life style options are more dependent upon, if not determined by, their conditions, if only because this generation of women did not have the freedom to exercise as much control over their contextual impingements as did the men. (p. 205)

Continuities in life styles were more apparent among the fathers, whereas the mothers were judged to have experienced more "role and other changes in their occupational and marital and parenting arenas" (p. 203).

Certainly simple continuity of a compatible marriage does not seem sufficient to explain the association between marital adjustment in early adulthood and life satisfaction in the later years, at least for women. All the men in our sample were married when interviewed at 70, but 51% of the women were single by that age. However, comparison of the correlations for the single and married women indicates no differences in the pattern of predictors (whether personal traits or aspects of the early marriage) of LSR at 70. Two possible, and not mutually contradictory, inferences from this finding are (1) young adults with the kinds of personal characteristics predictive of later life satisfaction are also more likely to have good marital relationships, and (2) a good marital relationship in young adulthood fosters or strengthens the kinds of personal characteristics we find to be predictive of high life satisfaction in the later years.

REFERENCES

Edwards, J., & Klemmack, L. Correlates of life satisfaction: A reexamination. *Journal of Gerontology*, 1973, *28*, 297–502.

Maas, H., & Kuypers, J. *From thirty to seventy: A forty-year longitudinal study of adult life styles and personality.* San Francisco: Jossey–Bass, 1974.

Macfarlane, J. W. Studies in child guidance. I. Methodology of data collection and organization. *Monographs of the Society for Research in Child Development*, 1938, *36*, (Whole No. 19).

Moss, H. A., & Susman, E. J. Longitudinal study of personality development. In O. G. Brim, Jr., & J. Kagan (Eds.), *Constancy and change in human development.* Cambridge: Harvard University Press, 1980.

Mussen, P., Eichorn, D. H., Honzik, M. P., Bieber, S. L., & Meredith, W. M. Continuity and change in women's characteristics over four decades. *International Journal of Behavioral Development*, 1980, *3*, 333–347.

Neugarten, B. L., Havighurst, R. J., & Tobin, S. S. Measurement of life satisfaction. *Journal of Gerontology*, 1961, *16*, 134–143.

Palmore, E., & Kivett, V. Change in life satisfaction: A longitudinal study of persons aged 46–70. *Journal of Gerontology*, 1977, *32*, 311–316.

Palmore, E., & Luikert, C. Health and social factors related to life satisfaction. *Journal of Health & Social Behavior*, 1972, *13*, 68–80.

Spreitzer, E., & Synder, E. Correlates of life satisfaction among the aged. *Journal of Gerontology,* 1974, *29,* 454–458.

Tyron, R. C. Identification of social areas by cluster analysis. *University of California Publications in Psychology,* 1955, *8*(1).

Warner, W. L., Meeker, M., & Eels, K. *Social class in American.* Chicago: Science Research Associates, 1949.

4

INTELLECTUAL DEVELOPMENT IN A LONGITUDINAL PERSPECTIVE

Georg Rudinger

FROM THEORY OF INTELLIGENCE TO A DEVELOPMENTAL VIEW

The theory of crystallized and fluid intelligence has a strong developmental appeal, if one remembers Cattell's investment theory (Cattell, 1963; Horn, 1960, 1978, 1980, 1982; Horn & Cattell, 1966) and the trajectories of crystallized (Gc), fluid (Gf) intelligence, visuo-motor flexibility, and so forth, reported by Schaie (1979) and Schaie and Hertzog (1983) (see also Baltes & Dittmann-Kohli, 1982; Baltes & Labouvie, 1973; Baltes & Schaie, 1974; Baltes & Willis, 1977; Baltes, Cornelius, Spiro, & Nesselroade, 1980; Willis & Baltes, 1980). In the last few years some researchers have come up with the idea of extending the theory of crystallized/fluid intelligence, which was developed within the Thurstonian–PMA tradition (Thurstone, 1938), to other concepts and test systems of intelligence, (e.g., to the Wechsler tests) (Birren, Cunningham, & Yamoto, 1983; Botwinick, 1977; Horn & McArdle, 1980).

As a consequence of a strict and classical trait-oriented perspective, we assume that old-age developmental change is solely *quantitative*, (i.e., changes only with respect to the level of the traits or, in other words, with respect to the means of the latent variables [factors]). In order to determine this hypothetical locus of change in a precise manner, we make a non-developmental point for invariance and stability of the other elements in the system of intelligence (i.e., in the structural area of our theoretical presuppositions concerning the constructs of fluid and crystallized intelligence). This assumption may be in some contradiction to empirical results presented and discussed by Baltes, et al., (1980); Birren, et al. (1983); Cunningham (1980, 1981); Horn (1978, 1982); Mandl and Zimmermann (1976); Oerter, Mandl, and Zimmermann (1974); and Reinert (1970).

But on the one hand one has to be aware of the limited section of the whole life-cycle throughout old age: 60–80 years covered with our assumption and the following study. In this essay we mainly refer to analyses of intelligence data (HAWIE/WAIS) from the Bonn Longitudinal Study of Aging (BLSA). On the other hand—in our opinion—one must clearly and distinctively separate the different sources of developmental change and the various facets of invariance and stability that have to be assumed from several theoretical viewpoints. If we behave as a classical "traitist," we have to make a point for stability and invariance at least on the level of constructs, instead of stressing change and variability, or even changes in variability. We are interested in the stability of interindividual differences (this is the only admissible variability, because it is a necessary one in this paradigm), and not at all interested in intraindividual changes and/or differences (see for these different viewpoints, Buss, 1974, 1979). These arguments are in accordance with the brilliant thoughts, advices, and designs presented by Baltes and Nesselroade (1973), Baltes and Schaie (1973), Baltes and Willis (1979), Bentler (1973), Horn and McArdle (1980), Jöreskog (1979), Nesselroade (1970, 1977), Rogosa (1979), Roskam (1976), and Schaie (1977).

The structural equation approach (Jöreskog & Sörbom, 1981; Bentler, 1980, 1983, 1984) offers good possibilities for this kind of separation into several components of stability and change, as shown by many recent studies (Cornelius, Willis, Nesselroade, & Baltes, 1984; Cunningham, 1980, 1981; Horn & McArdle, 1980; Jöreskog & Sörbom, 1976, 1977; Olsson & Bergman, 1977; Sörbom, 1976; and Weeks, 1980).

FROM DEVELOPMENTAL THEORY TO A TESTABLE MODEL

DESIGN OF THE BONN LONGITUDINAL STUDY OF AGING

The Bonn Longitudinal Study of Aging (BLSA) started in 1965 and ended with the seventh wave (measurement point) in 1980–81. For detailed information about the BLSA the reader may refer to Thomae (1976, 1983). The time-span of 15 years is partitioned into six phases by seven measurement points: 1965/66 (first measurement = I); 1966/67 (II); 1967/68 (III); 1969/70 (IV); 1972/73 (V); 1976/77 (VI); and 1980/81 (VII). On each occasion (I–VII), the Bonn team gathered about 1000 observations per person, but at present we confine ourselves to the HAWIE

(Hamburg Wechsler Intelligenz Test fuer Erwachsene—the German version of the WAIS). The HAWIE was administered throughout all occasions with the exception of the second (II).

We must not forget to mention the well-known attrition process that is typical and inevitable in a longitudinal, and particulary gerontological, study. In 1965 we started with 222 people and, in 1981, ended up with 48 persons. The drop-out rate (by experimental and biological mortality) was about 78% over 15 years.

In longitudinal analyses we can therefore include Occasions I, III, IV, V, and VI (i.e., at maximum we could deal with a five-waves situation, in which the waves are unequally spaced, such as I–III: 2 years; III–IV: 2 years; IV–V: 3 years; V–VI: 4 years; and I–VI: 11 years). Within this period of 11 years the sample decreased to the size of 81 persons.

It was our decision to give a report in the frame of this aforementioned situation mainly because it is interesting enough to speak about stability and change over a time-span larger than 10 years (see also Chaselon, Fennekels, Rudinger, & Zimmermann, 1984).

To summarize, our study is embedded within the following context: (1) Longitudinal study over 11 years with 5 waves, occasions, and measurement points; (2) Eighty-one Ss (aged 60–75 in 1965); (3) Ten variables (the HAWIE-subtests) at every occasion, which lead to a 50 × 49/ 2 correlation—respectively a 50 × 51/ 2 variance–covariance-matrix.

THE TWO-WAVES TRAIT MODEL

For the verbal presentation of the two-waves trait models it seems useful to us to refer to the graphical display in Figure 4.1.[1] Only two measurement points (I and VI: time-span 11 years), six subtests per occasion, and two latent variables (traits) per occasion are incorporated into this model. It deals with 12 observed variables (the selected HAWIE subtests) and two traits: the Gf and Gc constructs (for this kind of model see also Jöreskog, 1979; Jöreskog & Sörbom, 1976; Olsson & Bergman, 1977).

In Figure 4.1 and Table 4.2, the reader can find the relations between the HAWIE/WAIS-subtests (Y 1 = IN I, Y 2 = CO I, . . . ,Y 12 = OA VI) and the assumed latent variables, factors, constructs, or traits (ETA 1 = Gc I, ETA 2 = Gf I, ETA 3 = Gc VI, ETA 4 = Gf VI) on the one hand (*measurement model*) and a relation between the constructs (*structural model*) on the other.

---

[1]In Figure 4.1 the parameters to be estimated in this model are depicted with Greek and Arabic (the LISREL-computer-program abbreviations) letters. In the text and the tables we make use of the Arabic capital letter abbreviations for convenience.

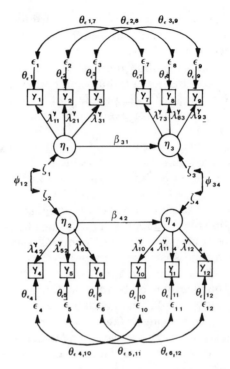

FIGURE 4.1 Graphical Display of the Trait-Model. In the text we use the LISREL-program labels instead of the Greek symbols. The relations are the following: λ = LY, η = ETA, β = BE, ψ = PS, θ = TE. The y-variables (=Y) represent the HAWIE-subtests: 1 and 7 = IN, 2 and 8 = CO, 3 and 9 = SI, 4 and 10 = DS, 5 and 11 = BD, 6 and 12 = OA.

The two mentioned prima facie nondevelopmental features are

1. Invariance of the measurement model over time. By making certain assumptions, constraints, and restrictions of the factor loadings and residual variances and covariances of the observed variables (see Bentler, 1973; Nesselroade, 1977) in a measurement model, different, variantly restrictive ways to define the concept of invariance are reached.

One can speak of an invariant *measurement model*

A. with respect to the invariant pattern of structural zeros (i.e., invariant pattern of LY = 0). (A.) is a necessary precondition for Facet (B.) (if structural [not numerical] invariance of the loading pattern is assumed = 1; otherwise = 0);

B. with respect to the numerical values of the corresponding nonzero LY parameters; LY i, j (time k) = LY i, j (time m) (if numerical equivalence/ invariance is assumed = 1, otherwise = 0);

C. with respect to the residuals of the observed variables (Y), TE i (time k) = TE i (time m) (i.e. if equal reliabilities are assumed = 1, otherwise = 0); and

D. with respect to the correlations of the residuals of the observed variables; one can put some constraints on these correlations (or groups of these correlations) (e.g., TE subtest i (time k), subtest i (time m) = TE subtest j, (time k), subtest j (time m), TE fk,fm = TE gk,gm, etc.) or specify them as unconstraint (if constraints = 1, otherwise = 0).

We therefore get a differentiated and hierarchical definition of invariance: The most restrictive—with reference to the above mentioned coding (1,0) of the assumptions—is described by the pattern 1 1 1 1 and the least restrictive in our context by the pattern 1 0 0 0. The "invariance-tree" has its "branches" depicted in Table 4.1.

2. Stability with respect to the structural model. Stability refers to the time-bound structural part of the intelligence model (i.e., to the theoretical relations between the constructs [BEtas and PSis]). Given the assumption of high stability, we expect high BE-values for the paths of crystallized intelligence at time 1 (ETA 1) to crystallized intelligence at time 2 (ETA 3), and analogously from Gf (1) (ETA 2) to Gf (2) (ETA 4). A numerically high value BE j i would indicate a reasonable predictability from ETA i to ETA j. So, further, it is our expectation that the residuals of ETA 3 and ETA 4,

TABLE 4.1

GRADES OF INVARIANCE OF MEASUREMENT MODELS

No. of model	Invariance pattern		Grades of invariance	
(1)		1 1 1 1	most	
(2), (3)	1 1 1 0	1 1 0 1	more	invariant
(4)		1 1 0 0	less	
(5)		1 0 0 0	least	
(6)		0 0 0 0	no	invariance
		A B C D		
		facet		

Facet A (structural zeros), B (numerical invariance of corresponding LY), C (equal reliabilities), D (constrained residual correlations-TE): 1 = yes, 0 = no. (1)-(6) number of the related LISREL-model.

respectively (i.e., PS 3 3 and PS 4 4) have low values (complementary to the BE 3 1 and BE 4 2 parameters).

We return to some problems inherent in this definition of stability in the third section of this chapter.

LISREL RESULTS FOR THE TWO-WAVES TRAIT-MODELS[2]

All the 11-year trait-models derived from our invariance and stability definitions and presented in Table 4.2, columns 1–4, show reasonably good fit indices (particularly the CHI SQ. and the CHI SQ./DF ratio). This fact holds even in the situation of rather restrictive assumptions (model (2)—1110 and model (1)—1111). In our opinion it is indeed a very strong hypothesis to postulate equal reliabilities over time (model 2), and additionally (as in model 1), equal residual correlations for the sets

TABLE 4.2

LISREL RESULTS FOR DIFFERENT VARIANTS OF THE TRAIT-MODEL (STANDARDIZED SOLUTIONS)[a]

				I–VI			
				(5) (1000)	(4) (1100)	(2) (1110)	(1) (1111)
ETA	1		(Gc I)				
LY	1	1	(IN)	2.046*	1.990*	1.955*	1.935*
LY	2	1	(CO)	1.087	1.363a	1.416a	1.427a
LY	3	1	(SI)	1.727	1.686b	1.654b	1.665b
ETA	2		(Gf I)				
LY	4	2	(DS)	1.721*	1.629*	1.695c	1.620*
LY	5	2	(BD)	1.817	1.883c	1.954*	2.057c
LY	6	2	(OA)	1.040	1.078d	1.101d	1.131d
ETA	3		(Gc VI)				
LY	7	3	(IN)	2.193*	2.247*	2.241*	2.213*
LY	8	3	(CO)	1.869	1.539a	1.622a	1.632a
LY	9	3	(SI)	1.874	1.904b	1.895b	1.905b
ETA	4		(GP VI)				
LY	10	4	(DS)	1.834*	1.863*	1.824c	1.736*
LY	11	4	(BD)	2.162	2.153c	2.102*	2.204c
LY	12	4	(OA)	1.230	1.233d	1.185d	1.212d

(*Continued*)

[2]The computations were performed at the RHRZ of the University of Bonn (IBM 367/168 and IBM 3081K).

TABLE 4.2 (*Continued*)

			I–VI			
			(5) (1000)	(4) (1100)	(2) (1110)	(1) (1111)
BE	3	1	0.939	0.945	0.941	0.938
BE	4	2	0.912	0.912	0.911	0.911
PS	1	1	1.000	1.000	1.000	1.000
PS	2	2	1.000	1.000	1.000	1.000
PS	3	3	0.119	0.107	0.115	0.120
PS	4	4	0.169	0.169	0.170	0.170
PS	1	2	0.659	0.646	0.644	0.620
PS	3	4	0.159	0.163	0.173	0.175
TE	1		1.190	1.236	1.394e	1.494e
TE	2		3.266	3.232	3.792f	3.733f
TE	3		2.052	2.096	2.307g	2.260g
TE	4		2.211	2.323	1.768h	2.064h
TE	5		3.038	2.933	2.492i	1.985i
TE	6		6.513	6.464	5.520j	5.570j
TE	7		1.565	1.530	1.394e	1.494e
TE	8		4.281	4.512	3.792f	3.733f
TE	9		2.467	2.365	2.307g	2.260g
TE	10		1.223	1.203	1.768h	2.064h
TE	11		2.127	2.135	2.492i	1.985i
TE	12		4.533	4.514	5.520j	5.570j
TE	1	7	0.306	0.266	0.286	0.400k
TE	2	8	0.681	0.571	0.526	0.400k
TE	3	9	0.408	0.417	0.444	0.400k
TE	4	10	0.338	0.374	0.364	0.677l
TE	5	11	1.307	1.261	1.207	0.677l
TE	6	12	0.351	0.333	0.360	0.677l
GOFI			0.847	0.793	0.765	0.762
AGOFI			0.729	0.664	0.660	0.680
RMSR			0.344	0.467	0.522	0.541
CHI SQ.			49.52	54.18	64.74	66.26
DF			44	48	54	58
p			0.26	0.25	0.15	0.21
CHI SQ./DF			1.12	1.13	1.20	1.14

[a]Rows of the table: LISREL parameters in the order and with the labels of the standard LISREL V/VI output. For reason of quick identification, the HAWIE-subtest labels are added. Columns of the table: I–VI = trait-model for the 11 year time-span (1965–1976).

The variants of the trait-model are indicated with reference to Table 4.1 (invariance tree) by numbers (5), (4), (2), and (1) (i.e. pattern 1000 1100 1110 1111). Star (*) and letters (a–k) are indicating the corresponding fixed (LY = 1.00) respectively constrained parameters. GOFI = goodness of fit index, AGOFI = adjusted GOFI, RMSR = root mean square residual.

of the observed Gc and Gf-variables, respectively. In the latter case, there is barely space for variability in the measurement model.

By involving other pairs of measurement points (I–V, III–VI, etc.), we tried to test the two-waves trait-model assumptions in different contexts. But here one has to be aware of the multiple testing problem. Nevertheless, for heuristic purposes, we proceeded the two-waves trait-model to any possible pair of two measurement points (i.e., we deal with another 9 two-waves trait-models). All the structural assumptions and the various restrictions of the original model (I–VI) remained unchanged. The results and the fit of the models for the other possible measurement pairs that are not reported here differ only slightly from those in Table 4.2.

CONSEQUENCES FOR THE DEVELOPMENTAL VIEW OF PSYCHOMETRIC INTELLIGENCE

Our intelligence model was conceptualized as a two-waves trait-model. It deals with six observed HAWIE-subtests and two latent variables (traits) for measurement point I (1965), and symmetrically for measurement point VI (1976).

The results give us strong evidence for the appropriateness of the a priori chosen measurement model (Information, Comprehension, Similarities—*crystallized intelligence*; and Digit Symbol, Block Design, Object Assembly—*fluid intelligence*) for the assumption of strong invariance of this measurement model over time and for the stability assumptions concerning the two constructs crystallized and fluid intelligence; the BE values indicate high stability. As a consequence of the quite high values of the parameters BE 3 1 (Gc I to Gc VI) = 0.94, and BE 4 2 (Gf I to Gf VI) = 0.91, the residuals of the latent variables (PS 3, PS 4) are relatively low. These results seem compatible with our expectations concerning stability of theoretical core variables, namely crystallized and fluid intelligence.

Nevertheless, it does not seem possible to abandon the correlation between the two residual components of the latent variables ETA 3 and ETA 4. Even though this residual correlation has a low numerical value (about 0.17), it contributes in a relevant, significant way to the fit of this type of trait model. If the residual correlation is removed, the goodness of fit drops drastically to inacceptable regions, regardless of the other features of the models presented up to this point. This may be considered as a drawback because one can argue that it should be the consequence of our theoretical assumption concerning high stability (i.e., almost perfect predictability) that the residual variances of the predicted latent variables should contain solely random noises. Random noises should be uncorrelated. However, our results are in contradiction to this view.

There is one exception: Model (3) (pattern 1101), not presented here in detail, delivers a reasonable fit. The pattern 1101 indicates a peculiar equality constraint pattern of the TE: unequal reliabilities, but equal correlations over time between the residuals of the set of Gc-variables (IN,CO,SI) on the one hand, and the set of Gf-variables (DS,BD,OA) on the other hand: TE [IN (time I), TN (time VI)] = TE [CO(I),CO (VI)] = TE [SI(I),SI(VI)]. This is analogous for the Gf-variables. It may be the gain of four degrees of freedom, compared to the mode of varying TE, that makes this model jump into a fairly acceptable probability region. This may be evaluated as some kind of trick, because it seems very hard to invent a theory for this extraordinary TE-constraint pattern.

There is one further problem: As far as we see, there is no direct chance to test any assumption about the correlations (r) or covariances (cov) between the latent variables, for example, COV (ETA 1, ETA 2) = COV (ETA 3, ETA 4), for a longitudinal design within the context of these trait-models, including the first wave. In our study these correlations r (Gc I, Gf I) and r (Gc VI, Gf VI) are very similar (0.65, and 0.70, respectively), but we could not test the equality hypothesis. However, the stability or change of these correlations is subject of the differentiation/integration hypothesis; therefore, it is of substantive interest to test hypotheses about stability and change of covariances between traits over time (Mandl & Zimmermann, 1976; Reinert, 1970). There is no question that this is possible in a *cross-sectional* multi-sample design by setting straightforward all PS's invariant (see Cunningham, 1980, 1981). But even the trait-model depicted in Figure 4.1 possesses some features for finding an answer to this question. By deleting the BETAS, setting free all PSis, and putting equality constraints on the PS 1 2, and PS 3 4, it should be possible to make explicit the assumption of equal covariances over time, including the first wave (for detailed derivations, see Andres & Rudinger, 1985). The clear cut twofold interpretation of our results still stands: An invariant meaning of the Gc, Gf constructs can be assumed, and an unchanged relative position of the older persons of our sample over a time-span of 11 years can be inferred—results that turn out to be very striking arguments for the justification of a trait-oriented perspective in evaluating developmental change in the field of psychometric intelligence.

ACKNOWLEDGMENTS

I would like to thank Friedrich Chaselon, Georg Fennekels, and Ejo Zimmermann for their invaluable assistance in data analysis, and give special thanks to Reinhold Kliegl and Johannes Andres for their critical comments and to Marlene Endepohls and Una Röhr-Sendelmaier for their helpful support in preparing the text.

REFERENCES

Andres, J., & Rudinger, G. Testing assumptions about covariances and correlations between latent variables in longitudinal designs. *Bonner Methoden—Berichte*, 1985, *2*(10).

Baltes, P. B., Cornelius, S. W., Spiro, A. III, Nesselroade, J. R., & Willis, S. L. Integration vs. differentiation of fluid-crystallized intelligence in old age. *Developmental Psychology*, 1980, *16*, 625–635.

Baltes, P. B., & Dittmann-Kohli, F. Einige einführende Überlegungen zur Intelligenz im Erwachsenenalter. *Neue Sammlung*, 1982, *22*, 261–278.

Baltes, P. B., & Labouvie, G. V. Adult development of intellectual performance: Description, explanation, and modification. In C. Eisdorfer, & M. P. Lawton (Eds.), *The psychology of adult development and aging*. Washington: American Psychological Association, 1973.

Baltes, P. B., & Nesselroade, J. R. The developmental analysis of individual differences on multiple measures. In J. R. Nesselroade & H. W. Reese (Eds.), *Life-span developmental psycholgy: Methodological issues* (219–251). New York/London: Academic Press, 1973.

Baltes, P. B., & Schaie, K. W. On life-span developmental research paradigms: Retrospects and prospects. In P. B. Baltes & K. W. Schaie (Eds.), *Life-span developmental psychology: Personality and socialization* (365–395). New York/London: Academic Press, 1973.

Baltes, P. B., & Schaie, K. W. Das Märchen vom Intelligenz-Abbau bei älteren Menschen. *Psychologie Heute*, 1974, *1*, 61–65.

Baltes, P. B., & Willis, S. L. Toward psychological theories of aging and development. In J. E. Birren & K. W. Schaie (Eds.), *Handbook of the psychology of aging*. New York: Van Nostrand-Reinhold, 1977.

Baltes, P. B., & Willis, S. L. The critical importance of appropriate methodology in the study of aging: The sample case of psychometric intelligence. In F. Hoffmeister & C. Muller (Eds.), *Brain function in old age*. Heidelberg: Springer, 1979.

Bentler, P. M. Assessment of the developmental factor change at the individual level. In J. R. Nesselroade & H. W. Reese (Eds.), *Life-span developmental psychology: Methodological issues* (145–174). New York/London: Academic Press, 1973.

Bentler, P. M. Multivariate analysis with latent variables: Causal models. *Annual Review of Psychology*, 1980, *31*, 419–456.

Bentler, P. M. Some contributions to efficient statistics in structural models: Specification and estimation of moment structures. *Psychometrika*, 1983, *48*, 493–517.

Bentler, P. M. *Theory and implementation of EQS: A structural equations program*. Unpublished program manual, preliminary version, University of California, Department of Psychology, Los Angeles, 1984.

Birren, J. E., Cunningham, W. R., & Yamamoto, K. Psychology of adult development and aging. *Annual Review of Psychology*, 1983, *34*, 543–575.

Botwinick, J. Intellectual abilities. In J. E. Birren & K. W. Schaie (Eds.), *Handbook of the psychology of aging*. New York: Van Nostrand-Reinhold, 1977.

Buss, A. R. A general developmental model for interindividual differences, intraindividual differences and intraindividual changes. *Developmental Psychology,* 1974, *19,* 70–78.
Buss, A. R. Toward a unified framework for psychometric concepts in the multivariate developmental situation: Intraindividual change and inter- and intraindividual differences. In J. R. Nesselroade & P. B. Baltes (Eds.), *Longitudinal research in the study of behavior and development* (41–59). New York/London: Academic Press, 1979.
Chaselon, F., Fennekels, G., Rudinger, G., & Zimmermann, E. J. Causal analysis of longitudinal intelligence data. *Bonner Methoden—Berichte,* 1984, *1*(1).
Cattell, R. B. Theory of fluid and crystallized intelligence: A critical experiment. *Journal of Educational Psychology,* 1963, *54,* 1–22.
Cornelius, S. W., Willis, S. L., Nesselroade, J. R., & Baltes, P. B. Convergence between attention variables and factors of psychometric intelligence. *Intelligence,* 1984, *7,* 143–152.
Cunningham, W. R. Age comparative factor analysis of ability variables in adulthood and old age. *Intelligence,* 1980, *4,* 133–149.
Cunningham, W. R. Ability factor structure differences in adulthood and old age. *Multivariate Behaviour Research,* 1981, *16,* 3–22.
Horn, J. L. Integration of structural and developmental concepts in the theory of fluid and crystallized intelligence. In R. B. Cattell (Ed.), *Handbook of Multivariate Experimental Psychology.* Chicago: Rand McNally, 1960.
Horn, J. L. Human ability systems. In P. B. Baltes (Ed.), *Life-span development and behavior* (Vol. 1). New York: Academic Press, 1978.
Horn, J. L. Concepts of intellect in relation to learning and adult development. *Human Intelligence,* 1980, *4,* 285–317.
Horn, J. L. The aging of human abilities. In B. B. Wolman (Ed.), *Handbook of developmental psychology.* Englewood Cliffs, NJ: Prentice Hall, 1982.
Horn, J. L., & Cattell, R. B. Refinement and test of the theory of fluid and crystallized general intelligences. *Journal of Educational Psychology,* 1966, *57,* 253–270.
Horn, J. L., & McArdle, J. J. Perspectives on mathematical/statistical model building (MASMOB) in research on aging. In L. W. Poon (Ed.), *Aging in the 1980s.* Washington: American Psychological Association, 1980.
Jöreskog, K. G. Statistical estimation of structure models in longitudinal-development investigation. In J. R. Nesselroade & P. B. Baltes (Eds.), *Longitudinal research in the study of behavior and development* (303–351). New York/London: Academic Press, 1979.
Jöreskog, K. G., & Sörbom, D. Statistical models and methods for test–retest situations. In D. N. de Gruijter & L. J. van der Kamp (Eds.), *Advances in psychological and educational measurement* (135–157). New York: Wiley, 1976.
Jöreskog, K. G., and Sörbom, D. Statistical models and methods for analysis of longitudinal data. In D. J. Aigner & A. S. Goldberger (Eds.), *Latent variables in socioeconomic models.* Amsterdam: North-Holland Publishing, 1977.
Jöreskog, K. G., & Sörbom, D. *LISREL V—analysis of linear structural relationship by the method of maximum likelihood.* Uppsala: University of Uppsala, Department of Statistics, 1981.
Mandl, H., & Zimmermann, A. *Intelligenzdifferenzierung.* Stuttgart: Kohlhammer, 1976.
Nesselroade, J. R. Application of multivariate strategies to problems of measuring and structuring long-term change. In L. R. Goulet & P. B. Baltes (Eds.), *Life-span developmental psychology: Research and theory* (193–207). New York/London: Academic Press, 1970.
Nesselroade, J. R. Issues in studying developmental change in adults from a multivariate perspective. In J. E. Birren & K. W. Schaie (Eds.), *Handbook of the psychology of aging* (59–69). New York: Van Nostrand-Reinhold, 1977.

Oerter, R., Mandl, H., & Zimmermann, A. Neue Befunde zur Differenzierungshypothese der Intelligenz—ein Nachgesang. *Zeitschrift für Entwicklungspsychologie und Pädagogische Psychologie*, 1974, *3*, 151–167.

Olsson, U., & Bergman, L. R. A longitudinal factor model for studying change in ability structure. *Multivariate Behavioral Research*, 1977, *12*, 221–241.

Reinert, G. Comparative factor analytic studies of intelligence throughout the human life-span. In L. R. Goulet & P. B. Baltes (Eds.), *Life-span developmental psychology: Research and theory*. New York: Academic Press, 1970.

Rogosa, D. Causal models in longitudinal research. In J. R. Nesselroade & P. B. Baltes (Eds.), *Longitudinal research in the study of behavior and development* (263–302). New York/London: Academic Press, 1979.

Roskam, E. E. Multivariate analysis of change and growth: Critical review and perspectives. In D. N. de Gruijter & L. J. van der Kamp (Eds.), *Advances in psychological and educational measurement* (111–133). New York: Wiley, 1976.

Schaie, K. W. Quasi-experimental research designs in the psychology of aging. In J. E. Birren & K. W. Schaie (Eds.), *Handbook of the psychology of aging* (39–58). New York: Van Nostrand–Reinhold, 1977.

Schaie, K. W. The primary mental abilities in adulthood: An exploration in the development of psychometric intelligence. In P. B. Baltes & O. G. Brim, Jr. (Eds.), *Life-span development and behavior* (Vol. 2). New York: Academic Press, 1979.

Schaie, K. W., & Hertzog, C. Fourteen-year cohort-sequential analyses of adult intellectual development. *Developmental Psychology*, 1983, *19*, 531–543.

Sörbom, D. A statistical model for the measurement of change in true scores. In D. N. de Gruijter & L. J. van der Kamp (Eds.), *Advances in psychological and educational measurement* (159–170). New York: Wiley, 1976.

Thomae, H. *Patterns of aging*. Basel: Karger, 1976.

Thomae, H. *Altersstile und Alternsschicksale*. Bern: Huber, 1983.

Thurstone, L. L. *Primary mental abilities* (Psychometric Monograph No. 1). Chicago, IL.: The University of Chicago Press, 1938.

Weeks, D. G. A second-order longitudinal model of ability structure. *Multivariate Behavioral Research*, 1980, *15*, 353–365.

Willis, S. L., & Baltes, P. B. Intelligence in adulthood and aging: Contemporary issues. In L. W. Poon (Ed.), *Aging in the 1980's: Psychological issues*. Washington, D.C.: American Psychological Association, 1980.

B

Process-Centered Studies

INTRODUCTION

This part includes three studies based on longitudinal data from the Bonn Study on Aging. All of them continue from the first general report, "Patterns of Aging" (Thomae, 1976). The first contribution by Fisseni deals with a fundamental aspect of the individual experience of ageing people, (i.e., the hardly translatable concept of "awareness of definiteness"). Fisseni operationalized this concept by searching the longitudinal data for expressions of "perceived unchangeability." His careful analysis resulted in the conclusion that "unchangeability is perceived more distinctly by subjects who under many aspects were restricted and limited in their life-space (low income, poor health status, or widowhood)." But he also discovered that perceived unchangeability has to be different from the attitude towards finitude. Although the concept of unchangeability provides some new insights, the process of ageing itself is so complicated that we cannot diagnose it by using these concepts in a central place.

The second study is of a totally different nature. While Fisseni's study concurred to a certain extent with the structure of the trait-centered studies, Insa Fooken's contribution selects a small number of women, studying them individually in a very intense way. This kind of investigation produces a lot of interesting data. It is fascinating to see how she obtains information about the subjective life-space, personality, coping styles, and other dominant concerns. She finds evidence of variability among old-aged women as well as of developmental growth-oriented change. She discovers the great impact of one's attitude towards the future. A positive attitude appears to be indicative of a successful pattern of aging. Women with a negative future perspective are more inclined to use a coping strategy of adaptation to the needs and desires of others. Women with a positive outlook towards the future are ready to cope actively with problems like housing, health, and family.

Insa Fooken also stresses the different coping styles. She believes that antecedents of these styles have to be traced back to former stages of life. This supposition brings back a problem mentioned earlier: Is old age only a consequence of all antecedents, that is, the proceeding stages of life, or can the personality change its own structure fundamentally? Here we are faced with a striking problem: Can old age bring a new perspective, new strategies, and perhaps a new personality make-up? The impression we get from these two Bonn studies, as well as from the following one by Olbrich, is that people shape their own coping style since some changes in that style are possible. These changes are adaptive in nature. But a real change of the personality during aging is a rare phenomenon. There is, as we said in the general introduction, discontinuity only within a context of continuity.

The third contribution in this section addresses the topic of coping in old age. Olbrich shows that neither a regression nor a growth-hypothesis can accurately describe age-related changes in coping. Rather, a reordering of priorities, a restructuring of plans and forms of behavior can be observed, as coping potentials and demands encountered by the aging individual change. Coping can be understood as a process of transaction between person and situation (Lazarus) or—when emphasizing the developmental perspective—as a changing need–press coordination (Thomae). Based on Thomae's theory of personality development (1951, 1970), a combination of paradigms of coping theory and developmental research is proposed. Using crystallization (*Verfestigung*) and fluidization (*Verflüssigung*) as core concepts, interactions between actual coping processes and diachronic developmental processes can be described. The meaning of these studies for the main theme of this book is obvious. The studies illustrate that, starting from an original theoretical conceptualization (Thomae's personality theory, 1951, 1970), very different pieces of research can be developed. Ageing appears to be a very distinct process, and the way people organize their personalities diverge widely. Because the antecedents play a major role in this context, it appears to be worthwhile to go into the middle years of the life-span when doing research on the life-span from a gerontological point of view.

J. M.

REFERENCES

Thomae, H. *Persönlichkeit: Eine dynamische Interpretation.* Bonn: Bouvier, 1951.
Thomae, H. Theory of aging and cognitive theory of personality. *Human Development*, 1970, 13, 1–16.
Thomae, H. (Ed.), *Patterns of aging.* Karger: Basel, 1976.

OLD AND FEMALE: PSYCHOSOCIAL CONCOMITANTS OF THE AGING PROCESS IN A GROUP OF OLDER WOMEN

Insa Fooken

INTRODUCTION: DATA FROM THE BONN LONGITUDINAL STUDY OF AGING

The Bonn Longitudinal Study of Aging (BLSA) started in 1965/66 and followed two cohorts of originally 221 women and men, who were born between 1890–1905, up until 1976/77. The subjects were guests of the Institute of Psychology at the University of Bonn for 4 to 5 days at each of the altogether six measurement points. Detailed interviews, behavioral ratings, tests for measuring intelligence, questionnaires, and assessments of physical health by an internal specialist were used (for further information on sampling procedures, description of sample, methods, etc., see Thomae, 1976, Chapters 1 and 2).

The sample of older women described in this essay is only part of the whole group of survivors that participated again at the time of the sixth measurement point in 1976/77. Included in the following analysis are 39 women of differing marital status (see Fooken, 1980a). The aim of the analysis carried out in this chapter is the comparison of women of differing marital status over time.

CONTROVERSIAL ISSUES ON THE OBJECT OF RESEARCH: WOMEN IN OLD AGE

As "objects" of social science/gerontological research, women in old age used to be subjected to prejudice or neglected to a great extent, respectively (Beeson, 1976; Giesen & Datan, 1980; Payne & Whittington, 1976; Sheehan, 1976). Thus, the concurrence of two specific social criteria, that is, of being old and being female (e.g., Hutchison & Lilienthal, 1980), turned out to be not only socially disadvantageous but helpful in making the persons in question appear as insignificant and devoid of interest to social scientists. If mentioned at all, the expressed views on the female aging experience are often distinguished by their absence of empirical evidence, outdatedness, and obstinate persistence. Only recently, Payne and Whittington (1976) analyzed data from the Duke Study and emphasized that most of the research evidence does not support popular stereotypes on aging women.

Unchangeability versus Developmental Change

Freudian theory depicts the old woman—referring to the woman beyond 30 years of age—as capable of no more development: She "staggers us by her psychological rigidity and unchangeability" (Freud, 1940, p. 144). Being in the Freudian element, Helene Deutsch characterizes the aging woman by anal-erotic features. William James (1980) notes the fixed character of women, which is unable to mature fully, and G. Stanley Hall (1922) finds the women at forty obsessed by attempts to cheat about her age. Hence we may infer that because becoming older is frightening, standstill is a more attractive and desirable alternative for women than development—a behavior for which they are also reproached. Classical authors, as well as social gerontologists using functionalistic role theory as a frame of reference, are often inclined to similar bias (Atchley, 1972; Blau, 1973; Clark & Anderson, 1967; Cumming & Henry, 1961). While describing the aging process as shifting from one role to the other, female and male aging experiences are compared under the heading "Who suffers most?" Comparisons between such claimed sex-linked equivalents as "male retirement" and "female widowhood" result in the formulation of the female experience as smoother, less problematic, and less significant (Beeson, 1976).

On the other hand, longitudinal studies, life-span oriented approaches, phenomenological research, and in-depth sociopsychological field studies are capable of proving quite an amount of developmental change in older women. Even psychologists following Jungian complex psychology extend the developmental phases of female experience far beyond wedlock and motherhood (Harding, 1971). Lowenthal, Thurnher, Chiriboga, and Associates (1975) demonstrate the experience of change in a group of women facing the post parental stage of the family life-cycle. Matthews (1979) explores the social world of older women in an institutional setting and provides proof of the adaptational and coping processes derived from situational change that facilitate development and growth. Giesen and Datan (1980) note the continuing emergence of competence due to life changes reported by older women.

All in all, there seems to be sufficient empirically based evidence for the supposition of developmental change in older women, as well as, of course, in male and other age groups (Thomae, 1979).

Decline versus Growth

For quite some time, being old has been regarded in gerontological science as a biologically defined state of deficiency. As a process, aging seemed to be identical with decline all along the way. Growth-oriented models of development like that of Erikson (1966), the developmental task concept of Havighurst (1972), or the cognitive theory of Thomae (1970) use "the integrated system of processes which is called the aging personality" (p. 2) as a frame of reference, thereby contributing to a way of viewing aging that defines it as more than a process of decay and deterioration. Similarly, for the same reason that old age might be regarded as a situation in which physical and partial social impairment is likely, the *focal task of old age* (Havighurst, 1972), a concept that implies a developmental "growth-aspect" (e.g., Jung, 1964), can be considered to be maintaining a balance between individual needs and a perceived life-situation, despite any possible decline of vital powers (Thomae, 1975, 1976). The application of the aforementioned theory to the case of older women supports the view of possible growth and competence. Widowhood, for example, may indeed be synonymous with the "shrinking circle" (Lopata, 1966) of family career, but it may also be regarded as a challenge to personal growth by requiring reconstruction of self-identity and social networks (Lopata, 1973a, 1973b). Analogous to this, the women in the study of Giesen and Datan (1980) expect to learn, develop, and become "better persons" as they grow older; they believe that "life brings change" and "change brings growth" (p. 71), and they distinguish themselves by competence and a variety of skills not usually associated with the traditional feminine characteristics of old age, such as incompetence, helplessness, destitution, and enfeeblement. Uhlenberg (1979) refers to the need for a reorientation of how the older woman's situation is assessed among social gerontologists; he notices a growing challenge to design ways to facilitate her engagement into socially constructive roles as the population of older women increasingly consists of relatively healthy, educated, non poor, and spouse less women.

General Norms versus Interindividual Variability in Patterns of Aging

Although longitudinal studies produce evidence of a growing amount of interindividual variability in old age (Thomae, 1976, 1979) the female aging condition has still been defined in a general, uniform way, seemingly determined by rather restrictive marital–family related roles (Atchley, 1972; Blau, 1973; Cumming & Henry, 1961; Duvall, 1971). Yet, there is no such thing as a typical old woman (Lehr, 1978). Women in old age differ not only by sociodemographic variables, but also by ways of perceiving and experiencing their specific life-situations and coping with "daily hassles" (Lazarus & Cohen, 1976). Although finding a high amount of stability and continuity as aging proceeded in their sample of women, Mussen, Eichorn, Honzik, Beiber, and Meredith (1980), for example, show the interindividual variability of intraindividual variation with regard to the important and central construct of life satisfaction. Similarly, Lopata's (1973a, 1975) demonstration of a variety of different styles to cope with widowhood obviously does not allow any generalized formula for the treatment of widows. Thus, women in old age may seem similar to one another only if compared with male contemporaries. A closer look at the same age and sex group reveals a variety of different life styles—a fact that seems especially important for social policy makers.

IMPLICATIONS FOR OUR OWN RESEARCH

Having followed the arguments cited above up until now, our own approach starts with the assumption that older women in the investigated sample exhibit developmental change, growth, and a certain degree of interindividual variability in their ways of becoming older. It is thus an approach that is differential and process-oriented as the individual constantly has to cope with situational change, and a combination of episodic and diachronic perspectives on developmental processes. Other implications are detailed below.

COGNITIVE THEORY AS A FRAME OF REFERENCE

Cognitive theory, as formulated by Thomae (1970), sees the "aging personality" as a system of processes integrated into an individual biography (Olbrich & Thomae, 1978). Cognitive representation of real life-situations, that is to say, the perceived life-space, accounts for interindividual variations in covert and overt behavior. Thus, it is the cognitive appraisal of a given situation, rather than just any evaluation, however objective, that "acts as the effective environment which . . . guides overt behavior." (Baldwin, 1969, p. 326). Being comparatively unbiased, this approach seems to provide a useful framework.

The life-situations of this sample of older women are explored, investigated, and described against the background of their individual biographies and without entertaining specific assumptions of how older women should be (see Beeson, 1976; Carlsson, 1972; Gubrium, 1975).

METHODOLOGICAL ASPECTS

The purpose of this study has been to do qualitative, rather than exclusively quantitative, research on older women. Thus, demands on the size of the sample, sampling procedures, generalizability of the results, and so forth, had to be reduced. What remains has to be regarded, on the one hand, as a small and selective sample of "survivors" but, on the other hand, as a sample that exhibits the advantage of an abundance of longitudinally obtained data.

To trace intraindividual and/or intragroup change, one has to contrast certain subjects or groups. According to the intention to compose homogenous groups, the grouping process might be done by either external (e.g., sociodemographic) variables or by other interesting (e.g. psychological) variables. In all, this attempt can be seen to be in accordance with the call for "small-N-methodologies" (Rudinger & Lantermann, 1978).

VARIABILITY AMONG WOMEN

As mentioned above, long-time social science/gerontological research has yielded little and/or misleading understanding of the female aging experience. There is reason to believe that this neglect/fallacy is associated with the usual failure "to study women as women rather than as 'not-men'" (Weinreich, 1977, p. 536); often enough discovered "differences" have been interpreted as existing "deficiencies" (Carlsson, 1972; May, 1966; Rudinger & Bierhoff-Alfermann, 1979). Yet, bearing in mind that to compare is a useful thing to do, the question ought to be "To whom shall we compare?" or "Who sets the standard for a group of older women)" (see also Payne & Whittington, 1976). The decision has been made in favor of studying the "female world . . . quite apart from its impact on the male world" (Bernard, 1981, p. 1) instead of comparing male and female experiences.

As early as 1921, Mathilde Vaerting claimed in her *Revision of the Psychology of Man and Woman* that comparisons between the sexes have to be regarded as invalid as long as men and women do not exist in identical social conditions. Weinreich (1977) concludes that the psychological processes of women ought to be viewed "in the context of differences *among women* rather than how like or unlike *men* women are" (p. 536). Our procedure comes close to Vaillant's (1977) approach as we, too, let our female subjects serve as their own foils. Thus, Lopata's (1973a) study on widowed women, for example, is able to convey deep insight into the experience of being widowed as a woman, mainly because she does not compare widowhood to widowerhood.

THE SIGNATURE OF MARITAL STATUS IN A SAMPLE OF OLDER WOMEN

As we have decided to compare homogenous groups, the question of which variable should be used as a grouping criterion is raised (i.e., which variable allows a reasonable differentiation among this sample of older women). The first choice is made in favor of an external variable (marital status structure) rather than a psychological one(e.g., ego-strength), because it would be easier for practitioners in the field of social gerontology to identify such classified groups. Secondly, the manifestation of marital status as a code implying considerable psychological facts seems to provide a good selectivity among the given sample. Considering the epoch these women were born in, one might state that the women of this generation, unlike their male contemporaries, are defined and define themselves in categories closely affiliated with marital/familial roles (Duvall, 1971; Lehr & Thomae, 1965; Levy, 1977). Thus, there is reason to believe that the manifestation of a given marital status (i.e., being either married, no longer-married, or never-married) refers to quite different experiences of one's life-situation. Skimming through some gerontological literature, one might get the opinion that the situation of married women is a taken-for-granted norm of female existence in old age, whereas so-called single women are looked upon as a deviant minority. Factually the reverse is true: Being married in old age is an exceptional state for women, while being single is the common thing. Beyond that, the label *single woman*—including divorced, widowed, and never-married women—proves to be inadequate as it seems to conceal the psychologically and sociologically interesting diversity among this social category (see Fooken, 1980b).

To apply to the sample in question, four subsamples of women differing by marital status have been constituted: Married Women; Never-Married Women; Recently Widowed Women, whose widowhood is in accordance to the so-called social clock (Neugarten, 1968); and Long-Time Widows, who have experienced their widowhood "off-time" (divorced Women cannot be included, because only two of the six divorced women of the original sample are left at the time of the sixth measurement point).

THE CURRENT STUDY

SAMPLE AND METHODS

Description of Four Subsamples

The following description lists some typical subsample characteristics of demographic and/or other relevant criteria.

1. Married Women. The subsample of the married women consists of 10 women (mean age at the time of the sixth measurement point: 75,7 years). During the time of World War I most of them were children or adolescents. After finishing their compulsory education, nearly all of them received no further educational qualification. Later employment was an exception among these women. However, since this time their financial circumstances (e.g., socioeconomic status) have to be regarded as satisfactory due to their husbands' positions. The majority of them live, together with their spouses, in rented apartments or flats in rather small towns. All of them have children, and most of them have grandchildren; they tend to live a certain geographical distance apart from their married offsprings. Their general health status, as rated by a physician, has decreased during the time of observation, but has to be seen as satisfactory and comparable with regard to the other women in the sample.

2. Never-Married Women. The nine women of the group of the Never-Married constitute the "oldest" subsample (mean age in 1976/77: 79,7 years). Mostly, they were young adults at the time of World War I. Two-thirds had educational and occupational training beyond the compulsory years, and all of them were employed women, either working in rather low service jobs or in higher helping/teaching professions. Their

financial situations improved over the time of investigation, with only three women reporting a relatively low income. Mostly, they live in large cities, alone in rented houses, flats, or homes for the aged, respectively. Quite a few of them live at a close distance to other relatives. According to the physician's rating, their health status has improved (!) significantly over the 12 years, but still proves to be comparable to the health situation of the other women of this sample.

3.   Recently Widowed Women. Eight women of the sample, after having been married for a very long time, were widowed 2 to 3 years before the sixth measurement point; thus, they were still married at the time of the first measurement point. Their mean age at the time of becoming widowed was 75,5 years, and the mean age in 1976/77 was 77,5 years, therefore emphasizing that these women tend to belong to the older cohort. Most of them completed compulsory schooling and had no further occupational training. Most of the time they worked exclusively as house-wives. Their financial situation was tense at the time of the first measurement point compared to the other group of Married Women, who were already rather well-off. Despite the reduction (down to 60%) of the Recently Widowed Women's formerly shared income before the death of their husbands, these women's financial circumstances have improved considerably during the 12 years of follow-up investigations.

At the time of the sixth measurement point most of the Recently Widowed Women live alone in rented apartments in big cities. All of them have at least two children and, except one, quite a number of grandchildren. They tend to live a small distance from at least one child. Compared with the physician's rating at the first measurement point, their health status seems to have slightly improved. Lastly, it seems noteworthy that there are some distinctions between the still-married group and this group of Recently Widowed women at the time they still were married, with the latter belonging to a slightly lower socioeconomic status and having more children.

4.   Long-Time Widowed Women. Twelve women of this sample have been widowed for an average of 28 years; the mean age at the time of the beginning widowhood was 49 years (half of these women lost their husbands in World War II). Their mean age in 1976/77 amounts to 75,8 years, which means that they tend to belong to the younger cohort. A small proportion of them went beyond compulsory schooling and received professional training. But even in this group of long-time single women employment has to be seen as an exception.

The financial situation of most of these women proved to be poor at the time of the first investigation, but has improved gradually. At the time of the last investigation, they seem to prefer living alone in rented flats in large cities. The size of their families is small, with two of them having no children, and three of them no grandchildren. The geographical distance between family members tends to be large. The physician's rating indicates a rather stable, satisfactory health status.

Statistical Methods

All interview information has been rated according to qualitative categories (rating scales); thus, all data are treated by "methods based primarily on the order relations among observations in a set of data" (Hays, 1969, p. 616) and analyzed by nonparametric statistical methods. Computed are:

1. Kruskall–Wallis analysis of variance by ranks in order to test intergroup variability.
2. Wilcoxon test for two matched samples in order to test intragroup variability.
3. Theta-based automatic-interaction detection (THETA-AID or THAID) by Morgan and Messenger (1973) to "predict" attitude toward the future. THAID is designed to identify an optimal model for explaining differences between cases with respect to a dependent variable, that is, to identify the underlying structure in the data (see Osiris III, 1973).

Generally, differences are not interpretated unless levels of statistical significance reach .05. If results of the two-order techniques prove to be significant at the level between .05 and .10 and are logically supportive of related findings, they are reported as trends.

RESULTS

A cognitively oriented differential psychology of aging as formulated by Thomae (1970, 1976) does not concentrate on specific behavioral aspects, but tries to comprehend the aging individual in his individuality and wholeness. This refers to one's being embedded in specific circumstances with specific ways of dealing with the environment, viewing the world in a specific way, and being determined by specific dominant concerns. Thus, the variables analyzed appear to represent in a comprehensive way the subject's life-span, that is, the sample's experiential and behavioral data with regard to certain important aspects of perceived life-space, personality data, coping styles, and dominant concerns. Most of the reported data are rating data assessed by the team of interviewers.

Significant group differences at the two measurement points in question in a cross-sectional analysis are reported, as well as intra group change within each group defined by the manifestation of marital status between the two measurement points.

Intergroup and Intragroup Variability at/between Two Measurement Points

One might conclude that the whole sample is homogenous, considering the fact that out of 176 cross-sectionally analyzed variables assessed in 1965/66 and 247 in 1976/77, only 26 or 36, respectively, turned out to differentiate in a sufficient way between the four subsamples. On the other hand, the longitudinal analysis of changes between the two measurement points within each subgroup suggests a slightly higher amount of variability. Thus, the question might be: What then is the evidence for inter- and intragroup variability?

MARRIED WOMEN

Differentiating Characteristics. In 1965/66, when most of their contemporaries were also married, the Married Women of this sample expressed a stronger feeling of being needed by family members than the women of the other subsamples. Family life seemed to provide a frame for outdoor activities (visiting restaurants, going on tours), whereas extrafamilial social orientations were hardly evident. The analysis of the women's coping styles identifies dependent behavior and so-called adjustment techniques, (mostly directed toward husband and children). The analysis of dominant themes of life reveals a rather low concern about extension and/or maintaining of personal interests. Twelve years later the majority of women, that is, the "norm" of their contemporaries, is widowed. One still finds a highly child-centered involvement but, on the other hand, decreasing activities within the familial role system; the perceived changes concerning family affairs are evaluated negatively. Subjectively rated health problems and a high degree of "neuroticism", implying psychosomatic symptoms, are more typical for the Married Women than for other groups. These women describe themselves as rather "modest/self-effacing" (Laforge & Suczek, 1955), and their coping styles still refer to adjustment and "relying-on-others" behavior. At the last measurement point, they are preoccupied with health and physical impairment and are concerned about perceived restrictions of social activities, while identifying themselves with aspects of former social life.

Intragroup Change. The attempt to determine intragroup change more precisely shows an increase of perceived restrictions in relating to health status and depressive reactions, less marital and familial satisfaction, feelings of being unnecessary and dependent, and a decrease of more extending orientations, such as leisure-time behavior and social activities. Yet, in spite of these "unfavorable" experiences, a slight increase in behavioral competence is noticed, including more achievement-related and less adjustment techniques compared to the expressed behavior of 12 years earlier.

NEVER-MARRIED WOMEN

Differentiating Characteristics. At the time of the first measurement point, most of these women were already retired. They were distinctive in their comparatively intensive extrafamilial social activities and their decisiveness in planning future residential circumstances. Their ways of coping can be characterized as achievement-related behavior. The analysis of dominant concerns shows them preoccupied with personal interests and identification with former professional life.

Twelve years later the Never-Married are noteworthy for the following characteristics: being together with relatives (mainly siblings and nieces/nephews), maintaining social contacts, entertaining guests, and reading books. They hardly feel stressed by health problems and/or psychosomatic symptoms. They cope by showing adjustment to the institutional aspects of their housing situations and are especially impressive in their obvious independence from other people. Their dominant concerns are directed toward religious affiliations and, again, toward identification with former professional and social life. They exhibit little concern about possible physical impairment.

Intragroup Change. Change within the group, regardless of the degree of contribution to intergroup variability, produces evidence for a reconstruction of the evaluation of perceived life-space and the existence of similar, yet less intensive, ways of coping.

The time after retirement can be regarded as a rather critical and restrictively experienced period of life; family life at that time turned out to be rather stressful. However, on becoming older, the Never-Married seem to experience more congruence between their desired and achieved goals, and more satisfaction with their given life-situation, while appearing, on the other hand, "free" and independent. A shift in the manifestation of their social activities seems to have taken place: a growing contentment with involvement in the increasing number of family affairs is accompanied by a (regretted) withdrawal from extrafamilial social activities.

RECENTLY WIDOWED WOMEN

Differentiating Characteristics. In 1965/66 the women of this subsample were still married, and their expressed role activities concentrated more on family concerns than on extrafamilial social life. They held a positive view of their past and personal memories. Their coping styles concerning "daily hassles" revealed achievement-related behavior as well as adjustment techniques. There were concerned about religious orientation and extension of personal interests. Thus, they are again similar to the other married group in their orientation towards family affairs, but they also differ slightly with regard to the importance of religious affiliation and personal interests. Despite having become widowed, these women reveal no signs of "deviant behavior" at the time of the later measurement point. In comparison with the other women they are noted for the amount of identification and ego-involvement directed toward their children and by activities in the mother role. Generally, perceived change in the family sphere is evaluated in a positive way. They seem to maintain a satisfying social life and do not feel very restricted by or concerned about health problems. They describe themselves as "modest/self-effacing," and their coping behavior is still dominated by adjustment techniques, although far less so than is characteristic of the Still-Married Women.

Intragroup Change.   Looking at the change that has taken place in the duration of this subsample, one is struck by the consistency, or even increase, of positive evaluations of daily life, and related behavior, respectively. These women are even more content with their family life over time. As concerns personality aspects, they seem to have become more open-minded and less rigid. Yet while there seems to be a high amount of stability concerning their dominant themes in general, tendencies to extend personal interests and social activities have decreased. Similar to this, readiness and alertness to cope seems to have diminished, despite it being characterized by less passivity and adjustment-oriented techniques.

LONG-TIME WIDOWED WOMEN

Differentiating Characteristics.   At the time of the first measurement point, the women of this subsample revealed a rather negative evaluation of their present life-situation. They were characterized by the feeling of being unnecessary, by perceived stress concerning their financial circumstances, and by inactivity with regard to social roles. Their recollection of the past was rather negative with the view of their former marriage life as the only extremely positive factor—possibly even a "glorification." They seemed to be interested in maintaining social contacts; yet, the readiness to cope with problems of the real life-situation has to be assessed as rather low.

Differentiating characteristics at the time of the sixth measurement point are different from those in 1965/66. Although activity in the mother role has decreased and ego-involvement directed toward children is low, readiness to deal actively with family problems has increased. There are comparatively high tendencies to express "neuroticism" or psychosomatic complaints, respectively, and to exhibit depressive reactions when health aspects are perceived as stressful. Yet the analysis of dominant concerns allows no specific characteristics, except that of religious affiliation, to be regarded as low among this subsample.

Intragroup Change. Although the search for differentiating characteristics among this subgroup yields evidence for rather negative evaluations of the given life-situations, the analysis of possible intragroup change reveals that the women involved are gradually more able to perceive some aspects of their life-space in a more positive way. With the exception of health-related events being viewed as more and more restrictive, the general feeling of well being seems to have improved. Higher satisfaction with their objectively improved economic status is expressed, and there is evidence of a stronger feeling of congruence concerning everyday life, along with an increase of extrafamilial social role activities. Personalitywise, they seem to be less characterized by "dogmatism" and "intolerance", and their concern about perceived restrictions of social activities is no longer predominant. The expressed coping styles with regard to the "daily hassles" refer to more achievement-related and socially oriented behavior.

SUMMARY

To summarize the results so far, it seems evident that the two cross-sectional analyses concerning data derived from two measurement points reveal distinctly differentiating criteria at each time of the two investigations.

In 1965/66 the four groups of this sample can be distinguished from each other according to their initiative and expressed activity in leisure, personal interests, and social participation, as well as by the evaluating process of their individual biographies. Twelve years later the "demarcation line" can be drawn according to family-related concerns and involvement, personality aspects, dissatisfaction/satisfaction with social life, perceived restrictions, and indoor-oriented leisure and social activities. Looking at coping styles, the groups of Still-Married and Later-Widowed Women reveal more adjustment and traditionally feminine, passive behavior than the single women at the time of the first measurement point—a differentiation that has diminished during the time of observation.

The analysis of intragroup variability yields evidence of a certain amount of intergroup differences in intragroup change: the Still-Married Women express more disturbance, the Never-Married exhibit growing stability and congruence, the Just-Widowed Women are rather consistent and stable in their ways of perceiving and coping, and the Long-Time Widowed Women partly overcome their formerly restricted life-situation and reveal a certain amount of competence. Thus, we may find evidence for variability among old-aged women as well as for developmental, growth-oriented change.

Attitude toward the Future: Differentiating between Satisfactory and Nonsatisfactory States of Being Old

Some other analyses (see Fooken, 1980) indicate that the specific manifestation of future-time perspective seems to be an important aspect of the pyschological construct life satisfaction. Thus, the purpose is to define subgroups even within the subsamples that sufficiently differentiate attitude toward the future, that is, express either a positive or a rather negative view of the time ahead. Hence, the interviewer's rating of the subject's expressed attitude toward the future is used as a central item (dependent variable). The selection of independent variables is made according to the demand for sufficient differentiation within each subsample and for adequate representation of important aspects of life-space, as well as of data on general experience, behavior, personality, coping styles, and dominant concerns. To further enhance the psychological comprehension of manifestation of attitude toward the future, characteristic variables of each subgroup are mentioned regardless of their predictive power concerning the dependent variable. What aspects of present life-space, personality, coping behavior, and dominant concerns manifest sufficient explanatory power?

1. MARRIED WOMEN

The quality of future time perspective is mainly associated with a general—meaning prospective and retrospective—attitude toward life as it is measured by the Riegel questionnaire (see Angleitner, 1976).

Negative View. A negative outlook on the time ahead and on life generally corresponds with low social participation in family and nonfamilial roles and with feelings of being unnecessary and hardly socially attractive. The women involved further reveal dissatisfaction with their daily life routine, perceiving it as eventless and monotonous despite a reported high amount of important events during the past 5 years. They

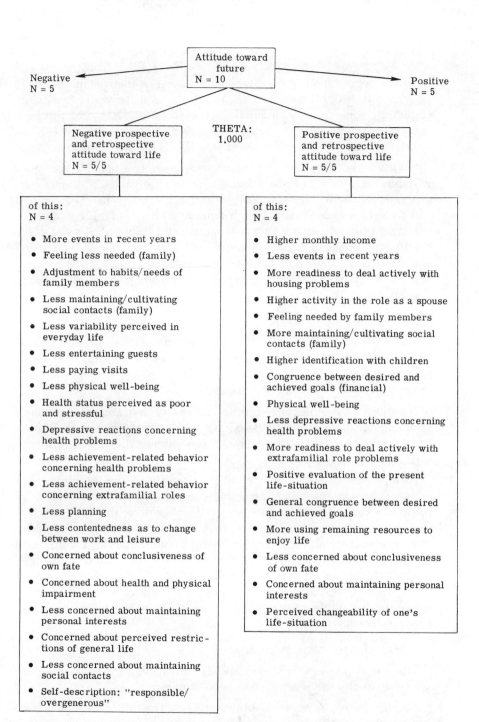

FIGURE 5.1 Multivariate analysis concerning attitude toward future (Married Women).

manifest depressive behavior when the rating of their health status is poor, and they don't seem to structure the time ahead with plans. They show little concern about maintaining personal interests, and although describing themselves as "responsible/overgenerous", still feel themselves determined by the conclusiveness (*Endgültigkeit*) of their own fate.

Positive View. Looking at the past and future in a positive way goes with high acceptance of one's present life-situation and a feeling of congruence between generally desired and achieved goals. The women mentioned here also reveal a high tendency towards family-related involvement (mainly directed toward spouse and children). A satisfactory health and financial situation seems to provide a framework for the maintenance of personal interests, the readiness to use remaining resources to enjoy life, and the perception of one's world as basically changeable.

2. NEVER-MARRIED WOMEN

The experience of the potential changeability of one's present life-situation and the way of relating the personality attributes "skeptical/distrustful" to oneself exhibit the high explanatory power of attitude toward the future within this subsample.

Negative View. A negative future time perspective and the experience of unchangeability are associated with the description of oneself as "skeptical/distrustful"; in general, these women reveal little effort to deal actively with aspects of housing, health, and social life.

Positive View. A positive look at the time ahead and the assessment of one's life-situation as changeable correspond with a self-image as being not very "skeptical/distrustful". Furthermore, these women distinguish themselves by planning their future time, cultivating fewer family-related social contacts, and having a higher monthly income, and physical well-being. Present acceptance of one's life-situation and a feeling of congruence between desired and achieved goals are high among these women, despite formerly expressed dissatisfaction with their decision to stay single and the description of their own behavior during the last decade as corrigible.

3. RECENTLY WIDOWED WOMEN

The perception of one's own fate as conclusive proves to be highly selective among the recently widowed women.

Negative View. A negative attitude toward the future and one's own fate go along with perceived unchangeability of one's life situation, a general negative attitude toward life, and the perception of everyday

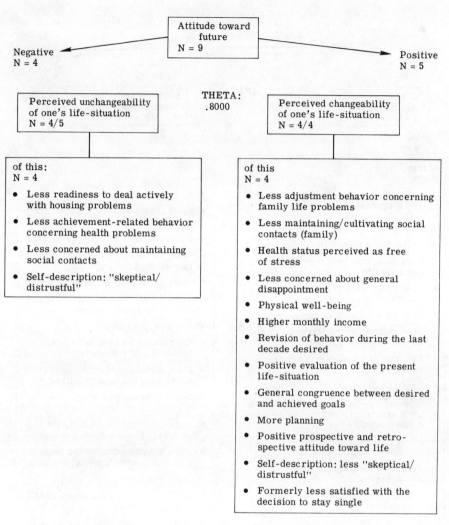

FIGURE 5.2 Multivariate analysis concerning attitude toward future (Never-Married Women).

life as eventless and monotonous. The women in this group do not feel needed by family members and do not seem concerned and interested in maintaining social contacts. Achievement-related behavior to improve the affected physical well-being is hardly recognizable. Generally, these women show little concern about maintaining personal interests and using their remaining resources to enjoy life, and yet they describe themselves as "less skeptical/distrustful."

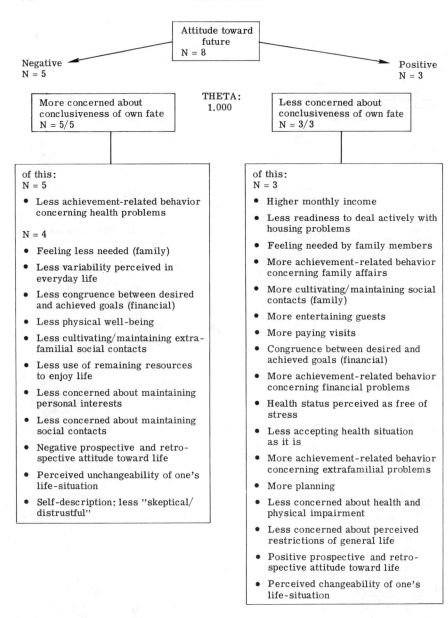

FIGURE 5.3 Multivariate analysis concerning attitude toward future (Recently Widowed Women).

Positive View. Not feeling determined by the conclusiveness of one's own fate and having a positive outlook toward the future appears to be associated with a positive attitude toward life and the expectancy of changeability of one's life-situation. Similarly, the Recently Widowed are differentiated by the degree to which they plan the time ahead; furthermore, they are characterized as feeling less restricted by financial, health, and social aspects than their "pessimistic" counterparts. Accordingly, they distinguish themselves by a higher monthly income, by perceiving their physical status as less stressful, and by being strongly involved in family and other social contracts.

4. LONG-TIME WIDOWED WOMEN

Using remaining resources and possibilities to make life enjoyable proves to be the best selective criterion with regard to predicting this subsample's attitude toward the future.

Negative View. Those long-time widows who reveal less concern about taking chances to make life more enjoyable and have a negative outlook toward the future also hold a negative view of life in general and feel dissatisfied when comparing their desired and achieved goals; they describe themselves as "skeptical/distrustful" and less "responsible/overgenerous". Their present life-situation, including everyday life, is perceived as restrictive, eventless and monotonous; no achievement-related behavior or social initiative to improve the unsatisfactory circumstances is revealed.

Positive View. A positive way of perceiving the time ahead and the readiness to use remaining resources to enjoy life correspond with active and self-initiated extrafamilial activity. The description of personality makes the involved women appear as "responsible/overgenerous" and less "skeptical/distrustful"; their general coping behavior in improving financial and health-related problems appears achievement-related. Their desired and achieved goals are congruent, and they look at life in a positive way, expressing no regrets for their behavior during the last decade. Generally, they perceive a high variability in everyday life and do not feel determined by the conclusiveness of their own fate.

SUMMARY

A summary statement concerning the kinds of results detailed above might emphasize the following aspects:

Interindividual variability can be expected even within each subsample. Therefore, an attempt was made to identify eight subgroups, with

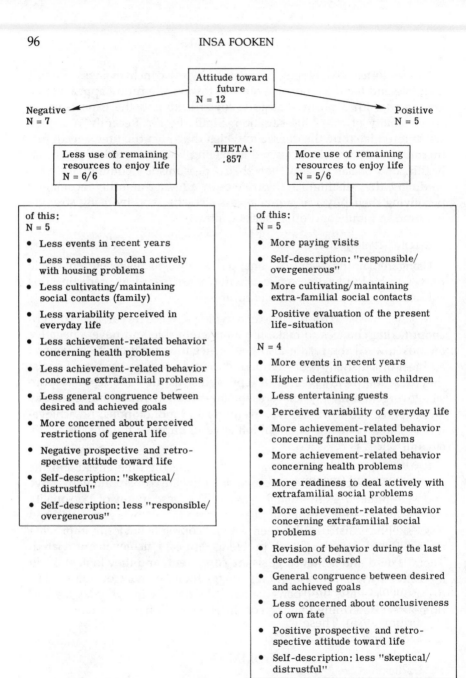

FIGURE 5.4   Multivariate analysis concerning attitude toward future (Long-Time Widowed Women).

four groups being slightly at risk because of expressing a negative outlook toward the future, and four groups expressing a satisfactory state of being old because of their ability to look at the time ahead in a positive way. According to this analysis, the subsample of Still-Married Women differ in regard to general attitude toward life and family-and health-related dissatisfaction/satisfaction; The two subgroups of Never Married Women are differentiated from one another by the amount of perceived restrictions or changeability, respectively, of their lives; the Recently Widowed Women differ according to the degree to which they feel determined by the conclusiveness of their own fate and to economic aspects; and the Long-Time Widowed Women are noted for the different amount of activity and readiness in dealing with personal and social interests.

CONCLUSION

With reference to other information on marital status structure and corresponding psychological data in old age, we might confirm the reported difficulties of married couples (see Payne & Whittington, 1976) who live a rather isolated and restricted social life in old age as compared to their contemporaries. Indications of "somatization" tendencies among the married women can be linked to similar findings that attribute complaints about health status to housewives rather than to employed women (see Waldon, 1980). As concerns marital satisfaction, there is evidence of a high correlation between life-satisfaction and marital involvement (meaning intensive couple-sharing activities). Referring to the so-called age grading of female dominance (Gutman, 1977), the results still indicate quite an amount of deference to the husband and reveal only slight hints of more active mastery; these are by no means, indications of exerted female power.

The Never-Married Women of the sample come close to other descriptions of never-married people in old age in gerontological literature. Agreement can be found in descriptions of their individuality, mastery of life in old age, and personal independence from popular stereotypes (Gubrium, 1975). These women are even prone to criticize their former decisions and behavior without quarreling about their fate and feeling totally determined by external circumstances. On the other hand, in contradication to the findings of Gubrium (1975) and Tunstall (1966), there is no evidence of their social isolation, the Never-Married Women of this study exhibit the most social activity of all the subsamples.

The study of Recently Widowed Women does not support the findings attesting to a high morbidity-rate and low morale in mourning women (e.g., Maddison & Viola, 1968; Bornstein, Clayton, Falikas, Maurice, & Robins, 1973). Similar to the old widows in the study of Heyman and Gianturco (1973), the women of this subsample are differentiated by the stability of their health ratings as well as general behavior and experiences. They come close to the type of widow Lopata (1973a; 1975) describes as a "traditional widow," that is, a woman who is embedded into satisfactory family networks. Furthermore, the synchronization of "normal status biography" (Levy, 1977) and personal experience, (becoming widowed "in time"), seems to enable these women to be psychologically prepared to accept the death of the spouse as well as their own status of widow. It might also be that a long and satisfying marriage provides a good opportunity to "survive" widowhood in old age.

On the other hand, the Long-Time Widowed Women experienced widowhood "off time" (Neugarten et al., 1968)—a fact which might account for the low morale of this subsample at the time when most of their contemporaries were still married. Growing into "normality," that is, not belonging to a minority group any more, seems to ease the burden and stigma of being a single woman in a couple-oriented society. It is the improvement of economic resources that's especially helpful in prompting these women to develop a "change potential" and use it in a constructive and satisfactory way.

In general, evidence is given for a variety of different "patterns of aging," which, above all, are accompanied by *satisfaction*, that is, by "maintaining a balance between individual needs and perceived life-situation" (Thomae, 1976). The antecedents, or genesis of "successful aging," have to be traced back to former stages of life, since *mastery potential* (evaluation of the past, general attitude toward life, and aspects of self-image) is regarded as powerful predictors of 'life-satisfaction' in old age. Thus, the "fate" of marital status does not explain or determine psychological well being in old age, although it might foster or hinder certain kinds of experiences. It is rather the way one has learned to match one's own aspiration level to the always-changing situational context that aids in coping with the (boring or comfortable) continuities and (dangerous or challenging) discontinuities that accompany the transition into old age.

REFERENCES

Angleitner, A. Changes in personality observed in questionnaire data from the Riegel questionnaire on rigidity, dogmatism, and attitude toward life. In H. Thomae (Ed.), *Patterns of aging* (68–80). Basel: Karger, 1976.

Atchley, R. C. *The social forces in later life: An introduction to social gerontology.* Belmont: Wadsworth Publishing Company, 1972.

Baldwin, A. L. A cognitive theory of socialization. In D. A. Goslin (Ed.), *Handbook of socialization theory and research* (325–345). Chicago: Rand McNally, 1969.

Beeson, D. Women in the studies of aging: A critique and suggestion. *Social Problems,* 1976, 3, 52–59.

Bernard, J. *The female world.* New York: The Free Press, 1981.

Blau, Z. S. *Old age in a changing society.* New York: New Viewpoints, 1973.

Bornstein, P. E., Clayton, P. J., Falikas, J. A., Maurice, W. L., & Robins, E. The depression of widowhood after thirteen months. *British Journal of Psychiatry,* 1973, 122, 561–566.

Carlsson, R. Understanding women: Implications for personality theory and research. *Journal of Social Issues,* 1972, 28, 17–32.

Clark, M., & Anderson, B. G. *Culture and aging.* Springfield, IL: Thomas Publisher, 1967.

Cumming, E., & Henry, W. E. *Growing old: The process of disengagement.* New York: Basic Books, 1961.

Deutsch, H. *Die Psychologie der Frau* (Vols. 1–2). Bern/Stuttgart: Hans Huber, 1953–1954.

Duvall, E. M. *Family development.* Philadelphia/New York: Lippincott, 1971.

Erikson, E. *Identität und Lebenszyklus.* Frankfurt: Suhrkamp, 1966.

Fooken, I. *Frauen im Alter: Eine Analyse intra- und interindividueller Differenzen.* Frankfurt/Bern/Cirencester: Peter D. Lang, 1980. (a)

Fooken, I., Biographische Faktoren des Altererlebens lediger und langjähriger verwitweter Frauen. *Zeitschrift für Gerontologie,* 1980, 13, 475–490. (b)

Freud, S. *Die Weiblichkeit: Vorlesungen 1915–1917* (Gesammelte Werke XV). London: Imago Publishing, 1940.

Giesen, C. B., & Datan, N. The competent older woman. In N. Datan and N. Lohmann (Eds.), *Transition of aging.* New York: Academic Press, 1980.

Gubrium, J. F. Being single in old age. *International Journal of Aging and Human Development,* 1975, 6, 29–41.

Gutman, D. The cross-cultural perspective: Notes toward a comparative psychology of aging. In J. E. Birren and K. W. Schaie (Eds.), *Handbook of the psychology of aging* (302–326). New York: Van Nostrand-Reinhold, 1977.

Hall, G. S. *Senescence.* New York: Appleton, 1922.

Harding, M. E. *The way of all women.* London: Rider, 1971.

Havighurst, R. J. *Developmental tasks and education.* New York: David McKay, 1972.

Hays, W. L. *Statistics for the social sciences.* London/New York: Holt, Rinehart & Winston, 1969.

Heyman, D. K., & Gianturco, D. T. Long-term adaptation by the elderly to bereavement. *Journal of Gerontology,* 1973, 28, 359–362.

Hutchison, S. L., Jr., & Lilienthal, R. A. Advisement to take risk: A study of attitudes toward the old. *International Journal of Behavioral Development,* 1980, 3, 19–26.

James, W. *The principles of psychology.* New York: Holt, 1980.

Jung, C. G. Über die Psychologie des Unbewussten (Gesammelte Werke VII). Zürich/Stuttgart: Rascher, 1964.

LaForge, R., & Suczek, R. The interpersonal dimension of personality: III. An interpersonal check-list. *Journal of Personality,* 1955, 24, 94–112.

Lazarus, R. S., & Cohen, J. B. *Theory and method in the study of stress and coping in aging individuals.* Paper presented at the W. H. O. Conference on Society, Stress, and Disease: Aging and Old Age, Stockholm, 1976, June.

Lehr, U. Die Situation der älteren Frau: Psychologische und soziale Aspekte. In U. Lehr (Ed.), *Seniorinnen: Zur Situation der älteren Frauen* (6–26). Darmstadt: Steinkopff, 1978.

Lehr, U., & Thomae, H. *Konflikt, seelische Belastung und Lebensalter.* Köln/Opladen: West-deutscher Verlag, 1965.

Levy, R. *Der Lebenslauf als Statusbiographie: Die weibliche Normalbiographie in makrosoziolo-gischer Perspektive.* Stuttgart: Enke, 1977.

Lopata, H. Z. The life cycle of the social role of housewives. *Sociology and Social Research,* 1966, *51,* 5–22.

Lopata, H. Z. *Widowhood in an American city.* Cambridge, MA: Schenkman, 1973. (a)

Lopata, H. Z. Self-identity in marriage and widowhood. *The Sociological Quarterly,* 1973, *14,* 407–418.

Lopata, H. Z. Societal factors in life-span disruptions and alternatives. In N. Datan and L. H. Ginsberg (Eds.), *Life-span developmental psychology: Normative life crises* (217–234). New York: Academic Press, 1975.

Lowenthal, M. F., Thurnher, M., Chiriboga, D., & Associates. *Four stages of life.* San Fran-cisco/Washington/London: Jossey–Bass, 1975.

Maddison, D., Viola, A. The health of widows in the year following the bereavement. *Journal of Psychosomatic Research,* 1968, *12,* 297–306.

Matthews, S. H. The social world of old women: Management of self-identity (Vol. 78). Sage library of social research. Beverly Hills/London: Sage, 1979.

May, R. Sex differences in fantasy patterns. *Journal of Projective Techniques and Personality Assessment,* 1966, *30,* 576–586.

Morgan, J. N., & Messenger, R. C. *THAID: A sequential analysis program for the analysis of nominal scale dependent variables.* Ann Arbor: The University of Michigan, Institute for Social Research, 1973.

Mussen, P., Eichorn, D. H., Honzik, M. P., Bieber, L., & Meredith, W. M. Continuity and change in women's characteristics over four decades. *International Journal of Behavioral Development,* 1980, *3,* 333–347.

Neugarten, B. L., Moore, J. W., & Lowe, J. C. Age norms, age constraints, and adult socialization. In B. L. Neugarten (Ed.), *Middle age and aging* (22–28). Chicago: The Uni-versity of Chicago Press, 1968.

Olbrich, E., & Thomae, H. Empirical findings to a cognitive theory of aging. *International Journal of Behavioral Development,* 1978, *1,* 67–82.

Osiris, III. *System and program description* (Vol. 1). Ann Arbor: The University of Michigan, 1973.

Payne, B. P., & Whittington, F. Older women: An examination of popular stereotypes and research evidence. *Social Problems,* 1976, *3,* 488–504.

Rudinger, G., & Bierhoff–Alfermann, D. Methodenprobleme in der Geschlecht-sunterschiedsforschung. In H. Keller (Ed.), *Geschlechtsunterschiede.* Weinheim/Basel: Beltz, 1979.

Rudinger, G., & Lantermann, E. D. Probleme der Veränderungsmessung in individuellen und gruppentypischen Entwicklungsverläufen. In R. Oerter (Ed.), *Entwicklung als le-benslänglicher Prozess* (178–227). Hamburg: Hoffmann und Campe, 1978.

Sheehan, N. Planned obsolescence: Historical perspectives on aging women. In K. F. Rie-gel and J. A. Meacham (Eds.), *The developing individual in a changing world* (59–68). The Hague/Paris: Mouton, 1976.

Thomae, H. Theory of aging and cognitive theory of personality. *Human Development,* 1970, *13,* 1–16.

Thomae, H. The "developmental task approach" to a theory of aging. *Zeitschrift für Ger-ontologie,* 1975, *8,* 125–137.

Thomae, H. *Patterns of aging: Findings from the Bonn Longitudinal Study of Aging.* Basel: Karger, 1976.

Thomae, H. The concept of development and life-span developmental psychology. In

P. P. B. Baltes and O. G. Brim (Eds.), *Life-span development and behavior* (Vol. 2, pp. 281-312). New York/San Francisco/London: Academic Press, 1979.

Tunstall, J. *Old and alone*. London: Routledge & Kegan, 1966.

Uhlenberg, P. Older women: The growing challenge to design constructive roles. *The Gerontologist*, 1979, *19*, 236-241.

Vaerting, M. *Neubegründung der Psychologie von Mann und Weib: Vol. 1: Die weibliche Eigenart im Männerstaat und die männliche Eigenart im Frauenstaat*. Karlsruhe i.B.: G. Braunsche Hofbuchdruckerei, 1921.

Vaillant, G. E. *Adaptation to life*. Boston: Little, Brown, 1977.

Waldon, I. Employment and women's health: An analysis of causal relationships. *International Journal of Health Services*, 1980, *10*, 435-454.

Weinreich, H. What future for the female subject? Some implications of the women's movement for psychological research. *Human Relations*, 1977, *30*, 535-543.

6

PERCEIVED UNCHANGEABILITY OF LIFE AND SOME BIOGRAPHICAL CORRELATES

Hermann-Josef Fisseni

INTRODUCTION

PERCEIVED UNCHANGEABILITY

"Old age is associated with death and dying as a matter of course" (Munnichs 1966, p. 5). Not identical with facing death or dying, but found in its vicinity, is the perception of one's situation as unchangeable: an experience here called "awareness of the definiteness of one's existence" (Erleben der Endgültigkeit der eigenen Existenz) or *perceived unchangeability*. This concept needs a detailed clarification. It refers to the process of becoming aware that one's existence is growing definite in an irreversible way, that one's future biography is fixed, and that one cannot expect significant changes.

Schultz (1939, p. 126) has described this perception or awareness (reported by many elderly persons) in the following way: decisive conditions of a person's situation are perceived to become unchangeable; the life course ahead is felt to be no longer a function of one's own potentials, but of obligations, responsibilities, and the necessity to dedicate oneself to family, work, and society. For many this perception is accompanied by fears and the experience of limitations or restrictions.

Elderly people, who are strongly aware of their life's unchangeability, scarcely "see" possibilities for a reordering or restructuring of their lifespace. The perception of unchangeability (or awareness of definiteness) thereby contradicts the belief in one's self-efficacy.

This experience may be illustrated by two biographical examples taken from Tismer. First, he reports (1969, pp. 62–69) about a woman, aged 75 (born 1889), who declared her whole life to have been made up of nothing but missed chances, and unrealized expectations: as an adolescent she was compelled by her parents to give up a profession she was eager to pursue (studying medicine); later she married a man who became an alcoholic and left her, without caring for his two children; and she raised a son and a daughter who were not able to keep up regular contact with her due to family and professional engagements. Second, Tismer describes (1969, pp. 102–108) a man, aged 64 (born 1901), who, from childhood up to his 30s was able to look for opportunities to enjoy life, but was thereafter forced to struggle for survival. As a child and adolescent he was coddled by his mother (as the only son out of four children). In his twenties he made a living as a photographer and was married. In his thirties, due to the economic situation in Germany and his deteriorating health (gastric trouble), he had to change his profession. He started running a grocery shop. Yet, as a consequence of increased gastric troubles and of his wife's illness, he gave up the shop and made his living by running a *kiosk*. Although he had begun receiving his disablement pension early (since 1962), the amount was very small (DM100 ca. U.S. $40–50) and he and his wife were dependent on social welfare.

The intention of this paper is to show the role of perceived unchangeability in an elderly person's conceptualization of his existence (i.e., to show the power of self-interpretation on perceptions and the construction of one's life-space). Such a concept has its place within the framework of a cognitive theory of personality.

COGNITIVE THEORY OF PERSONALITY

A cognitive theory of personality can be defined as a frame of reference that tries to clarify how an individual perceives the world around him (Baldwin, 1969; Kelly, 1955; Snygg & Combs, 1949; Thomae, 1968, 1970). In a cognitive theory percpetion is not considered to be a reaction to a stimulus, but an active selection and evaluation of stimulus input. This process is influenced by the individual's needs, expectancies, self-concepts, and coping or defense strategies.

As an example we refer to Thomae's cognitive theory (1968, 1970, 1979). In his view an individual structures his life by preferring and shaping certain dominant *themes* (Daseinsthemen), such as the establishing of harmony in life or the confrontation with disturbance in one's life conditions. The individual applies *techniques* (Daseinstechniken) of aggression, evasion, adjustment, or defense strategies in order to realize his dominant themes. This process more or less represents an individual's manner of self-conceptualization, described by Thomae (1970, pp. 4, 5, 8) in three *postulates* (Postulaten):

1. Perception of change rather than objective change is related to behavioral change.
2. Any change in the situation of the individual is perceived and evaluated in terms of the dominant concerns and expectations of the individual.
3. Adjustment to aging is a function of the balance between cognitive and motivational structure of the individual.

The first postulate introduces the decisive intervening variable of "perceived change," the second postulate relates perceptional and motivational aspects in the process of self-conceptualization, and the third postulate connects this process with "adjustment" as a criterion of successful aging.

In 1979 Thomae applied the cognitive theory of personality to perceived unchangeability (or the awareness of the definiteness of one's situation). This process implies four sets of variables: (1) transsituational determinants of behavior, (2) external situational conditions, (3) internal processes, and (4) external reactions.

Transsituational determinants refer to factors, such as generalized expectations, attitudes, beliefs, values, and structures of motives that are all acquired during a life-long process and channel an individual's behaviour; *External situational conditions* refer to objective factors confronting a person with limitations (e.g., socioeconomic factors); *internal processes* imply the comparison of the perceived objective factors with one's own expectations and the evaluation and selection of one's own reactions; and *external reactions* refer to what follows as an observable event, connected with the observable stimulus.

The central part of Thomae's model is the assumption that reactions to a situation originate from expectations, needs, and beliefs formed by an individual in a life-long process. The perception of unchangeability, therefore, is not interpreted as an objective process initiated by some stimuli, but as a formation of one's perceived life-space.

METHODS

SAMPLE

Our study's sample consisted of 81 elderly persons who were also participants in the Bonn Longitudinal Study of Aging (BLSA) from 1965 to 1977. The BLSA was initiated by Thomae in 1965, the purpose being to assess the individual world of elderly people in such a differentiated way as to allow for a variety of inter- and intraindividual comparisons by quantitative methods (Thomae, Angleitner, Grombach, and Schmitz-Scherzer, 1973, p. 361). Up to 1977, the BLSA included six measurement points (MP I to VI): 1965/66; 1966/67; 1967/68; 1969; 1972; and 1976/77.

Our sample was taken from two cohorts, born 1890–1895 and 1900–1905. It included more women than men, and more members of the younger than of the older cohort. Their health status, as judged by a physician, was satisfactory. Evaluations of monthly income, grade of school visited, and socioeconomic status, identified them as belonging to the middle class (Thomae, 1976). Further descriptions of the sample concerning some sociodemographic variables can be taken from Tables 6.1. and 6.2.

CORRELATES TO PERCEIVED UNCHANGEABILITY

In addition to sociodemographic factors 14 biographical variables and three mental test scores were analysed in this study and expected to be correlated with perceived unchangeability.

The information for the 14 biographical variables was derived from three interviews per measurement point, covering past, present, and future situations. Rating scales (from 1 to 9 or from 1 to 6) were used for measuring the information gathered. To explain this process more precisely, we outline the planning and design of the BLSA in greater detail.

TABLE 6.1

SAMPLE OF 81 PARTICIPANTS OF THE BONN LONGITUDINAL STUDY OF AGING (BLSA)[a]

	Men	Women	Sum
Cohort: 1890–1895	15	19	34
1900–1905	19	28	47
Sum	34	47	81
Grade of school visited (1 = low; 8 = high)			
M	3, 14	3, 17	
SD	1, 47	1, 47	
SES (1 = low; 5 = high)			
M	3, 05	2, 89	
SD	0, 74	0, 66	

[a]MP = Measurement Point, M = Mean, and SD = Standard Deviation.

TABLE 6.2

SMALL OF 81 BLSA PARTICIPANTS OVER 15 YEARS[a]

	MP I (1965/66)		MP IV (1969)		MP VI (1976/77)	
	Men	Women	Men	Women	Men	Women
Marital status						
Unmarried	0	9	0	9	0	9
Married	33	18	32	17	29	10
Widowed	—	16	1	19	5	26
Divorced	1	2	1	1	—	1
Living separately	—	2	—	1	—	1
Sum	34	47	34	47	34	47
Income (DM) (100 DM = 40–50 dollars)						
M	1023	696	1164	808	1887	1437
SD	508	413	780	575	882	873
Health status, as judged by a physician (1 = good, 5 = poor)						
M	2, 47	2, 71	2, 74	2, 90	1, 66	1, 78
SD	0, 70	0, 96	0, 76	0, 76	0, 70	0, 66

[a]MP = Measurement Point, M = Mean, and SD = Standard Deviation.

At each measurement point the subjects' assessment period was scheduled for 1 week (with the exception of measurement point V when, for financial reasons, only 4 days were available). Table 6.3 shows the procedure at each measurement point.

The schedule of our procedures demonstrates that we assigned the major part of our week with the subjects to interviews. This decision is explained firstly by the methodological preferences that can be traced in the Berkeley Studies (Jones, 1958) in the same way as they are in our own, and secondly, by the theoretical considerations, formulated in terms of a cognitive theory of personality (Thomae, 1968) or aging (Thomae, 1970), which place special emphasis on the nature of a behavior, as perceived by the individual, as the situation's dependent variable. Because our subjects were well motivated to cooperate in our study, their responses in the interviews can be regarded as valid cues to their perceptions of present, past, and future life-situations. On the other hand, we used intelligence and personality tests to get information on their psychological situations as objectively as possible. As cognitive and

TABLE 6.3
Weekly Schedule for Testing Program (BLSA)[a]

	MPI[b]	
Monday		informal meeting between staff and subjects
Tuesday	a.m.	interview on present life-situation, social participation, SES, etc.; daily round
	p.m.	medical examination
Wednesday	a.m.	life history interview (childhood, adolescence, young adulthood; life situation in 1948, 1955 and 1965)
	p.m.	free
Thursday	a.m.	testing procedures: WAIS, TAT, Z-test (short form of Rorschach), Riegel Scales
	p.m.	tour to the Rhine or Ahr Valley, behaviour ratings by the participating observers
Friday	a.m.	interview on future time perspective and expected living conditions including attitudes towards institutionalisation; Mierke psychomotor-performance test; measurement of variables in writing pressure.

[a]From Thomae 1976, p. 6.
[b]MPI = Measurement Point I (1965/66).

motivational aspects of behavior are interrelated to each other in a very complex manner, it was decided to introduce as many variables as possible; this would enable us to identify different patterns of aging and the cognitive, motivational, social, and biological correlates of these patterns. The design of the study was influenced by the author's experience as a psychological director of the German Longitudinal Study on Children (Coerper, Hagen, & Thomae, 1954; Hagen & Thomae, 1962) and by longitudinal studies on middle-aged white-collar employees (Lehr & Thomae, 1958), as well as on a sample of men and women born between 1885 and 1930 (Lehr, 1969; Lehr & Thomae, 1965). The final design was discussed with many colleagues from Bonn and other universities (Thomae, 1976, p. 7).

Biographical Correlates

The 14 biographical correlates that were introduced in this study may be commented upon in some detail.

   1. *General role activity* refers to the sum of activities in nine conventional roles, as conceptualized by Havighurst (1972): the roles of

parents, grandparents, kin, friend, acquaintance, neighbour, club member, spouse, and citizen.

2. *General role satisfaction* implies the subjective satisfaction found in these nine roles.

3. *Daily life* refers to a series of "normal" days, and to statements characterizing them on a continuum from "varying and stimulating" to "monotonous and altogether unattractive."

4. *Stress due to family* refers to reported difficulties in family life (spouse, relatives, or offspring).

5. *Contentment with the present* refers to the global situation, evaluated as positive or negative.

6. Attitude towards the future may be completely negative ("I do not expect anything good from the future") or highly positive ("I expect a lot of the future").

7. *Feeling needed by others* refers to the experience that other people (kin, acquaintance, offspring, or friends) are dependent on one's help under any aspect, or to the very opposite feelings: that one is of no use to anybody in any aspect.

8. *Housing problems* are related to the comfort of housing conditions, covering a continuum from a poor to a satisfactory amount of housing space and furniture.

9. *Worries about health* represent subjective judgments about one's health status.

10. *Quality and variability of mood* stem from behavior ratings by the staff, given at the end of each individual assessment (see Table 6.3: Thursday). The "quality of mood" was classified on a 9-point scale ranging from "depressive" to "elated," and the "variability of mood" was rated from "very stable" to "extremely unstable."

As was pointed out earlier, four biographical correlates belong to the so-called themes of life (*Daseinsthemen*) that are central topics in Thomae's cognitive personality theory. *Themes of life* are basic concerns and values that dominate one's life-space and contribute to its structure.

In our context, the relevant variables are

11. "confrontation or occupation with the finitude of life;"

12. "involvement in religious activities or thoughts;"

13. "being oppressed by one's health status (i.e., by physical stress);" and our key variable,

14. "perceiving the unchangeability of one's situation"—one of the basic concerns of the 'themes of life'.

The three *mental test scores*, introduced as correlates, stem from the German version of the WAIS (Wechsler-Adult-Intelligence Scale)—the so-called HAWIE (Hamburg-Wechsler-Intelligenztest für Erwachsene). The three scores represent the Total test, the Verbal part, and the Performance part. The statistics of the biographical and the test variables are quoted in Table 6.4, covering six measurement points (from 1965 to 1977).

STATISTICAL STEPS

The data of the biographical correlates were treated as ordinal measures. Therefore, all data were statistically analyzed by nonparametric methods, except for a global analysis of variance for the unchangeability scores. Johnson's Hierarchical Cluster Analysis (1967), Spearman's Rank Correlation, Mann and Whitney's U-Test, and Friedman's Two-Way Analysis of Variance were calculated.

The analysis included four steps. First, a global analysis of variance was computed using the unchangeability scores. Second, a cluster analysis was applied to all variables. Third, correlations were computed between perceived unchangeability and each of the correlates introduced. Fourth, the total sample was divided into 4 subsamples according to different scores for perceived unchangeability, and the subgroups were compared with each other.

RESULTS

PERCEIVED UNCHANGEABILITY
OVER SIX MEASUREMENT POINTS

The scores for perceived unchangeability show variation between subjects as well as between measurement points. As tested by an analysis of variance, both differences were significant. The results indicate that (1) the 81 participants differed in their perception of their situation as being unchangeable; (2) this intensity of perceiving unchangeability varied from measurement point I to VI; and (3) differences between subjects (SS) were more salient than differences between measurement points (MP). (ω [SS] = .20 vs. ω [MP] = .09). These results call for further analysis to investigate whether biographical correlates explain the variations found in the unchangeability scores (Tables 6.5 and 6.6).

MULTIVARIATE RELATIONSHIPS BETWEEN PERCEIVED
UNCHANGEABILITY AND OTHER VARIABLES

A hierarchical cluster analysis was computed, using the medians of each variable over measurement point I to VI. The analysis yielded three main clusters, each including subclusters that are neglected here.

TABLE 6.4

CORRELATES TO PERCEIVED UNCHANGEABILITY: 14 BIOGRAPHICAL VARIABLES AND 3 TEST SCORES (FROM WAIS)[a,b]

	Measurement points						
	1965/66 I	1966/67 II	1967/68 III	1969 IV	1972 V	1976/77 VI	Total I–VI
General role activity	5,08	4,25	5,27	4,87	5,20	5,02	4,95
(1 = low)	1,11	1,69	1,26	1,28	1,34	1,45	1,3
General role satisfaction	5,25	5,28	5,41	4,92	6,29	5,70	5,48
(1 = low)	1,20	1,13	1,15	1,41	1,12	0,80	1,19
Daily life: variable or monotonous	5,11	—	5,17	5,17	5,88	4,53	5,16
(1 = monotonous)	1,71	—	1,71	1,28	1,26	1,80	1,55
Feelings of being needed by others	5,53	5,47	5,38	5,11	—	7,78	5,73
(1 = not needed)	1,13	0,96	1,16	1,08	—	0,78	1,02
Housing problems	4,52	4,93	5,00	4,38	4,08	4,13	4,51
(1 = low)	1,14	1,43	1,42	1,01	0,94	1,06	1,17
Worries about health	4,33	4,15	4,38	3,64	5,92	2,15	4,39
(1 = low)	1,50	1,64	1,34	1,07	1,83	0,33	1,29
Stress due to family	5,08	6,59	5,02	3,76	5,06	4,54	5,03
(1 = low)	1,38	1,55	1,16	1,06	1,36	1,22	1,29
Contentment with the present	5,38	5,87	5,91	5,77	—	1,53	5,22
(1 = low)	1,35	1,11	0,94	1,04	—	0,57	1,00
Attitude towards the future	6,73	—	4,87	4,82	4,14	4,39	5,01
(1 = negative) (9 = positive)	1,35	—	1,60	1,42	1,01	1,48	1,37
Mood: quality (from elated to depressive)	5,97	5,71	5,72	5,68	5,69	4,34	5,51
(1 = depressive) (9 = elated)	1,83	1,16	1,05	1,03	1,09	1,09	1,21

(Continued)

TABLE 6.4 (Continued)

	Measurement points						
	1965/66 I	1966/67 II	1967/68 III	1969 IV	1972 V	1976/77 VI	Total I–VI
Mood: variablity (from very stable to very unstable)	6,43	5,78	4,01	3,93	4,20	3,34	4,64
(1 = stable)	2,01	1,19	0,42	0,36	1,15	0,57	0,95
Facing the finitude of one's life	4,37	4,33	4,20	4,20	4,70	5,10	4,50
(1 = low)	1,71	0,79	0,99	0,81	1,76	1,63	1,28
Religious involvement	5,56	5,17	4,88	4,18	4,32	3,92	4,66
(1 = low)	1,50	1,38	1,32	0,98	0,92	1,40	1,25
Being oppressed by physical stress	4,89	5,19	4,48	4,32	4,44	4,85	4,69
(1 = low)	1,43	1,59	1,50	0,75	0,78	1,57	1,27
WAIS							
Total	97,83	—	99,10	98,50	96,25	92,00	96,10
	9,33	—	10,31	10,50	11,13	13,52	10,96
Verbal part	53,19	—	53,19	53,00	52,17	52,38	53,05
	6,58	—	5,70	6,17	5,19	8,11	6,35
Performance part	44,21	—	45,38	45,25	45,10	40,40	44,30
	4,88	—	5,97	6,00	5,90	6,94	5,94

[a]Medians (above) and Semi-Interquartile Range (below).
[b]All scores were standardized with a mean of M = 5 and a standard deviation of SD = 2.

TABLE 6.5

PERCEIVED UNCHANGEABILITY (AWARENESS OF DEFINITENESS) IN THE MEDIAN
AND SEMI-INTERQUARTILE RANGE AT SIX MEASUREMENT POINTS[a]

| | Measurement points | | | | | | |
	I 1965/66	II 1966/67	III 1967/68	IV 1969	V 1972	VI 1976/77	Total
Med	4,88	4,48	4,25	4,21	4,47	5,24	4,61
SemQ	1,56	1,55	1,43	0,74	1,64	1,54	1,41

[a]Median = Med; Semi-Interquartile Range = SemQ; and Measuring Points = MP.

The results are reported in two figures, with Figure 6.1 schematizing
the three clusters, and Figure 6.2 representing the structure of the different clusters and subclusters in detail. The difficulty in cluster analysis
lies in the fact that no criterion exists for determining the number of
clusters and for differentiating the subclusters from each other.

In a cluster analysis the data are grouped according to the degree in
which their covariances are similar. Variables that are placed side by side
are correlated to a higher degree than those placed at a greater distance
from each other.

Cluster A consisted of nine variables:

marital status,
feeling needed by others,
finding one's daily life variable or monotonous,
number of children,
role satisfaction,
role activity,
contentment with the present,
attitude towards the future, and
mood (elated or depressive).

TABLE 6.6

PERCEIVED UNCHANGEABILITY (AWARENESS OF DEFINITENESS) ANALYSIS OF VARIANCE[a]

Source	SS	DF	MSS	F	ω	P
Between subjects	1259	80	15,74	2,79	.20	.01
Within subjects	2413	405	6,21			
Between MP	252	5	50,47	8,93	.09	.01
Residual	2261	400	5,65			
Total	3773	484	7,78			

[a]With repeated measures over six Measurement Points (MP).

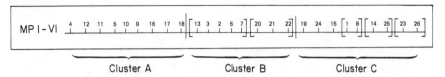

FIGURE 6.1   Cluster analysis of 26 Variables over six Measurement Points (MP). Comprehensive clusters are separated by a beam; smaller clusters by brackets. Meaning of numbers: 1, Age; 2, Income; 3, Sex (1 = Men, 2 = Women); 4, Marital status (1 = unmarried, 2 = married); 5, Number of children; 6, School; 7, SES; 8, Health status (physical); 9, Role activity; 10, Role Satisfaction; 11, Variability of daily life; 12, Feeling needed by others; 13, Housing Problems; 14, Worries about health; 15, Stress by family; 16, Contentment with the present; 17, Attitude towards the future; 18, Mood (from elated to depressive); 19, Variability of mood; 20, WAIS: Verbal part; 21, WAIS: Performance part; 22, WAIS: Total score; 23, Facing finitude; 24, Religious involvement; 25, Physical stress; 26, Perceived unchangeability.

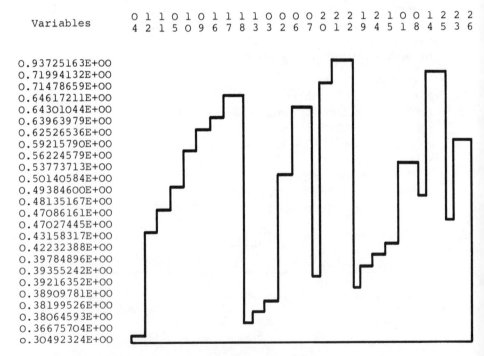

FIGURE 6.2   Cluster analysis of 26 Variables (the meaning of the numbers of variables is given in Figure 6.1). The numbers down the left-hand side are "similarity values associated with each clustering in the hierarchical representation" (Johnson 1967, p. 251).

Cluster B included eight variables:

housing problems,
sex,
monthly income,
grade of school visited,
socioeconomic status, and the
WAIS scores on
　the total test,
　the Verbal part, and
　the Performance part.

Nine variables were grouped in Cluster C:

variability (or instability) of mood,
religious involvement,
stress due to family,
age,
health status (as judged by a physician),
worries about health status (as judged subjectively),
being oppressed by physical stress,
facing finitude of life, and
perceived unchangeability.

We started by evaluating Cluster C, because it includes the variable of perceiving unchangeability. Unchangeability is placed side by side with facing the finitude of life; it is embedded in a context of variables that represent different kinds of immediately felt hardships (e.g., being oppressed by physical stress, being worried about one's health status, variability of mood, and stress from family). "From here it becomes clear that subjectively perceived 'definiteness' of one's situation is embedded in a context of experience which is characterized by a negative tuning." (Thomae 1979, p. 446).

We have pointed out the close relationship between unchangeability and finitude, but we consider the two variables to be two different aspects of viewing one's life-situation: one aspect is related to death and dying (finitude) and the other to the perceived unchangeability of life.

Cluster B includes variables that describe the socioeconomic status of a person: sex, education (school visited, intelligence), and economic factors (SES, income, housing problems). These variables are placed at a greater distance from unchangeability, indicating that the latter may likewise be molded by socioeconomic factors.

As to Cluster A, we are inclined to see in its nine variables determinants that prove their influence over a longer period of a biography.

Factors like marital status, number of children, playing and enjoying one's roles, the degree of being integrated in a social context, and attitudes towards present and future life-situations are interpretable as determinants of long-termed influence.

In order to analyze more precisely the nature of the 3 clusters, we considered the bivariate correlations between unchangeability and the biographical correlates.

BIVARIATE RELATIONSHIPS BETWEEN UNCHANGEABILITY AND OTHER VARIABLES

Rank correlations (Spearman's rho) between unchangeability and each of the biographical and test variables at each measurement point were computed.

As can be seen in Table 6.7, higher scores for unchangeability from measurement point I to VI were continuously found to be related to the female sex, housing problems, being oppressed by physical stress, depressive and instable moods, low confidence regarding the future, monotony in daily life, and an intensive experience of one's own finitude. Unchangeability scores for measurement IV to VI were correlated with age, income, health status (as judged by a physician), intensive religious involvement, and low role activity (obviously, these relationships became stronger over time). High unchangeability scores for measurement point I to III were connected with high socioeconomic status (SES), great stress due to family, and low contentment with one's present life-situation (these relationships seem to have become weaker over time).

More clearly here than in the cluster analysis, perceived unchangeability appears to be embedded in a pattern of experiencing limitations of one's life.

Continuing the analysis, we divided the total sample into 4 subsamples, according to their different scores for perceived unchangeability.

COMPARISON OF SUBSAMPLES WITH DIFFERENT UNCHANGEABILITY SCORES

According to the cluster and correlation analysis, higher unchangeability scores were found in the neighbourhood of higher scores of certain other variables. This effect shows up more clearly if subsamples are selected whose subjects have a similar pattern of perceived unchangeability within the groups, but a different pattern between the groups. In compliance with this criterion, the total sample was divided into subsamples (1) according to high or low intensity of perceiving unchangeability (i.e., according to high or low scores for unchangeability); and

TABLE 6.7

Correlations between Perceived Unchangeability and Other Variables (Spearman's rho) at Six Measurement Points (MP)

Variables	I	II	III	IV	V	VI
			MP			
Age	0	−4	0	12	26	57
Sex (1 = M, 2 = W)	19	19	19	17	39	30
Income	−8	—	−7	−16	−29	−30
Marital status (1 = unmarried, 2 = married)	11	18	5	17	−12	−1
Children	−4	—	—	—	—	4
School (1 = low grade)	17	0	27	25	16	31
SES (1 = low)	24	26	25	9	1	0
Health status (physician's judgment) 1 = good	−10	−6	19	22	25	25
Role activity (1 = low)	−8	−13	−18	−7	−30	−26
Role satisfaction (1 = low)	0	−10	−27	−8	−18	1
Daily life: variability (1 = monotonous)	−13	—	−21	2	−40	−20
Feeling needed (1 = not needed)	7	−23	6	−13	—	26
Housing problems (1 = low)	5	34	11	2	30	22
Worries about health (1 = low)	15	9	0	26	17	10
Stress due to family (1 = low)	21	22	14	−5	5	−12
Contentment with present (1 = low)	−35	−37	−6	−11	—	12
Attitude towards the future (1 = negative)	−32	—	−22	−22	−18	−45
Mood: from elated to depressive (1 = depressed)	−34	−25	−27	−8	−29	−16
Variabililty of mood (1 = stable, invariable)	19	34	21	28	5	24
Facing finitude (1 = low)	40	24	48	27	72	38
Religious involvement (1 = low)	3	4	11	2	43	21
Being oppressed by physical stress (1 = low)	31	19	25	26	39	42
WAIS: Total	05	—	37	13	−11	−19
Verbal part	06	—	34	15	−02	−15
Performance part	05	—	26	10	−15	−20

(2) according to high or low consistency of these scores over the six measurement points.

The *intensity* criterion was each individual's median of unchangeability scores for measurement point I to VI, as compared to the median of the total sample. The median of the total sample was 4,61 (see Table 6.5). Individuals with a higher median formed the group of higher intensity in perceived unchangeability.

The *consistency* criterion was each individual's coefficient of variability for unchangeability scores from measurement point I to VI, as compared to the coefficient for the total sample. (If V stands for coefficient of variability, SD for standard deviation and M for arithmetic mean, then V = SD/M.) The lower the coefficient of variability, the lower the variation within a series of data and the higher the consistency. The coefficient of variability for the total sample was 0,253. Individuals with a lower coefficient formed the group with higher consistency in perceived unchangeability.

Combining the two criteria, four subgroups were created:

1. Subjects of Subsample A had low medians of unchangeability scores, but high coefficients of variability; perceived unchangeability over the six measurement points was neither intensive nor consistent.
2. Subjects of Subsample B had high medians of unchangeability scores as well as high coefficients of variability; perceived un-

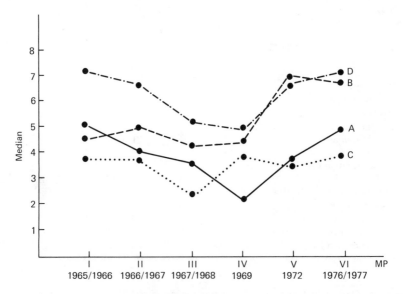

FIGURE 6.3 Perceived unchangeability in 4 subsamples at 6 measurement points (MP). Group A: Low intensity, low consistency of unchangeability perceived; B: High intensity, low consistency; C: Low intensity, high consistency; D: High intensity, high consistency.

changeability over six measurement points was intensive, but not consistent.

3. Subjects of Subsample C had low medians of unchangeability scores and low coefficients of variability; perceived unchangeability over six measurement points was consistently insignificant (the unchangeability scores were low at measurement point I and remained low until measurement point VI).

4. Subjects of Subsample D had high medians of unchangeability scores and low coefficients of variability; perceived unchangeability over six measurement points was consistently intensive (The unchangeability scores were high at measurement point I and remained high until measurement point VI).

The discrepancies in perceived unchangeability between the four subsamples are shown in Table 6.8 and Figure 6.3. The four subgroups may also be characterized by certain sociodemographic variables (see Table 6.9).

The subgroups with low unchangeability scores (low intensity) were contrasted to the subgroups with high unchangeability scores (high intensity) by the following variables (from Table 6.9):

Low-intensity groups (A and C)	High-intensity groups (B and D)
More married subjects	More unmarried subjects
Higher income	Lower income
Better health status	Poorer health status

Such key variables show the influence that socioeconomic factors have on the perception of one's situation as changeable or unchangeable.

Comparisons of biographical and test correlations of the four subsamples, result in the following pattern (Table 6.10):

Subgroup A is characterized by:

lower unchangeability scores, varying from MP I to VI,
lower scores for finitude,
higher income,
lower SES,
lower school index,
better health status (physician's judgment),
lower WAIS scores,
higher scores for religious involvement,

TABLE 6.8

PERCEIVED UNCHANGEABILITY IN 4 SUBSAMPLES AT 6 MEASUREMENT POINTS[a]

Subsamples of perceiving unchangeability		N	1965/66 I	1966/67 II	1967/68 III	1969 IV	1972 V	1976/77 VI	Total I-VI
A	Less intensively	23	5.00	4.00	3.75	2.33	3.88	4.93	4.01
	Not consistently		0.50	1.50	1.08	1.07	1.58	1.54	1.22
B	Very intensively	18	4.50	5.00	4.30	4.50	7.00	6.83	5.49
	Not consistently		2.00	1.98	1.70	0.83	2.65	1.25	1.74
C	Less intensively	19	3.86	3.90	2.42	3.94	3.83	3.93	3.70
	Very consistently		1.00	0.35	1.15	0.33	0.92	1.19	0.82
D	Very intensively	21	7.10	6.63	5.25	4.94	6.67	7.00	6.28
	Very consistently		1.27	1.13	0.44	1.19	0.43	0.96	0.96

[a]Median (above) and Semi-Interquartile Range (below).

TABLE 6.9

FOUR SUBSAMPLES HAVING DIFFERENT UNCHANGEABILITY SCORES[a]

	A		B		C		D	
	Men	Women	Men	Women	Men	Women	Men	Women
Cohort: 1890–1895	6	6	4	4	5	8	4	10
1900–1905	7	4	3	7	2	4	3	4
Sum	13	10	7	11	7	12	7	14
Marital status at MP VI:								
Unmarried	1	8	2	10	2	8	4	12
Married	12	2	5	1	5	4	3	2
Income								
MP I–VI at I-VI-VI	1136		916		1134		756	
	768–973–1824		875–768–1195		822–1024–1847		528–656–1237	
School visited (1 = low; 8 = high)	2.21		3.49		3.08		2.34	
SES (1 = low; 5 = high)	3.02		3.10		3.06		2.89	
Health judged by a physician (1 = good; 5 = poor)								
at MP I–VI	2.22		2.62		2.37		2.44	
at I–IV–VI	2.29–2.64–1.35		2.91–3.25–1.72		2.56–2.50–1.65		2.44–2.89–2.05	

[a] MP = Measurement Point. MP I–VI = Median over MP I to VI; MP I–IV–VI = Scores at MI I (1965), at MP IV (1969), at MP VI (1977).

TABLE 6.10

CORRELATES TO PERCEIVED UNCHANGEABILITY IN 4 SUBSAMPLES (A, B, C, D) OF THE TOTAL SAMPLE[a]

	A			B			C			D		
	I	I-VI / IV	VI	I	I-VI / IV	VI	I	I-VI / IV	VI	I	I-VI / IV	VI
General role activity	5.2	5.8 / 5.3	5.0	5.1	4.8 / 4.4	5.5	5.2	5.7 / 5.0	5.2	4.8	4.9 / 4.7	4.4
General role satisfaction	6.3	5.9 / 5.7	6.0	6.0	5.8 / 4.8	5.6	5.7	5.5 / 4.0	5.3	5.5	5.0 / 4.6	5.6
Daily life: variable/monotonous	6.0	4.9 / 5.6	4.4	4.5	4.7 / 5.5	5.5	6.6	6.0 / 6.7	6.3	6.2	4.7 / 5.8	4.3
Needed by others	5.8	5.9 / 5.7	7.6	5.3	5.1 / 4.8	2.5	5.9	5.9 / 5.7	5.8	5.6	5.5 / 5.9	7.5
Housing problems	4.0	4.0 / 3.7	3.6	4.8	4.8 / 4.5	4.1	3.4	4.4 / 4.6	4.3	4.9	4.8 / 4.4	4.4
Worries about health	5.4	4.2 / 3.9	2.2	5.2	4.6 / 4.8	2.1	5.6	4.5 / 4.8	2.1	5.3	4.4 / 4.3	2.2
Stress with family	5.4	5.1 / 3.7	5.0	4.5	4.5 / 2.5	3.8	4.7	5.2 / 3.4	5.6	6.2	5.0 / 3.7	4.1
Contentment with present	6.7	5.4 / 6.6	2.5	6.5	5.2 / 6.5	2.7	6.4	5.5 / 6.6	2.3	5.3	4.7 / 6.3	3.1
Attitude towards future	6.9	5.4 / 5.6	5.9	6.8	4.8 / 5.2	5.2	6.7	5.5 / 5.9	5.9	5.9	4.5 / 5.4	5.0

Mood: from depressive to elated		5.9			4.7			5.6			4.8	
	6.2	5.7	5.6	5.2	5.7	5.1	6.1	5.9	5.3	5.4	5.2	5.1
Mood: stable to unstable		4.2			4.6			4.9			5.0	
	5.9	4.8	3.3	6.0	5.0	3.4	7.8	5.0	3.4	8.1	5.0	3.4
Facing finitude		4.3			4.6			4.2			5.2	
	4.6	4.1	5.7	4.2	4.5	6.0	4.3	4.8	5.7	4.9	5.2	6.3
Religious involvement		4.7			5.0			4.6			4.3	
	6.6	5.0	4.6	5.7	4.5	4.9	4.7	4.9	4.6	3.6	4.7	4.6
Being oppressed by physical stress		4.5			4.7			4.6			5.1	
	4.2	3.9	4.3	4.5	3.9	6.2	4.4	4.4	4.4	4.0	4.3	4.4
WAIS:		92			96			103			97	
Total	94	94	87	99	92	89	103	109	98	95	99	97
Verbal part		51			52			57			52	
	54	51	50	52	51	49	59	59	55	53	52	55
Performance part		42			43			47			45	
	42	42	38	45	43	37	48	49	43	44	47	41

[a]In the cells are medians at Measurement Point (MP) I, IV, and VI (below), that is, in 1965, 1969, 1977, and a median of six Measurement Points (above).

lower physical stress,
higher confidence in the future,
higher contentment with the present,
rather elated mood,
rather stable mood,
variability in daily life,
stronger feelings of being needed by others,
lower stress due to housing problems,
fewer worries about health,
higher degree of stress due to family,
higher degree of role activity, and
higher role satisfaction.

Subgroup B is characterized by:

higher unchangeability scores, varying from MP I to VI,
higher scores for finitude,
lower income,
higher SES,
higher school index,
poorer health status (physician's judgment),
lower WAIS scores,
higher scores for religious involvement,
higher physical stress,
lower confidence in the future,
lower contentment with the present,
rather depressive mood,
more invariability of mood,
more monotony in daily life,
weaker feelings of being needed by others,
higher stress due to housing problems,
more worries about health status,
lower stress due to family,
lower role activity, and
higher role satisfaction.

Subgroup C is characterized by:

lower unchangeability scores, and this consistently from MP I to VI,
lower finitude scores,
higher income,
higher SES,
better health status (physician's judgment),
higher WAIS scores,

lower religious involvement,
lower physical stress,
higher confidence in the future,
higher contentment with the present,
rather elated mood,
more variability of mood,
less monotony in daily life,
stronger feelings of being needed by others,
lower stress due to housing problems,
more worries about health status,
higher stress due to family,
higher role activity, and
lower role satisfaction.

Subgroup D is characterized by:

higher unchangeability scores, and this consistently from MP I to
  VI,
higher scores for finitude,
lower income,
lower SES,
lower school index,
poorer health status (physician's judgment),
higher WAIS scores,
lower religious involvement,
higher physical stress,
lower confidence in the future,
lower contentment with the present,
rather depressive mood,
more monotony in daily life,
weaker feelings of being needed by others,
higher stress due to housing problems,
fewer worries about health status,
lower stress due to family,
lower role activity, and
lower role satisfaction.

The four groups were compared by Friedman's nonparametric Two-Way Analysis of Variance and by the Mann–Whitney U-Test. The main differences are found between the two low-intensity groups (A and C) as compared to the two high intensity groups (B and D). This can be seen in the following comparisons:

Low-intensity groups (A and C)	High-intensity groups (B and D)
Higher quota of men	Higher quota of women
Lower scores for finitude	Higher scores for finitude
Higher income	Lower income
Better health status	Poorer health status
Lower physical stress	Higher physical stress
Higher confidence in the future	Lower confidence in the future
Higher contentment with present	Lower contentment with present
Rather elated mood	Rather depressive mood
Stronger feelings of being needed by others	Week feelings of being needed by others
Lower stress due to housing problems	Higher stress due to housing problems
Higher stress due to family	Lower stress due to family
Higher role activity	Lower role activity

In order to estimate the importance of this difference, we compared the consistently low groups (A and B) with the consistently high groups (C and D).

Low consistency groups (A and B)	High consistency groups (C and D)
Lower WAIS scores	Higher WAIS scores
Higher religious involvement	Lower religious involvement
Less variability of mood	More variability of mood
Higher role satisfaction	Lower role satisfaction

Evaluating the two comparisons, the contrast of intensity proves to be more decisive than the contrast of consistency. Therefore we are inclined to conclude that decisive conditions favouring the perception of the unchangeability of one's life-situation are in such shortcomings and hardships as were found in Subsamples B and D: lower income, poorer health status, etc. In these kinds of conditions the finitude of life is realized more intensively. Certainly this fact accounts for the high correlation between the two variables. But we should not confound these two variables.

In order to test the findings stated so far, we selected two single cases from Subgroup C (low unchangeability scores, consistently from MP I to VI) and two cases from Subgroup D (high unchangeability scores, consistently from MP I to VI). We compared a man and a woman from each subsample, contrasting those biographical correlates that proved

TABLE 6.11

UNCHANGEABILITY SCORES OF FOUR SUBJECTS, TWO FROM SAMPLE C AND TWO
FROM SAMPLE D AT SIX MEASUREMENT POINTS (MP)[a]

Subsample		MP I 1965/66	II 1966/67	III 1967/68	IV 1969	V 1972	VI 1976/77	Mean standard deviation
C	Male	2	2	0	0	1	1	1.5 0.5
	Female	0	2	1	0	1	1	1.25 0.43
D	Male	5	5	4	4	4	4	4.33 0.47
	Female	6	6	6	4	6	6	5.67 0.75

[a]1 = low.

to be relevant to the contrast between the two low-intensity groups (A and C) and the two high-intensity groups (B and D). Does the same pattern turn up in the single cases, too?

First we report the unchangeability scores for the six measurement points. As can be seen from Table 6.12, the two subjects of Subgroup C differ from the two subjects of Subsample D in a similar way to how the two low-intensity samples differ from the two high-intensity samples.

Subjects of Sample C	Subjects of Sample D
Both: married	Male: married at MP I widowed at MP VI Female: divorced
Higher income	Lower income
Better health status (male of C compared with male of D; female of C with female of D)	Poorer health status
More confidence towards the future	Less confidence towards the future
More contentment with present	Less contentment with present
Rather elated mood	Rather depressive mood
Feeling needed by others more strongly	Feeling needed less strongly
Less stress due to housing problems	More stress due to housing problems
More role activity	Less role activity
Awareness of finitude	Awareness of finitude weaker/stronger

TABLE 6.12

COMPARISON OF FOUR SUBJECTS (TWO BELONGING TO SUBSAMPLE C AND TWO TO D): INDIVIDUAL VALUES OF BIOGRAPHICAL VARIABLES DISCRIMINANT BETWEEN SUBSAMPLES A AND C AND B AND D

Variables	Subsample C						Subsample D					
	Male (No. 1629)			Female (No. 2621)			Male (No. 1725)			Female (No. 2704)		
Measurement point	I-VI	IV	VI	I-VI	IV	VI	I-VI	IV	VI	I-VI	IV	VI
Cohort	1900–1905			1900–1905			1890–1895			1890–1895		
Marital status	Married		Married	Married		Married	Married		Widowed	Divorced		Divorced
Income	1500	1580	2000	2000	2150	2500	1000	1140	1500	202	335	802
Health status (Physician's judgment) 1 = good	2	3	1	2,2	3	2	2,2	3	2	3	4	2
Physical stress (1 = low)	2,2	—	—	1,8	2	2	1,6	2	2	4,3	5	4
Attitude toward the future (1 = negative, 9 = positive)	6,8	8	8	6,0	7	6	4,0	4	6	2,7	2	5
Contentment with present (1 = low)	7,0	8	—	5,0	6	—	4,0	3	1	2,7	3	3
Mood (1 = depressed, 9 = elated)	6,0	6	6	5,2	6	5	3,8	4	2	4,5	5	7
Feeling needed by others (1 = not needed)	7,3	6	—	7,3	6	7	7	7	9	5,7	3	8
Housing problems (1 = low)	3,0	7	2	1,8	1	1	3,2	1	4	4,5	3	3
Stress with family (1 = low)	3,3	3	1	7,5	7	9	4,2	4	1	5,3	3	7
Role activity (1 = low)	6,1	5	7	4,8	5	4	4,0	3	4	4,1	4	4
Facing finitude (1 = low)	1,5			2,0			2,7			4,8		

An analysis of four single cases leads to similiar results, as does the comparison of the two high-intensity (B and D) and two low-intensity (A and C) groups. Subjects with higher unchangeability scores suffer from shortcomings to a higher degree than do subjects with lower unchangeability scores. This result supports the findings gathered by contrasting the total sample.

SUMMARY AND INTERPRETATION

In a sample of 81 participants of the BLSA from 1965 to 1977, the *perceived unchangeability of life* (awareness of definiteness, or *Endgültigkeit des eigenen Daseins*) was studied. Perceived unchangeability refers to viewing and evaluating one's life in such a way as to selectively consider its limitations and restrictions. In order to reveal the biographical setting of this perception, 25 variables—sociodemographic, attitudes, and behavior ratings—were introduced in the study. The statistical analysis proceeded from a multivariate survey (cluster analysis) to a more detailed consideration (comparison of 4 subsamples, supplemented by case-study). Gradually it became clear that life's unchangeability was perceived more distinctly by subjects who, under many aspects, were restricted and limited in their life-space (e.g., by low income, poor health status, or widowhood). We do not consider this perception a kind of, or a result of, maladjustment, but rather—following a cognitive theory of personality—an interpretation of one's life-situation.

Objective factors, such as low income or widowhood, are "objectively" perceived as sources of disappointment, but it is the cognitive representation and interpretation of those factors that provokes disappointment. Cognitive representation is moulded by subjective expectations, needs, or self-concepts, and serves, in itself, as a cue for shaping expectations, needs, or self-concepts.

In this sense, perceived unchangeability becomes one "theme of life" (Daseinsthema according to Thomae) that influences one's self-interpretation, or self-conceptualization. If a host of variables is found to be highly correlated with perceived unchangeability (e.g., low contentment with the present, low confidence towards the future, rather depressive mood), we interpret them to be different or differentiated ways of spelling out this special theme of life.

ACKNOWLEDGMENTS

I should like to express my deep appreciation to Professor Dr. Erhard Olbrich for his contribution in discussing and correcting this essay.

REFERENCES

Baldwin, A. L. A cognitive theory of socialization. In D. Goslin (Ed.), *Handbook of socialization theory and research* (325–345). Chicago: Rand McNally, 1969.

Baltes, P. B., & Goulet, L. R. Status and issues of a life-span developmental psychology. In L. R. Goulet & P. B. Baltes (Eds.), *Life-span developmental psychology: research and theory* (3–21). New York: Academic Press, 1970.

Bühler, Charlotte. *Der menschliche Lebenslauf als psychologisches Problem* (2nd ed.). Leipzig: Hirzel/Göttingen, 1959.

Bühler, Charlotte, & Massarik, F. (Eds.). *The course of human life.* New York: Springer, 1968.

Coerper, C., Hagen, W., & Thomae, H. *Deutsche Nachkriegskinder.* Stuttgart: Thieme, 1954.

Fisseni, H. J. Perceived Life Space: Patterns of consistency and change. In Thomae, H. (Ed.), *Patterns of Aging* (93–112). Basel: Karger, 1976.

Fisseni, H. J. Einstellung und Erleben der Endlichkeit des Daseins. *Zeitschrift für Gerontologie,* 1979, *12,* 460–472.

Fisseni, H. J. Erleben der Endgültigkeit der eigenen Situation: Biographische Aspekte. *Zeitschrift für Gerontologie,* 1980, *13,* 491–505.

Grombach, H. H. *Konstanz und Variabilität von Persönlichkeitsmerkmalen.* Unpublished doctoral dissertation, University of Bonn, 1975.

Hagen, W., & Thomae, H. *Deutsche Nachkriegskinder.* München: Barth, 1962.

Havighurst, R. J. *Developmental tasks and education* (3rd ed.). New York: McKay, 1972.

Johnson, C. Hierarchical Clustering Schemes. *Psychometrika,* 1967, *32,* 241–254.

Jones, H. E. Consistency and change in early maturity. *Vita Humana,* 1958, *1,* 43–51.

Kelly, G. A. *The psychology of personal constructs.* New York: Norton, 1955.

Kastenbaum, R., & Cosla, P. T. Psychological Perspectives on Death. *Annual Revue of Psychology,* 1977, *28,* 225–249.

Lazarus, R. S. Cognitive and coping processes in emotion. In B. Weiner (Ed.), *Cognitive views of human motivation.* New York: Academic Press, 1974.

Lehr, Ursula. Attitudes towards the future in old age. *Human Development,* 1967, *10,* 230–238.

Lehr, Ursula. Frau im Beruf. *Eine psychologische Analyse der weiblichen Berufsrolle.* Frankfurt: Athenäum, 1969.

Lehr, Ursula. Der ältere Mensch in der Familie. *aktuelle gerontologie,* 1975, *5,* 539–550.

Lehr, Ursula. Die Situation der älteren Frau—psychologische und soziale Aspekte. *Zeitschrift für Gerontologie,* 1978, *11,* 6–26.

Lehr, Ursula. Intervention im Rahmen der Gerontologie. In Ursula Lehr (Ed.), *Interventionsgerontologie.* Darmstadt: Steinkopf, 1979.

Lehr, Ursula. Alterszustand und Alternsprozesse: biographische Determinanten. *Zeitschrift für Gerontologie,* 1980, *13,* 442–457.

Lehr, Ursula. Die Bedeutung der Lebenslaufpsychologie für die Gerontologie. *aktuelle gerontologie,* 1980, *10,* 257–269.

Lehr, Ursula, & Dreher, G. Determinants of attitudes towards retirement. In R. J. Havighurst, J. Munnichs, B. L. Neugarten, & H. Thomae (Eds.), *Adjustment to retirement: A cross-national study* (116–137). Assen: Van Gorcum, 1969.

Lehr, Ursula, & Olbrich, E. Ecological correlates of adjustment to aging. In H. Thomae (Ed.), *Patterns of aging* (81–92). Basel: Karger, 1976.

Lehr, Ursula, & Schmitz-Scherzer, R. Survivors and Nonsurvivors: Two Fundamental Patterns of Aging. In H. Thomae (Ed.), *Patterns of aging* (137–146). Basel: Karger, 1976.

Lehr, Ursula, & Thomae, H. Eine Längsschnittuntersuchung bei 30–40 jährigen Angestellten. *Vita Humana,* 1958, *1,* 100–110.

Lehr, Ursula, & Thomae, H. *Konflikt, seelische Belastung und Lebensalter.* Opladen: Westdeutscher Verlag, 1965.

Munnichs, J. *Old Age and Finitude.* Basel: Karger, 1966.

Olbrich, E. Hilfestellung bei einem neuen Lebensabschnitt. *Ärztliche Praxis,* 1980, *22,* 1073–1078.

Olbrich, E., & Thomae, H. Empirical findings to a cognitive theory of aging. *International Journal of Behavioral Development,* 1978, *1,* 67–82.

Rudinger, G., & Lantermann, E. D. Soziale Bedingungen der Intelligenz im Alter. *Zeitschrift für Gerontologie,* 1980, *13,* 433–441.

Schmitz–Scherzer, R. *Freizeit und Alter.* Unpublished doctoral dissertation, University of Bonn, 1969.

Schultz, I. H. Das Endgültigkeitsproblem in der Psychologie des Rückbildungsalters. *Zeitschrift für die Gesamte Neurologie und Psychiatrie,* 1939, *167,* 117–126.

Simons, H., Mehler, D., & Erlemeier, N. Aspekte der psychologischen Anpassung im höheren Lebensalter. In *Deutsche Gesellschaft für Gerontologie* (Vol. 1, pp. 215–223). Darmstadt: Steinkopf, 1968.

Snygg, D., & Combs, A. W. *Individual behavior: A new frame of reference for Psychology.* New York: Harper, 1949.

Thomae, H. *Das Individuum und seine Welt.* Göttingen: Hogrefe, 1968.

Thomae, H. Theory of aging and cognitive theory of personality. *Human Development,* 1970, *13,* 1–16.

Thomae, H. The developmental-task-approach to a theory of aging. *Zeitschrift für Gerontologie,* 1975, *8,* 125–137.

Thomae, H. *Patterns of Aging.* Basel: Karger, 1976.

Thomae, H. Altern und Lebensschicksal. *Zeitschrift für Gerontologie,* 1980, *13,* 421–432.

Thomae, H. Personality and Adjustment to Aging. In J. E. Birren & R. B. Sloane (Eds.), *Handbook of Mental Health and Aging* (285–309). Englewood Cliffs, NJ: Prentice-Hall, 1980.

Thomae, H. *Alternsstile und Altersschicksal. Ein Beitrag zur Differentiellen Gerontologie.* Bern: Huber, 1983.

Thomae, H., Angleitner, A., Grombach, H., & Schmitz–Scherzer, R. Determinanten des Alternsprozesses. Ein Bericht über die Bonner gerontologische Längsschnittstudie. *actuelle gerontologie,* 1973, *3,* 359–377.

Thomae, H., & Kranzhoff, U. Erlebte Unveränderlichkeit von gesundheitlicher und ökonomischer Belastung. *Zeitschrift für Gerontologie,* 1979, *12,* 439–459.

Tismer, K. G. *Untersuchungen zur Daseinstechnik älterer Menschen.* Unpublished doctoral dissertation, University of Bonn, 1969.

Weiner, B. (Ed.). *Cognitive views of human motivation.* New York: Academic Press, 1974.

Wittkowski, J. *Tod und Sterben: Ergebnisse der Thanatopsychologie.* Heidelberg: Quelle und Meyer, 1978.

COPING AND DEVELOPMENT IN THE LATER YEARS: A PROCESS-ORIENTED APPROACH TO PERSONALITY AND DEVELOPMENT

Erhard Olbrich

TRAIT-CENTERED AND PROCESS-ORIENTED APPROACHES TO THE STUDY OF PERSONALITY DEVELOPMENT

THE TRAIT-CENTERED APPROACH

The most common approach to the study of personality and personality development seems to be *trait-centered* (Costa & MCrae. 1976). Thomae (1980), in a review on personality development in old age, states that a major group of researchers still accepts Guilford's (1959) definition of personality as a "unique pattern of traits" and does research in accordance with such a view. In analyses of trait-centered research on personality development, however, one seldom finds descriptions of changing patterns of traits. Most often differences between single trait measures are presented as evidence of personality development. The actual process of change is not a subject for this type of work: change is only inferred from differences between repeated (ipsative) measures, or even from cross-sectionally assessed data that confound age with cohort differences.

It is not only this disregard of changing patterns of traits and the lack of emphasis on change that casts doubts on the use of the trait centered approach for the study of personality development. Workers interested in development over long periods of the biography, or even over the full life-span, are also concerned with the construct of trait. They ask questions like these:

1.   Are traits constructs that remain identical over long periods of life? It is doubtful that a variable like extraversion in a 6-year-old child is identical to extraversion in a 45- or 60-year-old adult. Traits may not only undergo qualitative change over biographical time, but also over generations and over historical time (see Schaie, 1965).

2.   Do traits remain identical over different situations? Authors like Mischel (1968, 1979) Endler and Magnusson (1976), Magnusson and Endler (1977), or Lantermann (1980) have directed our attention to situation-specific inconsistencies of behavior. In encounters with different demands, interactions between person and situation change, and the concept of a stable trait loses some of its explanatory power. Again, such a question can be widened, and the identity of traits over groups and cultural settings can be doubted.

3.   Is it justifiable to assume identity of traits across individuals? This question does not intend to deny all the evidence presented by psychometric work in personality research and in diagnostics on the usefulness of traits. The question should rather make us aware of all the variance that cannot be explained by trait measures. The work on states or idiographic research has informed us that there exist dimensions of personality that are idiosyncratic in their meaning. It can be assumed that the individual history of a person contributes to his subjective definition of himself, and to individual definitions of any situation encountered by him. This leads to the critical question below.

4.   Concerning research practice, we must ask if we can assume identity of operationalizations of traits and of assessment techniques over researchers and over studies.

From the work of Mischel or Lanterman (1980) we have learned to criticize trait models for their underestimation of situation-specific inconsistencies in behavior. We also have to criticize them for their disregard of the discriminative facility of the human actor. "This discriminative facility contributes much to the adjustment of the person, whereas rigid across-situational consistency of behavior may cause conflict or maladjustment" (Thomae, 1980, p. 293).

THE PROCESS-ORIENTED APPROACH

In contrast to trait-oriented approaches, *process-oriented* views are closer to offering direct insights into processes of development, as well as into processes of adaptation. They have a long tradition in psychoanalytic theory, which conceives of personality as a system of forces that motivates behavior and development—often in a conflicting manner—and of adjustive and co-ordinating mechanisms.

But it is not only psychoanalytic theory that has favored a process-oriented view. Cognitive conceptualizations of human adaptation (e.g., Lazarus, 1966, 1980; Lazarus, Averill, & Opton, 1974) have described personality processes and discussed developmental consequences. A behavioral–descriptive theory of personality and personality development that is also process-oriented was developed by Thomae (1951); it defines much of the theoretical framework of this chapter. Thomae suggested to conceive of *personality* as a system of processes. These can be biological, cognitive, emotional–motivational, or—concerning person-environment interactions—social-interactional or physical-interactional. All these processes are integrated into a system that we call personality. Personality processes regulate actual adaptive functions. Besides the actual processes that are usually studied by personality psychology, processes of change over time are studied in a diachronic perspective by developmental psychology. Diachronically (i.e., over time), personality processes are integrated into a biography.

Thomae conducted research in natural situations, trying to identify actual (i.e., rather short lasting) personality processes as well as diachronic (i.e., extended over time) developmental processes. Often, stressful episodes were chosen for study, since these seem to allow a rather clear identification of personality processes. The perception of biologically, physically, and socially, or psychologically challenging or threatening situations seems to have a higher chance of becoming behaviorally relevant than the perception of "normal" situations or of demands close to the adaptation level of the person. Quite similarly, students of development have chosen periods of transition, critical life-events, hassles, crises, or other situations that require new forms of adaptation in order to study diachronic change of adaptational processes. To put it more specifically: A combination of coping research and of developmental research brings together the actual study of personality processes and the diachronic study of change.

In order to link the actual or episodic perspective with the diachronic perspective, the concepts of *crystallization* and *fluidization* are proposed. If a person repeatedly encounters specific demands, and if his behavior proves to meet these demands effectively, a crystallization of the episodic processes leading to adaptation is assumed to occur. On the other hand, frequent experiences of inadequate behavior are not likely to consolidate processes leading to such maladaptive actions.

Whenever new demands have to be met, one or several of the whole set of processes have to be rendered fluid—thus making development feasible. Processes that have become crystallized over time can again become fluid through actual demands that require change. On the other hand, actual processes depend on former, and more or less crystallized, ones. Personality development in Thomae's theory is conceptualized as a process of interaction between actual and formerly crystallized processes.

Studying the interaction between actual and diachronic adaptive processes requires a theoretical framework that can combine paradigms of personality research with those of developmental research. Here, theories of coping are discussed as possible explanations of actual adaptation. *Actual adaptation*, refers to processes that usually lead to some form of new, often even productive, adaptation. This is one point that relates them to *development*. The broader concepts of crystallization and fluidization, and the interaction between actual and diachronic processes, are of particular theoretical importance for the bridging of personality and developmental research—in other words, for the explanation of actual as well as diachronic adaptive processes. Before we turn to the question of whether active/productive personality processes can be observed in the later years of life, a brief survey of different conceptualizations of the coping process are given.

COPING AND ITS RELEVANCE FOR DEVELOPMENT: CONCEPT AND THEORY

PSYCHOANALYTIC THEORY

One of the best known roots of coping research is psychoanalysis. *Psychoanalytic ideas* have influenced our understanding of personality processes and of processes of development since the beginning of this century (Freud, 1905). They have quite obviously become incorporated in neoanalytical conceptualizations, but also in cognitive and behavioral conceptualizations of coping, and are outlined briefly.

Sigmund Freud, already in his therapeutic work, identified mechanisms of the ego that regulate instincts and affects in the adult years; these mechanisms develop from early childhood on. Freud felt that some of such mechanisms could be pathological; others, however, could be productive in function. In 1936, his daughter Anna Freud (Freud, 1936) systematically described and classified the defense mechanisms of the ego. She was quite explicit in stating that some of the ego defenses are normally observed during specific periods of transition (e.g., during adolescence). They are understood as frequent and often productive programs for the solution of conflicts between id-impulses and norms of the super-ego or of the social environment.

NEOANALYTIC THEORY

Later, *neoanalytical theory* emphasized conscious control mechanisms more strongly. A helpful distinction between defensive and coping processes was proposed by Blos (1962) and more clearly by Kroeber (1963) and Haan (1963). These authors felt the need to conceptually "represent the rational, logical, wise, civil, loving, playful and sensual aspects of people's ego actions" (Haan, 1977, p. 36), and to distinguish such coping modes from more defensive ones.

> Coping involves purpose, choice, and flexible shift, adheres to intersubjective reality and logic, and allows and enhances proportionate affective expression; defensiveness is compelled, negating, rigid, distorting or intersubjective reality and logic, allows covert impulse expression, and embodies the expectancy that anxiety can be relieved without directly addressing the problem. (Haan, 1977, p. 34).

In Haan's view coping is an adaptive ego process, integrating cognitive and motivational as well as social, moral, and value orientations of the person. All these are usually elicited through new demands. Defense is likely to occur when the person encounters demands that go beyond his capacities. Developmental consequences of defending are assumed to be disruptive in nature; they do not represent the individual's adaptive potentials, but rather distort them. Developmental consequences of coping, in contrast, are discovered in more effective programs or person–environment interactions. These represent the individual's ego resources. In accepting this view, it becomes quite explicit that challenging or threatening demands, life transitions, or even crises or conflicts are prerequisites for coping. These should not, however, exceed an individual's capacities or resources.

COGNITIVE CONCEPTION

Richard S. Lazarus' (1966, 1974, 1980) "cognitive conception" has probably contributed most to our knowledge of coping. An important basis of his work was his own research on stress, where from "its humble beginnings as a footnote to stress theory, the concept of coping has grown to occupy a central place in current theoretical models of stress and emotion." (Roskies & Lazarus, 1980, p. 45). Lazarus, in his earlier work on stress and performance as well as in his more recent work on stress and health, found effects of stress to be facilitative and impairing. A panel report on psychological assets and modifiers of stress presented by the Institute of Medicine and by the National Academy of Science (Cohen et al., 1982) states that

> individuals who have faced severe life stressors also may find that they have increased self-esteem, are able to perform better in similar situations at a later time, learn empathy, or can take advantage of new opportunities. Certain stressors are inevitable throughout the life course, yet most people do not appear to suffer from adverse effects. (Cohen et al., 1982, p. 153)

If a stressful demand leads to growth, temporary difficulty or trauma is a function of (1) the pervasiveness and persistence of the stressor, (2) the timing of the event, (3) the individual's personal resources available for dealing with the stressor, (4) the opportunities available to act on the environment and to receive social support (Dunkel–Schetter & Wortman, 1981), and (5) the meaning given to the experience (Benner, Roskies, & Lazarus, 1980). In accordance with theoretical conclusions reached after a review of the literature on stressful occupations, an interaction between situational demands, personal resources, and social support is emphasized. Cognitive representations of these factors and their appraisal seem to be the relevant factors determining the outcome. In general, scientists and practitioners in the fields of personality and clinical psychology have developed the conviction that, more than the stressful impact itself, it is the way people cope with stress that is important for their adaptation, their health, and their development (Coelho, Hamburg, & Adams, 1974; Goldfried, 1977; Meichenbaum, 1977; Murphy & Moriarty, 1976; Filipp, 1981; Moos, 1976, 1977; Kaplan, 1983). Understanding coping processes seems to contribute more to an explanation of outcomes than does an analysis of the stressful situation.

Lazarus has developed a transactional model of coping. He conceives of the person as an active organizer of the stress experience and as an active responder to a demanding environment. In a transaction between stressor and person, the two influence eath other. Such a transactional conceptualization "offers a new level of discourse in which separate variables are now lost or changed" (Lazarus, 1980, p. 37). On the common level of cognitive representation and cognitive appraisal, situational components and personal factors seem to meet. "Because appraisal is a function of both situational and personal variables, this unit expresses the transaction between the person and the environment in terms of the cognitive processes by means of which a given type of person processes and evaluates information about the environment" (Lazarus et al., 1974, p. 307).

Although these are interwoven in reality, we can conceptually distinguish primary, secondary, and tertiary appraisal. *Primary appraisal* is basically an evaluative perception and a judgment of what a demand means to the person. In *secondary appraisal* this is brought together with the individual's resources for dealing with the demands. Secondary appraisal can be compared to a cognitive extrapolation of how personal means (resources) can be employed to meet aspired goals and, respectively, to reach foreseen effects of planned actions. Reappraisal (*tertiary appraisal*) then, refers to a new perception and evaluation that becomes feasible after possible reactions to the encountered demands have been constructed.

Coping is called for whenever habitualized programs of behavior are insufficient to meet a demand. If coping results in mastery of the demand, it contributes to the development of new behavioral programs. Failure, on the other hand, will have adverse effects on cognitive functioning, performance, health, morale, and self-esteem. The crucial role of the coping process in actual adaptation and in development has been emphasized in personality theory as well as in clinical work, in studies on critical life events, and in developmental work on periods of transition. It is agreed that knowledge of perception and subjective representation of stressing demands, together with knowledge about the individual's potentials to control and to deal with these demands, is of great value for the explanation of adaptive and developmental possibilities. Although seldom dealt with, the topic of coping in old age seems to be an important one for theory and for practice.

BEHAVIORAL–DESCRIPTIVE CONCEPTUALIZATION

The behavioral–descriptive conceptualization of coping was developed by Hans Thomae (1951, 1968, 1984). This author proceeded from detailed observations of everyday behavior and development in normal, nonclinical populations. He recognized that behavior is usually thematically structured and that individuals act in meaningful ways. *Themes* result from specific constellations of environmental pressures and personal needs, but these do not interact mechanically. Thomae, rather, speaks of open thematic structures (i.e., he realizes that personal potentials for perceiving and experiencing come into play as do personal intentions and tendencies toward self-realization). In thematically structured behavior, motivation does not only aim at better homeostasis; growth tendencies and development are often incorporated into interactions between environmental press and personal needs.

A second important concept is that of *Daseinstechniken* (coping techniques). These describe instrumental techniques used by the individual in order to attain a thematically defined goal behavior. Thomae (1984) distinguishes techniques of performance and adaptation, as well as defensive, evasive, aggressive, and other techniques. They are used in accordance with the individual's perceptions of situational demands as well as of his personal needs and resources. *Daseinstechniken* are coordinated within the whole framework of meaningful behavior set by a person's themes. In Thomae's theory, prospective elements are part of the factors determining adaptation and development. Thematic regulations and coping techniques are concepts describing processes. They are core concepts in a process-oriented theory of personality and personality development. Parallels between these concepts and Lazarus' conceptualizations of environment–person transactions should be noted.

OTHER CONCEPTUALIZATIONS

Other conceptualizations of the coping process can be mentioned briefly; they are not elaborated upon since little or no research conducted on coping in old age has been guided by them. Schönpflug and his associates (1979) have proposed a biocybernetic conception of the coping process: following stress or dysregulation of behavior, a reprogramming, respectively a development of new regulatory processes, can begin that may lead to a new form of behavior organization. *Psychobiological* and *learning theoretical conceptions* have recently been described by Weinberg and Levine (1980), Frankenhäuser (1980), and Miller (1980). All these conceptualizations convey an active-organism model. They emphasize productive adaptation and development instead of mere drive reduction and striving for homeostasis. They describe processes instead of static variables as important for transactions and behavior. Cognitive constructions and preconstructions (plans) of behavior are emphasized. Success or failure of adaptation and development appear, in part, as functions of coping. The important question now is how coping develops over the adult years and what changes in coping can be observed with aging.

COPING AND AGING: THEORY

There is little literature on coping in the later years. Many of the available studies were not intended to analyze age changes of coping processes. Frequently, data result from clinical observations, but an interpretation of this material together with insights gained in the few systematic studies (cf. Lazarus & Olbrich, 1983; McCrae, 1982; Thomae, Lehr, & Schmitz-Scherzer, 1981; Renner & Birren, 1980; Pfeiffer, 1977;

Lieberman, 1975) give an overview and a preliminary answer to the above-posed question.

THE REGRESSION HYPOTHESIS

McCrae (1982) proposes to distinguish two different hypotheses on age changes of coping. One is the *regression hypothesis*, stated, for example, by Pfeiffer (1977) in his work on psychopathology and social pathology in aging. It purports that with increasing age, failures to adapt to challenging or threatening demands will occur more frequently. Pfeiffer proceeds from the proposition that the demands to which older people have to adapt differ substantially from those faced by younger adults: The elderly have to deal with more frequent and maybe more severe losses (of persons, relationships, work and roles, recognition, mobility, and health) and have to cope with the necessity to remain active and retain functions. These are tasks aimed at keeping up behaviors that are "successful" and adaptive in the younger and the mid-adult years. In addition to these, and quite different from them, is another task to be dealt with, the identity review.

Presenting data on adaptation to the various losses, Pfeiffer concentrates on those approximately 15% of the elderly who suffer from some moderate to significant form of psychopathology, and who indeed often fail to adapt. He concedes that "some older persons continue to use the entire range of adaptive mechanisms," but many return to the use of more primitive mechanisms that are defensive often by nature. "Thus, unmodified anxiety, depression–withdrawal, projection, somatization, and denial are the preponderant mechanisms used" (1977, p. 651). Pfeiffer specifies that only "in those instances where failure of adaptation has occurred, the mechanism outlined are used with great regularity." We should add that regression does not occur in those aged who have successfully adapted to the taxing demands encountered in their life. Universal, that is, overindividual, and general, or over-situational, evidence for a regression hypothesis cannot be presented.

Gutman (1977; 1980) is sometimes quoted as another proponent of the regression hypothesis of coping. As active mastery diminishes with age and passive or even magical mastery becomes prevalent, coping capacities seem to decrease. But we must be aware that this can be called a regression only so far as performance and mastery of achievement-related demands are concerned. This is, of course, the case in working life and, more generally, in a technologically oriented society. Gutman himself presents evidence that judgment, wisdom, and contemplative functions do not deteriorate with age. So again no general evidence of a regression hypothesis is found. Rather, its dependence on a restricted emphasis of specific values has become evident.

THE GROWTH HYPOTHESIS

The second hypothesis is the *growth hypothesis*. It was advanced by Vaillant (1977). This author observed that immature defense mechanisms such as projection, schizoid fantasies, passive–regressive behavior, and acting-out decrease with age, whereas mature mechanisms such as altruism, humor, sublimation, and anticipation increase. Vaillant bases the growth hypothesis on data gathered in his study of a healthy and well-adapted group of mid-adult men.

Other studies fail to discover correlations between age and the successful adaptation to the stresses of life in late adulthood. All in all, we find neither general nor universal evidence of age changes in coping, be it growth or regression. Such evidence probably cannot be gained, if the active view of coping developed by Lazarus, as well as by Thomae, is correct. In this view, an individual perceives, cognitively appraises and represents, and then processes the demands of a specific situation. Thus, differentiations between individuals' perceptions and personal resources to deal with the demands of subjectively appraised stressful demands must be developed, also taking into account that situations vary considerably. In the next part of this chapter some data on differences in demands encountered during different periods of the adult life-cycle, and some changing coping potentials in old age, are reported. These provide evidence for the differential position taken here.

AGE-RELATED CHANGES IN STRESSORS
AND DEMANDS

Age-related changes in stressors and demands have been reported in work on normative and nonnormative transitions encountered during the family life-cycle and the working life (cf. Datan & Ginsberg, 1975; Kohli, 1978; Olbrich, 1983). McCrae (1982) reports that older people have to deal with a disproportionately larger number of "exit events" than younger persons, who have to adjust to more "entrance events." After comparing data from subjects between 24 and 91 years of age, McCrae summarizes that challenges decrease with age, losses occur at all ages with about equal frequency, and threats increase (the latter are most often related to health). Folkman and Lazarus (1980) found that older participants in their sample, who were between 45 and 64 years of age, reported more health-related hassles, while younger people more often mentioned work and family-related episodes.

COPING POTENTIALS

Looking at personal coping potentials, some of the best information available comes from the work of McCrae (1982). His cross-sectional comparisons of coping styles did not reveal evidence for either the regression or the growth hypothesis. McCrae corrected his data for different stressors encountered during the single periods of the life-span and concludes: "These analyses again offer no support for the regression hypothesis, but they partly support the growth position . . . none of the theoretically mature mechanisms shows a cross-sectional decline, whereas some of the theoretically immature mechanisms do. There was, however, no evidence that the use of theoretically mature mechanisms increased with age" (1982, p. 457).

In the Quayhagen and Quayhagen (1982) study, older people scored lower on problem solving coping styles and higher on negative affectivity. Help-seeking did increase between 40 and 70 years, and more for men than for woman. No differences were found for other coping variables. Lesser, Lazarus, Wilson, Cohler, Schweon, Kasanick, & Fox (1981) found more psychotic defense mechanisms among demented elderly, but no age effects for normal subjects. In the Gleason, Karuza, and Zevron (1981) study, older participants assumed less responsibility and used more mechanisms by which they relied on others and profited from their support and discipline. Kirscht and Rosenstock (1979) explicitly emphasized the differential perspective when reporting that older persons with a greater belief in internal control had the more efficient coping style. It seems worthwhile pointing out that lack of social support and reduced attributions of personal control seem to gain more and more relevance as aging continues.

Considering the differences reported so far, we have to be aware that samples of the studies varied widely with respect to age, socioeconomic status, education, and other demographic indices. Moreover, measures and techniques for the assessment of coping were not comparable. Most importantly, the theoretical framework of many of the studies was not made explicit. The theoretical basis for the study of age-related changes in coping in general has not been worked out clearly. A process-oriented approach is seldom followed. But the fact that different results were obtained supports our view that neither situational nor personal variables alone can satisfactorily explain coping, which is better understood as an ongoing transaction between situational demands and an actively perceiving, appraising, and acting individual.

Transactions between Situation and Person

When we conceive of coping as transactions between situation and person, we are required to direct our attention to the "unit" of situational demands and personal resources that are cognitively represented and, on this level of representation, form the basis for an individual's plans of action and ensuing behavior. The effects of psychological factors involved in cognitive representation and in coping should be emphasized more than has been done before today. There is knowledge of the fact that objectively identical demands are differently perceived by different persons (cf. Roskies & Lazarus, 1980: Olbrich & Thomae, 1978). There is also evidence that over the lifetime a reordering of priorities, a relegation of no longer relevant roles to the periphery of importance, and an investment into activities more in tune with present commitments occurs (Lazarus & Olbrich, 1983). Differences in coping processes between persons and between periods of lifetime must be recognized in order to come to a better understanding of person-processes and their development. An understanding of age-specific processes, of course, has to take into account changes in aging people's sensory, motor, intellectual, and motivational capacities (cf. Birren & Schaie, 1977; Salthouse, 1982). These directly influence processes of coping, but also come into play in cognitive representations of coping resources, in appraisal, and in plans of action.

Social Influences

Besides coping potentials of the person, social influences must be considered. Work on cognitive behavior modification has frequently shown that processes of perceiving and appraising demands can be influenced as well as the planning of behavior (cf. Meichenbaum, 1977; Baade, Borck, Kroebe, & Zumvenne, 1980). Cognitive strategies and processes of problem solving can be improved in educational programs (Labouvie-Vief & Gonda, 1976; Plemons, Willis, & Baltes, 1978; Willis, Blieszner, & Baltes, 1980). Such a form of social influence on cognitive adaptive processes has been shown to be effective even in areas that are usually regarded as strongly susceptible to age-related deficits, namely fluid intellectual functions. In other studies it was shown that coping strategies that dampen or eliminate disturbing emotional responses to challenging or threatening situational demands can be taught (Roskies & Lazarus,

1980; Baade et al., 1980). Psychoanalytic techniques of therapy or counseling are recommended by McLean (1979) as a kind of "Rolls Royce" on a person's way to more effective functioning. They strengthen ego processes, improve accurate recognition of situational demands as well as of one's own resources, and facilitate coordinated use of cognitive, affective, moral, and social schemas of the person (Haan, 1977). This, too, emphasizes the view of an active individual.

However, it is not only exacting techniques such as these, usually applied by trained professionals, that have been shown to be effective in strengthening coping skills. Everyday helpful interactions and social support measures also seem to influence coping. House (1981) or Dunkel-Schetter and Wortman (1981) offer hypotheses concerning the effects of instrumental, informational, emotional, and appraisal support. Social appraisal support relates directly to personal coping. It refers to help given in order to adequately interpret an encountered demand and to exchanges during the ventilation of cognitive and affective experiences that also serve to validate that these experiences are understood by others who are or have been in a similar situation. In its cognitive elements, appraisal support is related to informational support. This incorporates the giving and receiving of accurate information about demands as well as about older persons' capacities to deal with them. Informational support of coping in old age works on an individual but also on a collective level. The latter, for example, is the level of the gerontologist who informs on older people's capacities, thereby often fighting against the stereotypes contained in a deficit model of aging (Lehr, 1977).

COPING AND AGING: RESULTS FROM THE BONN LONGITUDINAL STUDY ON AGING

Data from the Bonn Longitudinal Study on Aging (BLSA) permit the longitudinal examination of the transaction between situational demands and behavior in old age. A sample that was fairly representative of the social middle class of Western Germany ($n = 222$) was studied between 1965 and 1981. Participants were born between 1890 and 1910. Psychological, social, medical, and ecological variables were assessed at seven measurement points, and extensive interviews, observations, and medical examinations were made in an attempt to represent the real life situation of the elderly. Each of the assessment periods lasted about 1 week. In a 3-hour interview, a fairly complete account of stresses in the following areas was given: health, income, housing, family, and occupation. Participants were also asked to describe how they had perceived the various stresses and how they had reacted to them. A recent book by Thomae (1983) gives a full description of the study.

THE PERCEPTION AND COGNITIVE REPRESENTATION OF DEMANDS

In his cognitive theory of personality and aging, Thomae (1970) formulated three postulates. The first says that the perception of change, rather than the objective change, is related to behavioral change. Using data on health status (objective assessments made by a physician), subjectively experienced stress due to health problems (a subjective rating), and health-related activities, Olbrich and Thomae (1978) were able to test the hypothesis that path coefficients from objective health scores (such as degree of heart insufficiency or degree of sclerosis) on health-related activities are smaller than path coefficients from stress experienced due to health on health-related activities. Results of path analyses confirmed this hypothesis. Quite similarly, the objective variable "monthly income" had a very small influence on subjective "satisfaction with life," whereas the cognitively represented degree of "stress due to economic restrictions" had a great influence on the older persons' present life satisfaction.

These results confirm that subjective perceptions of demands are not isomorphical representations of objectively present demands. Rather, it is the active role of the perceiving subject in the transaction between situation and person that becomes evident.

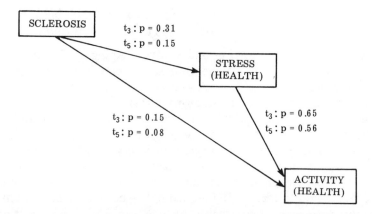

FIGURE 7.1 Influences from "Sclerosis" on the cognitive representation of the health situation ("Stress [Health]") and on health-related behavior ("Activity [Health]").

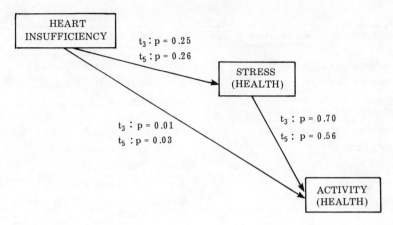

FIGURE 7.2 Influences from "Heart Insufficiency" on the cognitive representation of the health situation ("Stress [Health]") and on health-related behavior ("Activity [Health]").

COPING STYLES AND THEIR DEVELOPMENT

Within the BLSA a system of categories was developed in order to describe coping styles (*Daseinstechniken*). This system was used in order to score interview information. Figure 7.3 presents patterns of coping with occupational problems in 1948 (retrospective accounts) and 1965 (actual descriptions). Only data from men born between 1890 and 1895 are presented. Although participants probably reconstructed their information about 1948 when interviewed in 1965, thereby distorting it (see Field, 1981), the following picture that emerges from Figure 7.3 seems psychologically meaningful.

In 1948 there was a currency reform in Germany (i.e., everybody lost most of his savings and had only 40 DM to start anew). So people had to use chance opportunities in their jobs and, of course, in other areas, such as the black market. The average pattern of coping seemed to require more adjustment to institutionalized aspects of the situation (e.g., finding out about governmental compensations for damages suffered during the war). On the other hand, people could not follow an evasive pattern of behavior; they had to build up a new career, that is, activate achievement-related behavior. Identification with the goals and/or the successes of children and grandchildren was able to become stronger in 1965, after the situation had changed occupationally as well as in regard to the family situation of participants, who were between 70 and 75 years of age at that time.

A comparative analysis of adjustments made in 1966 and in 1976 sug-

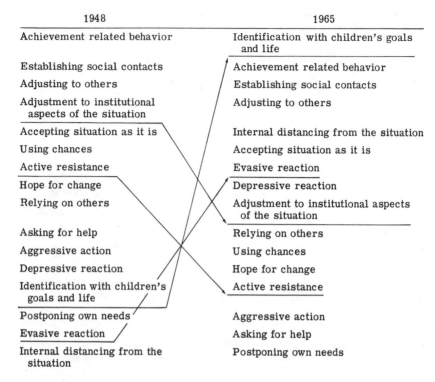

1948	1965
Achievement related behavior	Identification with children's goals and life
Establishing social contacts	Achievement related behavior
Adjusting to others	Establishing social contacts
Adjustment to institutional aspects of the situation	Adjusting to others
Accepting situation as it is	Internal distancing from the situation
Using chances	Accepting situation as it is
Active resistance	Evasive reaction
Hope for change	Depressive reaction
Relying on others	Adjustment to institutional aspects of the situation
Asking for help	Relying on others
Aggressive action	Using chances
Depressive reaction	Hope for change
Identification with children's goals and life	Active resistance
Postponing own needs	Aggressive action
Evasive reaction	Asking for help
Internal distancing from the situation	Postponing own needs

FIGURE 7.3 Styles of coping with regard to occupational problems (arrows indicate significant differences in rank-order of coping style: translated from Lehr, 1977).

gests that participants cognitively restructured their situation and developed different patterns of reaction to the demands encountered in their occupational, economic, family, and health-related life. A full account of the analyses is given in Thomae (1983). Here, it is the area of health-related problems that is dealt with briefly.

Health-Related Problems

As can be seen in Figure 7.4, degrees of subjectively perceived stress and of coping increased with regard to health. There was, however, a decrease in these parameters with regard to the economic situation and housing problems. Stress due to the family situation did not change. The parallels between subjectively experienced change in stressful demands and personal efforts to successfully deal with these demands deserve to be mentioned. They present evidence of an interplay between demands encountered in a 10-year period of life and the person's responses to these demands.

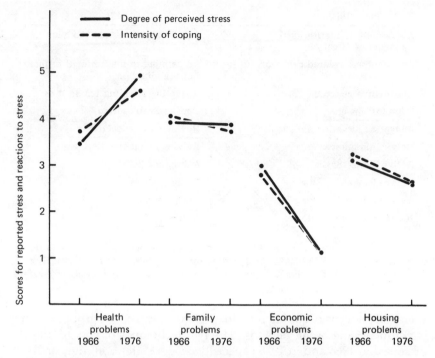

FIGURE 7.4   Degree of perceived stress (———) and coping with stress (— — —) in different areas of life.

Comparisons of preferred and less preferred styles of coping with health problems encountered over the seven measurement points of the Bonn Longitudinal study on Aging seem to indicate that the aging persons structured their situation in a way that allowed them to meaningfully deal with even loss and failure. We have to add that objective health problems of the sample increased over the years 1966–1976. Data from medical examinations show that vision, hearing, and mobility became increasingly impaired. Symptoms of heart insufficiency and of sclerosis as well as high blood pressure were significantly more frequent in 1976 than a decade before.

Before interpreting the types of reaction to health problems, we have to explain that each person showed an idiosyncratic pattern of *Daseinstechniken* when dealing with the respective demands, for many style scores were low. But differences became evident when *Daseinstechniken* were rank-ordered, and shifts from earlier to later times of assessment were analyzed. Data in Figure 7.5 show evidence of a considerable consistency in reactions to health problems. This seems to indicate that

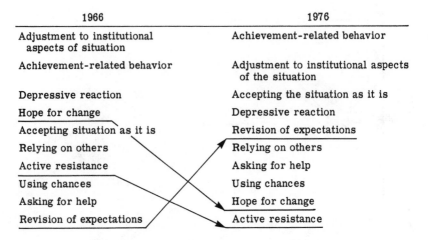

1966	1976
Adjustment to institutional aspects of situation	Achievement-related behavior
Achievement-related behavior	Adjustment to institutional aspects of the situation
Depressive reaction	Accepting the situation as it is
Hope for change	Depressive reaction
Accepting situation as it is	Revision of expectations
Relying on others	Relying on others
Active resistance	Asking for help
Using chances	Using chances
Asking for help	Hope for change
Revision of expectations	Active resistance

FIGURE 7.5   Rank order of the 10 most important styles of coping with health-related problems in 1966 and 1976 (data from all participants of the BLSA, reprinted from Thomae, Lehr, & Schmitz-Scherzer, 1981). Significant differences in ranks are indicated by arrows.

averaged patterns of coping remain quite constant for our group of rather well-functioning aging persons. The two techniques of coping that are preferred in 1966 and in 1976 especially deserve attention; they are both forms of active behavior. "Adjustment to the institutional aspects of the situation" in the area of health behavior refers to a range of activities, from finding the best doctor or getting the best treatment to endeavors directed at getting the most out of health insurance or efforts to find financial support for recreation in a spa, and so forth. It is also includes active adjustments to the regulations of a hospital or rehabilitation center. "Achievement-related behavior" is defined by any expenditure of energy or effort in order to obtain a goal. This could be work in one's garden because it is "healthy," physical activities, or efforts recommended by one's physician.

Irrational reactions, such as "Hope for change" apparently lost their relevance over the decade observed, since they may have turned out to be ineffective in dealing with health-maintaining demands in older age. Another *Daseinstechnik,* "Active resistance," shifted from Rank 7 in 1966 to Rank 10 in 1976. This indicates that resistance against recommendations to take medical examinations (e.g., to undergo surgery) was given up. The aging persons were also less resistant to a diet recommended to them, or to advice concerning reduction of alcohol or cigarette consumption.

Familial Problems

Concerning problems in family life, it must be explained that these were scored when, for example, the person had to encounter harsh or unfriendly behavior by the spouse or another family member, when children's marital or economic problems had to be worked through, or when coping with grandchildren's school or job problems. Familial stress can also be related to loss of contact or to tensions arising from too much contact.

The most frequent form of coping with family-related stress in 1966 was an "adjustment to the needs and/or peculiarities of others." This refers to adaptation of one's expectancies and desires to those of another person (e.g., a rather egocentric husband). It is a meaningful response in social interaction, but is, of course, seldom observed in coping with health-related stresses. Differences between scores obtained in 1966 and in 1976 reflect that the aging persons of the BLSA were able to obtain a better balance between adjustments to their own and to other persons' needs.

"Identification with the aims of children and grandchildren" is a form of adaptation in which the aging person introjects plans, future perspectives, aspirations, or worries of offspring, and regulates his behavior in accordance with these introjected standards. This technique increases over the 10-year period of observation and certainly contributes much to the solving of conflicts with children. Often, however, the elderly's own interests are sacrificed for the sake of others'.

Aside from several minor shifts in the rank order of reactions between 1966 and 1977, more sizable ones were observed with regard to "Active resistance" and "Relying on others." But, in general, a remarkable degree of consistency in the ranking of *Daseinstechniken* over the 10-year period could be observed. Achievement-related behaviors, as well as relying on others, became more important in 1976. Caregiving, financial contributions to children's households, and gifts to the children increased, but elderly parents likewise relied on their social environment when they needed help.

CONCLUSIONS

Information about *Daseinstechniken*, or coping styles, as reported in the last paragraph of this essay describes ways or programs used by a person when dealing with stressful demands. It is process-oriented information telling about the "how" of adaptive endeavours. When assessed longitudinally, it permits a description of the interacting actual and diachronic adaptive processes.

Our data convey that older people do cope. In other words, those processes activated when the individual has to face threatening, challenging, or otherwise taxing demands can be observed in old age. We have found evidence for the assumption that cognitive processes play a major role in coping. This confirms for our aged sample what has already been stated for adolescents and mid-life adults (Lazarus, 1966; 1974; 1980). Cognitively represented demands are no isomorphic representations of the taxing situations encountered; rather they are representations partly constructed by an actively perceiving and appraising individual.

We can generally interpret our participants' styles of coping as meaningful activities. Plans for action and actions themselves seem to effectively relate personal potentials to situational demands. In most areas studied, active styles of coping prevailed; they appeared to be adaptive.

Turning to the diachronic perspective, we also observe a meaningful restructuring of forms of behavior over time. It is not quite appropriate to speak of a consistency of coping styles in aging—although we could claim consistency of its efficiency. Rather, with changing demands encountered, the aging person responds with forms of behavior that try to accomplish what is in the scope of his coping capacities. There is an over-time transaction between situational demands and personal resources that seems to be continuously coordinated by the coping person. In other words, forms of behavior are determined by person- and situational-factors.

There is no direct evidence of the interaction between actual and developmental processes in the data reported: such an interaction can be inferred only. In idiographic research, and before all in biographical studies, participants report about interactions between crystallized and actual processes. Yet it still requires ideas and efforts to design studies that can prove such complex interactions in individual and universal, specific and general, and actual, as well as diachronically crystallized, form.

REFERENCES

Baade, F. E., Borck, J., Kroebe, S., & Zumvenne, G. *Theorien und Methoden der Verhaltenstherapie.* Mitteilungen der DGVT: Sonderheft II, 1980.

Benner, P., Roskies, E., & Lazarus, R. S. Stress and coping under extreme conditions. In J. E. Dimsdale (Ed.), *Survivors, victims, and perpetrators: Essays on the Nazi holocaust* (219-258). Washington, D.C.: Hemisphere, 1980.

Birren, J. E., & Schaie, K. W. *Handbook of the psychology of aging.* New York: Van Nostrand, 1977.

Blos, P. *On adolescence.* New York: The Free Press, 1962.

Coelho, G. V., Hamburg, D. A., & Adams, J. E. (Eds.). *Coping and adaptation.* New York: Basic Books, 1974.

Cohen, F. et al. Panel report on psychosocial assets and modifiers of stress. In G. R. Elliott & C. Eisdorfer (Eds.), *Stress and human health: Analysis and implications for research* (147–188) New York: Springer, 1982.

Costa, P. T., & McCrae, R. R. Age differences in personality structure: A cluster analysis approach. *Journal of Gerontology,* 1976, *31,* 5654–570.

Datan, N., & Ginsberg, L. H. (Eds.). *Life-span developmental psychology: Normative life crises.* New York: Academic Press, 1975.

Dunkel-Schetter, C., & Wortman, C. B. Dilemmas of social support: Parallels between victimization and aging. In S. B. Kiesler, J. N. Morgan, & V. K. Oppenheimer (Eds.), *Aging: Social change* (349–381). New York: Academic Press, 1981.

Endler, N. S., & Magnusson, D. (Eds.). *Interactional psychology and personality.* Washington, D.C.: Hemisphere, 1976.

Filipp, S. H. (Ed.). *Kritische Lebensereignisse.* München: Urban und Schwarzenberg, 1981.

Folkman, S., & Lazarus, R. S. An analysis of coping in a middle-aged community sample. *Journal of Health and Social Behavior,* 1980, *21,* 219–239.

Frankenhäuser, M. Psychobiological aspects of life stress. In S. Levine & H. Ursin (Eds.), *Coping and Health* (203–223). New York and London: Plenum, 1980.

Freud, A. *Das Ich und die Abwehrmechanismen.* Wien: Internationaler Verlag, 1936.

Freud, S. *Drei Abhandlungen zur Sexualtheorie.* Wien: Deuticke, 1905.

Gleason, J., Karuza, J., Jr., & Zevon, M.A. *Personal responsibility in coping.* Paper presented at the Meeting of the Gerontological Society of America, San Diego, CA, 1981, November.

Goldfried, M. R. The use of relaxation and cognitive relabeling as coping skills. In R. B. Stuart (Ed.), *Behavioral self-management: Strategies, techniques and outcome* (82–116). New York: Brunner and Mazel, 1977.

Gutman, D. The cross-cultural perspective. In J. E. Birren & K. W. Schaie (Eds.), *Handbook of the psychology of aging,* (302–326). New York: Van Nostrand, 1977.

Gutman, D. Observations on culture and mental health in later life. In J. E. Birren & B. Sloane (Eds.), *Handbook of mental health and aging* (429–447). Englewood Cliffs: Prentice Hall, 1980.

Guilford, J. P. *Personality.* New York: McGraw-Hill, 1959.

Haan, N. Proposed model of ego functioning. Coping and defense mechanisms in relation to IQ change. *Psychological Monographs,* 1963, *77,* No. 8.

Haan, N. *Coping and defending.* New York: Academic Press, 1977.

House, J. S. *Work Stress and social support.* Menlo Park, CA: Addison-Wesley, 1981.

Kaplan, H. B. (Ed.). *Psychosocial stress: Trends in theory and research.* New York: Academic Press, 1983.

Kirscht, J. P., & Rosenstock, I. M. Patient's problems in following recommendations of health experts. In G. C. Stone, F. Cohen, & N. E. Adler, *Health psychology: A handbook.* San Francisco: Jossey-Bass, 1979.

Kohli, M. *Soziologie des Lebenslaufs.* Darmstadt/Neuwied: Luchterhand, 1978.

Kroeber, T. C. The coping functions of the ego mechanisms. In R. White (Ed.), *The study of lives.* New York: Atherton, 1963.

Labouvie-Vief, G., & Gonda, J. N. Cognitive strategy training and intellectual performance in the elderly. *Journal of Gerontology,* 1976, *31,* 327–332.

Lantermann, E. D. *Person, Situation und Handlung*. München: Urban und Schwarzenberg, 1980.

Lazarus, R. S. *Psychological stress and the coping process*. New York: McGraw-Hill, 1966.

Lazarus, R. S. The stress and coping paradigm. In L. A. Bond & J. C. Rosen (Eds.), *Competence and coping during adulthood* (28–74). Hanover: University Press of New England, 1980.

Lazarus, R. S., Averill, J. R., & Opton, E. The psychology of coping: Issues of research and assessment. In G. V. Coelho, D. A. Hamburg, & J. E. Adams (Eds.), *Coping and adaptation* (249–315). New York: Basic Books, 1974.

Lazarus, R. S., & Olbrich, E. Problems of stress and coping in old age. In M. Bergener, U. Lehr, E. Lang, & R. Schmitz-Scherzer (Eds.), *Aging in the eighties and beyond* (272–287). New York: Springer, 1983.

Lehr, U. *Psychologie des Alterns*. Heidelberg: Quelle und Meyer, 1977.

Lesser, L., Lazarus, L., Wilson, R., Cohler, B., Schweon, C., Kasanik, A., & Fox, J. *Psychological defense mechanisms in normal and demented elderly*. Paper presented at the meeting of the Gerontological Society of America, San Diego, CA, 1981, November.

Lieberman, M. A. Adaptive processes in later life. In N. Datan & L. H. Ginsberg (Eds.), *Life-span developmental psychology: Normative life crises* (135–159). New York: Academic Press, 1975.

Magnusson, D., & Endler, N. S. *Personality at the crossroads: Current issues in interactional psychology*. New York: Wiley, 1977.

McCrae, R. R. Age differences in the use of coping mechanisms. *Journal of Gerontology,* 1982, *37*, 454–460.

Meichenbaum, D. *Cognitive behavior modification*. New York: Plenum Press, 1977.

McLean, A. *Work stress*. Reading: Addison Wesley, 1979.

Miller, N. E. A perspective on the effects of stress and coping on disease and health. In S. Levine & H. Ursin (Eds.), *Coping and health* (323–353). New York and London: Plenum, 1980.

Mischel, W. *Personality and assessment*, New York: Wiley, 1968.

Mischel, W. On the interface of cognition and personality. *American Psychologist,* 1979, *34*, 740–754.

Moos, R. (Ed.). *Human adaptation: Coping with life crises*. Lexington: Heath, 1976.

Moos, R. (Ed.). *Coping with physical illness*. New York: Plenum, 1977.

Murphy, L. B., & Moriarty, A. E. *Vulnerability, coping and growth*. New Haven and London: Yale University Press, 1976.

Olbrich, E. Normative übergänge im menschlichen Lebenslauf: Entwicklungskrisen oder Herausforderungen? In S. H. Filipp (Ed.), *Kritische Lebesereignisse* (123–138). München: Urban und Schwarzenberg, 1981.

Olbrich, E. übergänge im Jugendalter. In, R. Silbereisen & L. Montada (Eds.), *Entwicklungspsychologie: Ein Handbuch in Schlüsselbegriffen* (89–96). München: Urban und Schwarzenberg, 1983.

Olbrich, E., & Thomae, H. Empirical findings to a cognitive theory of aging. *International Journal of Behavioral Development,* 1978, *1*, 67–84.

Plemons, J., Willis, S., & Baltes, P. Modifiability of fluid intelligence in aging: Short term longitudinal training approach. *Journal of Gerontology,* 1978, *33*, 224–231.

Pfeiffer, E. Psychopathology and social pathology. In J. E. Birren & K. W. Schaie (Eds.), *Handbook of the psychology of aging* (650–671). New York: Van Nostrand, 1977.

Quayhagen, M. P., & Quayhagen, M. Coping with conflict: Measurement of age-related patterns. *Research on Aging,* 1982, *4*, 364–377.

Renner, V. J., & Birren, J. E. Stress: Physiological and psychological mechanisms. In,

J. E. Birren & R. B. Sloane (Eds.), *Handbook of mental health and aging* (310–336). Englewood Cliffs: Prentice Hall, 1980.

Roskies, E., & Lazarus, R. S. Coping theory and the teaching of coping skills. In P. O. Davidson & S. M. Davidson (Eds.), *Behavioral medicine* (38–69). New York: Brunner and Mazel, 1980.

Salthouse, T. L. *Adult cognition*. New York: Springer, 1982.

Schaie, K. W. A general model for the study of developmental problems. *Psychological Bulletin, 1965, 64,* 92–107.

Schönpflug, W. Regulation und Fehlregulation im Verhalten: I and II. *Psychologische Beiträge, 1979, 21,* 174–202 and 597–621.

Thomae, H. *Persölichkeit*. Bonn: Bouvier, 1951.

Thomae, H. *Das Individuum und seine Welt*. Göttingen: Hogrefe, 1968.

Thomae, H. Theory of aging and cognitive theory of personality. *Human Development, 1970, 13,* 1–16.

Thomae, H. Personality and adjustment to aging. In J. E. Birren & R. B. Sloane (Eds.), *Handbook of mental health and aging* (285–309). Englewood Cliffs: Prentice Hall, 1980.

Thomae, H. *Alternsstile und Altersschicksale*. Bern, Stuttgart, Wien: Huber, 1983.

Thomae, H. Formen der Auseinandersetzung mit Konflikt und Belastung im Jugendalter. In E. Olbrich & E. Todt (Eds.), *Probleme des Jugendalters* (89–110). Heidelberg: Springer, 1984.

Thomae, H., Lehr, U., & Schmitz-Scherzer, R. Research on aging in behavioral sciences in the Federal Republic of Germany. *Zeitschrift für Gerontologie, 1981, 14,* 204–223.

Vaillant, G. E. *Adaptation to life*. Boston: Little Brown, 1977.

Weinberg, S., & Levine, S. Psychobiology of coping in animals: The effects of predictability. In S. Levine & H. Ursin (Eds.), *Coping and health* (39–59). New York and London: Plenum, 1980.

Willis, S., Blieszner, R., & Baltes, P. Intellectual training research in aging: Modification of performance on the fluid ability Figural Relations. *Journal of Educational Psychology, 1981, 73,* 41–50.

III

SOCIAL, INTERGENERATIONAL, AND THEORETICAL STUDIES

INTRODUCTION

This section includes contributions of a different kind. In the first three (Maas; Fiske & Chiriboga; Troll & Stapley) the social component and intergenerational differences and relationships are obvious. And although Coleman and McCulloch's contribution is mainly psychological, the social aspects appear to be very powerful too. These four studies cover various aspects of life-span research: the discussion of longitudinal experiences (Maas), the connection of ongoing longitudinal research to new social-cultural tendencies (Fiske and Chiriboga), the review and discussion of diachronic data on the social network in family-research (Troll et al.), and the reconsideration of original cross-sectional data with data from a second observation (Coleman and McCulloch). We can derive some general points from these studies.

The comments of Maas on research on adulthood and old age are clearly justified. We should not restrict ourselves to certain stages or periods of life without taking into consideration the whole individual biographies of the respondents. But it will take time for life-span psychology and sociology to achieve the standards that developmental psychology (child psychology) has already achieved. The point of view of a life-span psychologist or sociologist assures that they will look for concepts that can be applied to childhood as well as to the middle and later years. Notions or concepts, such as attachment, competence, and commitment, can be studied over the total life-span. The interplay of cultural, social, and individual change is well exposed in Fiske and Chiriboga's contribution. At the same time, the different generations give a diachronic vista, making the contributions of many life-span researchers modest. Are we only writing contemporary history? As we discover unexpected connections, we can also be of value for other, coming generations.

157

In any case, the finding that stress does not necessarily result in less enjoyment is a good example of the significance of this kind of research. Fiske and Chiriboga point to other interesting findings. The differentiation between normative and nonnormative events is striking. The young newly divorced people show that social context can also have a negative impact; they have experienced a major loss, which was not in accordance with their own expectation, built up by the societal meaning (evaluation) of the marriage event. And a final, but very important, finding, also found in other research (Lehr & Thomae, 1965) may be stated thusly: Because older people have experienced more, and frequently more severe, stress, they become less likely to be preoccupied with relatively minor stresses.

Coleman and McCulloch's contribution also accommodates the biological component in some of the major psychiatric diagnoses. However, their contribution is a psychological one, they more strongly stress the interplay of social and personal values. Their data show a rather negative attitude of the aged towards modern society, indicating different coping strategies: either acceptance of these new values or successful retreat from them. For the adoption of the latter, the aged have to have a positive self-image.

In addition, Coleman and McCulloch stress a possible generation gap. In doing so, they put forward a very fundamental question: If we are to take this generation gap seriously, will there be a relatively important problem between representatives of the different generations? We also ask ourselves whether life-span research, rather than generations-research, is possible. In this context, it is self-evident that methodological questions arise, as, for instance, in the value of case studies, the advantages and disadvantages of quantitative versus qualitative research, and so forth.

It is obvious that the above-mentioned four studies add a host of ideas to our thoughts on life-span research. Together they cover all different stages of life. They increase the awareness of a very complex subject that life-span science will further study. For example, Bengtson and Kuypers elaborate their well-known social breakdown syndrome (1973), simultaneously proposing a very useful model that should be tested in future research.

These various contributions show how various researchers in the field are working within the framework of the life-span. It is impossible, and at the same time unnecessary, to try to summarise all these different views, data and considerations. Whether they are youth- or age-oriented, they are proof of the vivid world of a life span science. These scholars have become aware of the fact that old age cannot exist without a childhood and that to understand older people we need knowledge about their youth and middle years. Life-span science is not new, but it means a way of looking at human behavior from a different point of view. It puts the human being on a life-line, and what is more attractive and inspiring than to follow and understand a human being from birth to death?

J. M.

REFERENCES

Kuypers, J. A., & Bengtson, V. L. Social breakdown and competence: A model of normal aging. *Human Development*, 1973, *16*, 181–201.

Lehr, U., & Thomae, H. *Konflikt, seelische Belastung und Lebensalter.* Köln, Opladen: Westdeutscher Verlag, 1965.

THE DEVELOPMENT OF ADULT DEVELOPMENT: RECOLLECTIONS AND REFLECTIONS

Henry S. Maas

INTRODUCTION

Looking backward because of one's interest in the future is a strategy familiar to developmentalists. Less familiar—or at least less public—are the reflections of developmentalists themselves as they review their own experiences and studies in the field. In accord with research conventions, Occam's razor or the law of parsimony, and other such disciplining dicta, reflections that may seem tangential are excluded from research reports. This essay, though not written with an excess of self-indulgence, is derived from my musings about three developmental studies I did in the 1960s and early 1970s, as well as some professional involvements in the late 1940s and 1950s. The results of my second thoughts are questions about the present course of development of adult development—questions addressed in my 1980s life-course book (Maas, 1984).

The current state of the art is one of great activity and expanding commitments. Social Science Research Council (SSRC) reports indicate that many sciences and other academic disciplines are joining the adult development network, presumably to participate supportively in its young life. But social networks also impose constraints, and dense networks may inhibit radical changes in a life-course. Should policy-committed adult developmentalists plan a large-scale, practically oriented research program, "pure" scientists in the network or on a funding committee might disapprove and obstruct the proposal. Academic newcomers, such as zoologists, ethologists, and primatologists are joining human developmentalists to study, among other things, "parenting and offspring development" and particularly "brain and behavioral development in relation to parenting"—problems viewed not only "cross-time" and across cultures, but also "cross-species" (Social Science Research Council, 1980b, p. 62). On the other hand, there were policy-oriented economists at a 1980 SSRC workshop on the use of panel data for life-course research, and cardiologists at a 1980 SSRC conference on life-course stress (both seminars were sponsored by the SSRC Committee on Life-Course Perspectives on Middle and Old Age). In still another pattern involving new disciplines in developmental problems, Glen Elder works closely with social historians, to understand the impact of past social events on the personal development of cohorts of people who experienced, for example, the 1930s depression or similar large-scale assaults (Elder, 1981). Marjorie Fiske's concern with interrelationships between social change and personal change leads her into social philosophy (Fiske, 1980). And, more broadly, the social sciences are joining forces with the humanities to draw on "analytic approaches utilized in literary criticism, linguistics, philosophy, religion, and hermeneutics." This rapprochement with the humanities arises out of "a growing disenchantment among social scientists with the explanatory adequacy of models borrowed from the natural sciences" (Social Science Research Council, 1980a, p. 54). We are indeed witnesses to an expanding and otherwise changing universe.

Each discipline is, of course, both a set of lenses to view the world and a somewhat separate language to describe and explain it—or at least one fragment or aspect of it. Each discipline has its own central concerns and preoccupations and its specialized purposes. However, as intellectually stimulating as are the inevitable flow of new ideas from wide-ranging cross-discipline studies, are we going to suffer Tower-of-Babel-type communication problems? Within the context of a wasteful society in which more and bigger are considered better than few and smaller, what disadvantages should be anticipated, and perhaps obviated as adult development becomes a new growth industry? Or do I misinterpret the signs? Am I "generation-gapping"?

A mere three decades ago, such an explosion of interest in the adult development of *Homo sapiens* could not have been even dreamed of. During the few years preceding and following 1950, when I made the transition from doctoral student to assistant professor, the terra incognita between adolescence and Robert Havighurst's ideas on successful aging (Havighurst, 1953) was vast. The theoretical and unresearched chasm between life's first two decades and old age was tenuously bridged by Erik Erikson's eight stages of man (Erikson, 1950) and by students of culture-and-personality and socialization, for whom social class was a key concept. The Guidance Study longitudinal data at Berkeley's Institute of Child Welfare had been accumulated only through the subjects' teen years. These thick files suffered an inevitable analysis lag, so that findings on adolescence were just beginning to emerge. Moreover, the Berkeley developmental field was still primarily a psychological and anthropometric one. Only at Chicago, as I recall, were there incursions of a broader interdisciplinary nature especially in the sociological and anthropological perspectives of Allison Davis and Havighurst (1946; Havighurst, 1952a, 1952b), Lloyd Warner (1952; Warner, Meeker, Eels, 1959), and the younger generation of Bernice Neugarten and her colleagues (1946, 1957).

In all this early groping, the place of theory for orienting inquiry was uncertain. For example, I recall a 1950's attack on Berkeley's Harold E. Jones and Nancy Bayley by a young Iowa learning theorist at a small Chicago child development conference; the Iowan derided California's atheoretical approach to longitudinal data collection—a conflict between members not only of different schools of thought but also of different generations. A quarter century later, as Berkeley's systematically gathered but theoretically uncommitted data are patterned into a series of contributions to the literature on adulthood and old age, I wonder whether 1930's theory might not have ultimately narrowed, through its data screenings, the range of possible findings in the 1970s and 1980s. The utility and limitations of changing theory for the orientation of data collection in longitudinal studies need more thorough review than they seem thus far to have been given.

If theory failed to provide strong direction in the early days of the Berkeley Guidance Study, practice-based clinical perspectives did give structure to the inquiry. The design, with its experimental and control groups, was intended to provide evidence of the effects of "child guidance." In keeping with the influences of the 1920's child guidance movement in the United States, reflected in the founding of Institutes of Child Welfare to study child development at Iowa, Minnesota, Berkeley, Yale, and Teachers College Columbia, early longitudinal research—whether it be Arnold Gesell's (1947) at Yale or Jean Macfarlane's (1938) at Berkeley—was, in large measure, a practically directed enterprise. I return to this issue in regard to adult development in the final section of this essay.

THREE STUDIES AND THREE ISSUES

The workings of any field of inquiry become clearest, I believe, during the course of one's own empirical research. Since I want to draw some metafindings from three developmental studies in which I was engaged, I very briefly outline them.

Study 1 was an assessment of young adults in their early twenties who had been separated from their families in infancy or early childhood (under five). The separation occurred during World War II, when they were placed for a year or more in one of three British wartime residential nurseries. The nurseries had been set up as part of a national program to protect the young from the Nazi bombing of London. This arrangement, quite incidentally, provided an opportunity to study, through a natural experiment, the long-term effects of early childhood separation and group care when the separation was not preceded by intense psychosocial disarray in the families from which the children came.

The then-existing theory on the sequelae to early childhood separation had been sufficiently developed by John Bowlby (1951) and others to give prescriptions for the design of research aimed at testing the validity of such a theory's predictions. This selection of variables left primarily operational problems to an investigator. These included the difficult task of locating appropriate persons for follow-up study after 15–20 years. Thus, in this study, theoretically proposed life-course continuities between early childhood and young adulthood, over roughly a 20-year span, were under investigation. Deviant or pathological developments in young adulthood were anticipated, but were not found, for those separated at age 2 or older. I spent a busy academic year (1960–1961) in London tracking down, interviewing, and testing 20 young adults and their parents, with data-collection help in the field by a University of London colleague. I call Study 1 The Adult Adjustment Study (Maas, 1963a, 1963b).

Major findings of Study 1 were that "early childhood separation [from family] and preschool residential care, at least from about age two on, are not themselves *sufficient* antecedents to a seriously troubled or troublesome young adulthood" (Maas, 1963b, p. 72). Study of such psychological variables as attachment capacities and competence in social roles was coupled with consideration of contextual differences among the three residential nurseries. Social development seemed to be fostered by continuities in personnel and values between the children's home neighborhood and the residential nursery to which they were evacuated.

Study 2 was an examination of the relationships between capacities for intimacy in young adults of about age 30 and the nature of their peer relationships in later childhood or preadolescence. The theory of interpersonal development proposed by Harry Stack Sullivan (1953) suggests that a critical period appears between the ages of about 8½ and 10 or 11 years. During that period, the preconditions for closeness in adult relationships include the formation of a close same-sexed friendship, a linkage with someone Sullivan calls a "chum." Parallels to this formulation on development in childhood appear in the work of a Piagetan (Nielsen, 1951) and psychoanalytically oriented researchers (Isaacs, 1937; Bornstein, 1950). During this critical period of sex homogeneity in friendships, the first close bond between peers provides a presumably necessary matrix for later openness and compassion in close relationships. An adulthood characterized by distance or the avoidance of close relationships is, hypothetically, more likely to develop when there has been no preadolescent chum.

To test this two-part paradigm linking adult intimacy and preadolescent peer relations, the longitudinal records of 44 Berkeley Guidance Study adults were contrasted. An important facet of adult life was studied on the assumption that childhood preconditions could be programmatically modified if support was found for the proposition (capacities for adult intimacy assumed to be a desirable state). At the least, a contribution might be made to theory on human social development into the young adult years, covering about a 25-year span of early life. While the data did not support the central hypothesis on chumship and intimacy, the results did provide some interactional patterns warranting further study. I call Study 2 The Adult Intimacy Study (Maas, 1968).

Evidence in Study 2 shows that although both aloof and warm adult males had preadolescent chums, the men who had little capacity for warmth or intimacy in their thirties had experienced a souring and rupturing of their chumships in preadolescence. By contrast, none of the males who became warm and intimate adults had similarly spoiled preadolescent chumships. Other differences in the age and sex composition of play groups suggest that warm males, compared with aloof males, developed greater preadolescent capacities for reciprocity and collaboration. Preadolescent differences between warm and aloof adult women, while being less striking, were the greater number of playmates and more acceptance of boys as playmates among the former and more evidence of preadolescent feelings of boredom and loneliness among the latter.

Study 3 started out from the young adult data on parents in the Berkeley Guidance Study longitudinal files and searched for continuities into old age (about age 70). Drawing on interviews from the early 1930s on, when the parents were initially about age 30, Joseph Kuypers and I launched a series of reinterviews and tests with all of the 142 parents accessible to us in the late 1960s. The new data collection and analysis

were slanted to parallel the early data with which they were to be compared, although we thought and reported in terms of the 1960s' ideas
about life styles and personality unknown in the 1930s. I refer to this
third study as The Aging Parents Study (Maas & Kuypers, 1974). (The
findings of this booklength report are too extensive for summary here,
but the final section of this essay presents a few of the study's discov-
eries.)

In currently contemplating Studies 1 and 2, I am struck by what I call
the childlessness of adult development (the first issue to be discussed
below). In regard to all three studies, my motives and commitments,
tucked well out of view in the study reports, seem now to be matters
that should somewhere have been made explicit. This is a second issue
I address because of its relevance to the development of adult development. Finally, all three studies and especially the third (on aging parents) evoke second thoughts about theory on continuities over the life-
span and the complex matter of practical or policy problems as a starting
point for inquiry into human—and particularly adult—development. The
final section of this essay discusses this issue.

THE CHILDLESSNESS OF ADULT DEVELOPMENT

The Adult Adjustment Study (Study 1) and The Adult Intimacy Study
(Study 2) are based on separate mini-theories of development in infancy
and early and later childhood and are predictive of developmental deficits manifest in adult behavior. The study (on adult adjustment) grew
out of formulations on what was then called, in perhaps accusatory if
not sexist fashion, maternal deprivation. These formulations were derived initially from clinical observations and then from systematic study,
mostly in the 1940s by psychiatrists who were concerned with the prevention and treatment of psychopathology. Subsequently theory on
early childhood separation was more rigorously tested and detailed by
a large contingent of child psychologists (mostly developmental). What
has now come to be known as *attachment theory* is emerging not only as
a child development mini-theory but also as a life-span concept (Kahn
& Antonucci, 1980). The growing curiosity of adult developmentalists
regarding social networks and social supports over the life-course makes
the emergence of attachment as a life-span concept timely and of promising utility (Maas, 1984, pp. 58-79).

This sketch of the history of a developmental mini-theory, from the
practical concerns of pathologists, through the academic interests of child
developmentalists and into the larger realm of the life-span perspective,
describes a pathway along which I believe other orienting ideas in adult

development might profitably travel. To do so, childhood must reenter adult developmentalists' awareness. I have at least three reasons for believing this pathway to be a good route: (1) To discover how early antecedent and subsequent human conditions or potentials are related over the life-course, developmental ideas of childhood should normally be considered in the process of planning studies in adult development; (2) Questions arising out of early pathology or other kinds of human problems that call for practical attention are more likely, as foci for research, to provide returns to the world of social policy—an essential purpose for such research, I believe, in a time of increasingly limited resources; and (3) All the logic of science (as well as pedagogy) presses us to proceed from the known to the unknown. In this context, the knowns are better defined in early life's developments; the less well-boundaried and charted regions remain in the later years. For example, the development of the disengagement theory in the late 1950s and 1960s (Cumming & Henry, 1961), properly linked with early childhood separation theory of the 1940s and early 1950s, could have advanced similarities and sharpened differences between both perspectives. Attachments provide the very young with secure bases for explorations. Do attachment losses among elderly people help to explain their reduced exploration, withdrawal and disengagement? Might such thinking have hastened and illuminated research on widowhood?

The reciprocal nature of early separation as reflected in the suffering or filial deprivation among parents (Jenkins, 1972) could probably have been discovered sooner. And life-span continuities, such as were found in Study 3 (on aging parents), might have proliferated, for "more than any other mothers' cluster, most of the uncentered (57 percent) [out of the 21 in the sample] lost a parent in their preadult years" (Maas & Kuypers, 1974, p. 92).

For many specialists in aging and adult development, childhood remains a terra incognita. As little as 3 decades ago, the reverse was true but for good reason. There was precious little known about the long stretch of life beyond adolescence. Since that time, however, some students of aging have entered the developmental "family" with a grievance against their child development kin, who are seen to have gotten too much public recognition or funding. And this rivalry seems to persist to the detriment of the whole family's well-being.

For example, writing on the later years of life, Ronald P. Abeles and Matilda White Riley remark with implicit criticism, "Social scientists concerned with human development have traditionally focused their greatest attention upon infancy, childhood, adolescence, and early adulthood," although in the same paragraph they seem to deplore the "major tendency . . . to study discrete age groups in relative isolation" (1977, p. 1). In the same vein, from Pennsylvania State University comes a 1981 textbook called *Adult Development and Aging* and subtitled *A Life-Span Perspective* (Hultsch & Deutsch, 1981). Its 25-column, 9-page Subject Index includes not a single entry on childhood or infancy—merely on "child-rearing" and, appropriately enough, on "childlessness." The brief text passage on child-rearing or parenting gives no attention at all to children's influences on adults; there is apparently little awareness of child development in current life-span perspectives focused on the adult years. How are conceptual linkages to be made between the earliest and later phases of human life?

Rare, indeed, are efforts like those of Toni Antonucci to struggle with attachment as a unifying life-span concept, from infancy through old age (1976). But there are a host of processes having their origins in the early years that reverberate all through adulthood. Being attuned to even the grossest understandings of infancy, no newcomer to adult developmental studies (on the socioeconomic life-cycle) could make so naive an observation as that "between ages 16 and 24, more changes and significant events take place for most people than in any other comparably short span of years". How can the transformations between birth and age 2 remain outside the awareness of someone professing an "interest in research that encompasses much or all of a persons's lifetime" (Peterson, 1978, p. 29)?

My necessarily brief plea is not for more longitudinal studies of cohorts of the young to be followed from birth to maturity and beyond. It is rather for more designs of inquiries on the adult years, including concepts relevant to the social development of children and youth as well as of young adults, the middle aged, and old people, so that the life-span can be understood in its obviously ongoing flow (from beginning to end). Included in my own framework of concepts, which have organized the book *People and Contexts: Social Development from Birth to Old Age* (Maas, 1984), are not only the developing social capacities, but also the environments or contexts that foster or impede the expression and elaboration of these capacities. Thus, in addition to attachment and the context of supportive networks, are curiosity and manipulative competencies. They are combined with the more or less responsive environments that can—or cannot—be explored and coped with, whether they be in infancy and youth or in old age (when the prostheses of responsive environments determine in large measure the levels of competence). Capacities for reciprocity and collaboration are as dependent on cognitive development as on the caring and sharing milieus in which preadolescents are growing up (i.e., the play groups and neighborhoods of the boys and girls in my Study 2 on chumships and later capacities for intimacy). But reciprocity and collaboration, like capacities for productive work and intimacy, are equally relevant to an understanding of middle age, its life-course transitions, and the development of a wide-ranging sense of social responsibility. A sense of social responsibility orients some privileged people in midlife to exercise their power in social and political causes in collaboration with, or in the interests of, underprivileged others. The genesis of such later life development may lie in early life conditions. So long as adult development chooses to work in isolation of its child development counterpart, we shall not know. The conceptual and operational schism between child and adult development reveals a woeful negation of life-span commitment in both camps.

THE PURPOSES AND COMMITMENTS OF DEVELOPMENTALISTS

I can be somewhat briefer on the second issue, developmentalists' purposes and commitments. These determine, to a large extent, the questions developmentalists choose to pursue and the methods they may use in this pursuit. In a collection of essays by sociologists on what motivates their inquiries and the "subjective side" to their methodologies, the differences are considerable—from George Caspar Homans's primarily intellectual curiosity and "compulsion" to bring some large-scale order out of chaotic wholes, to Llewellyn Gross's early concerns about "the awesome and often destructive consequences of human inequality" (Horowitz, 1969, pp. 13–69). Similarly, Lee Rainwater says "the relationship of sociology to social problems was at the heart of my initial interest," but then he moves to a balanced position: "A sociology which strives so hard for relevance and application that there is no play for pure curiosity must inevitably use up its intellectual capital; a sociology in which application is either rejected or considered 'dirty work' better delegated to other professions like social work or planning runs the very real risk of losing touch with the reality its theories are supposed to encompass" (Horowitz, 1969, p. 99). Although I like the rational balance of this statement, in hard times priority-setting is likely to require even firmer guidelines. Moreover, questions generated by a concern for policy or application need not signify a curiosity that is impure.

Study 1, the London study of young adult adjustment after early childhood separation and group care, followed a large inquiry into the conditions of children in foster care in nine counties across the United

States in the late 1950s (Maas & Engler, 1959). We discovered, among
other things, that children who were in foster families moved about or
were replaced in care much more frequently than children in group or
congregate care, although the importance of continuity in care-taking
and residential stability for young children seemed well documented.
Of course, the developmentally relevant contexts of group care are obviously multivariate, facilities ranging from small and child-centered to
large, impersonal, and differing along many other dimensions. But John
Bowlby's (1951) warnings homogenized all group care as unhealthy for
the young; he thus accelerated the closing down of many institutions
or their conversion in name, if not completely in function, to residential
treatment homes. My London study of young adult adjustment was thus
an effort to see whether, given variations in kinds of group care, the
evidence of pathology in young adulthood, in fact, followed predictions.
I could foresee how the London findings on young adult adjustment
might contribute to welfare policy decisions affecting many children's
lives. Practice assumptions are a useful starting point for research.

Similarly, having worked with children and youth in small groups,
and having then done a series of field studies of pre- and early adolescent groups (Maas, 1950, 1951, 1954), I approached Study 2 (on adult
intimacy) with hopes that it might contribute simultaneously to developmental theory and to group programs for the young. It seemed important that the antecedent or independent condition—the presence of
a close preadolescent friend or confidant—be a "variable" in the orbit
of children's services and primary socialization agents, (one that they
might planfully influence), and that the subsequent condition of adult
intimacy be based in a socially desirable human capacity. One study of
research utilization indicates that the surest route to research use is to
test "assumptions embedded in current policy," and come up with findings that "challenge the status quo" (Weiss & Bucuvalas, 1980, p. 255).

By that criterion, only Study 1 is acceptable. The second study, on
adult intimacy and preadolescent peer relations, was designed in response to the lures of Berkeley's longitudinal files and my curiosity about
the validity of Sullivan's theory of interpersonal development (Sullivan,
1953). The surest way for developmental research to be useful is to plan
for its use in the design. The use may not be immediate, but, rather
implemented at the end of a research program or in a set of cross-val-
idating studies. Applications should be planned for, at least ultimately,
in the design of adult development studies, as discussed in the final
section of this essay. Without research designs, the explicit purpose of
which is to provide findings usable in the real world, and without developmentalists' commitments to such purpose, useful results would be

a matter of mere happenstance—or rare serendipity. The plan for utility, of course, in no way diminishes a study's potential for contributing to general theory or knowledge. But one must, nevertheless, work harder at the design stage, committed to a double purpose, rather than to merely one of them.

THE UTILITY OF ADULT DEVELOPMENT AND AGING STUDIES: "IF" THEORY AND "THEN" POLICY

Developmental research findings lend themselves especially well to preventive policies and programs when undesirable sequelae follow preventable or modifiable antecedents. In fact, preventive work is dependent on predictive formulations that stipulate certain modifiable conditions as generating certain consequences. For example, one developmental study reveals that widows find initial support among married friends while grieving during their "crisis phase," but from other widows later, after about a year and a half and in their "transition phase" (Bankoff, 1980). Human service workers in programs aiming to help widows should find such formulations useful. "If" other widows are helpful after the initial intense mourning has dissipated, "then" the timing and composition of supportive groups for widows are well oriented by relevant research findings.

Study 3, of aging parents (Maas & Kuypers, 1974), revealed a number of potentially useful formulations linking early adult antecedents and problems in old age. For example, women concerned about health problems in old age tend to be the same women who have had a continuity of somatic difficulties over their adult years, beginning in young adulthood. The implication for early health care is apparent, although I describe below an intervening variable that Glen Elder's (1980) LISREL reanalysis of our data reveals. To cite another example of useful findings, the mothers in two lifestyle clusters who evidence the highest life satisfaction in old age were not happy in their family roles as young adults; but in midlife and later years became happily involved in occupations or social organizations. By contrast, among the least satisfied in old age are another cluster of mothers who were completely and very contentedly engaged as wives and mothers all through their early and middle adult years. Their lives were completely family centered, but in old age they seem bereft. The obvious preventive implication is that young women ought not put all their eggs in the family basket—a basket that overturns in later years. Not only the changing life-course of friendships (Brown, 1981), but also the mental health significance of peer relations and extra-familial network involvement in adult life are well documented in the research literature. In short, to prevent or reduce specifiable and undesirable sequelae in old age, developmental and especially longitudinal studies may provide lifestyle guidance for young adults.

Yet note that such findings and their implicit prescriptions offer little to those who are currently in trouble. As Jerome Kagan observed in discussing the continuities perspective of developmentalists, "Connectedness tempts one to look always for historical explanations and to dismiss the significance of recent or concurrent forces. . . . Faith in connectedness blunts our motivation to change the present [and] clouds our vision of local irritants that are difficult to remove" (Kagan, 1980, p. 69). This is a possibility we should be sensitive to. And if, as Paul Baltes (Baltes, 1980, p. 6) proposes, life-span studies aim, beyond describing and explaining, to contribute to the "modification (optimization) of developmental processes" (Baltes, 1980, 66), developmentalists should be able to do more than offer the kinds of broad, post hoc proposals Kuypers and I provide in our final "Issues and Implications" chapter (Maas & Kuypers, 1974). Such proposals, unplanned for in initial designs, may later become ridiculously obvious, although findings reveal theoretically nice complexities. For example, Glen Elder's reanalysis of our data on health reaffirms the linkage of women's "early signs of ill health" and "bodily preoccupations some 40 years later" (Elder & Liker, 1980, p. 19). The association is strengthened for those low socio-economic status mothers who also suffered "economic deprivation" in the 1930s. Among the higher status women who "were tested by the pressures and tensions of heavy income loss during the 1930s" and were strengthened by such adversity, their subsequent health in old age is unrelated to their 1930s health. From such an interaction formulation, all one can propose as instrumental is an early adult avoidance of serious money-shortage strains; however, years of hard work and expense in large-scale studies are not needed to discover the damaging effects on people who are living in poverty! If we are seriously committed to the utility of findings as one of our purposes in adult development and aging research, we should reconsider how we plan studies.

For such ends, developmental theory and research designs should aim for associations among conditions, some of which provide leverage for policy purposes (e.g., manipulable antecedents and feasible options, clarity about alternative sequelae from differing preconditions, and questions about the development of undesirable states). But relatively little adult development research seems to be concerned with ultimate modifiabilities. Studies of normal personality constancies and changes over time, though of considerable interest to many, offer little to work from practically, especially at the levels of abstraction in which generalizations enter bodies of relevant theory. The following is an example of this: "Consistency [of personality] is most obvious for personality characteristics that are endowed with positive cultural and societal valences" (Moss & Susman, 1980, p. 590). Taking achievement motivation as one example, to what course of action or policy proposals might such a generalization, if valid, lead us? Without designs that stipulate policy aims, the yield is likely to remain slim.

Forces affecting the direction of our curiosities in selecting a research problem or program have nowhere, to my knowledge, been adequately studied. To engage in inquiries that provide practical payoffs as well as theoretical gains, there are some simple tests to apply to the questions or hypotheses that entice us. Before beginning any study, we typically consider the array of anticipated or alternate findings—X, Y, and/or Z. We should then ask: "if" we discover X, "then" what are the policy implications, and "if" we discover Y, "then" how do the policy implications differ? And to what extent are such policy implications realizable in the short-run? Are they feasible only in the long-run, or most unlikely even in the foreseeable future? Our answers to such questions should influence our choice of, and decision to proceed with, a study program.

In the adult development field, research on stages of adaptation to widowhood, in the work of Lopata (1977) and more recently, Bankoff (1980), nicely illustrates policy-relevant studies. "If" widows are at Stage A in their efforts to cope with loss of a spouse, "then" these are appropriate supportive social network and other contextual arrangements; but at Stage B, different kinds of people prove helpful. In a world of increasing economic stringencies, diminishing natural resources, and much human pain, developmentalists have some social responsibility to earn their funding by helping, through such formulations, to reduce human suffering.

REFERENCES

Abeles, R. P., & Riley, M. W. A life-course perspective on the later years of life: Some implications for research. *Annual Report*. New York: Social Science Research Council, 1976–1977.

Antonucci, T. Attachment: A life-span concept. *Human Development*, 1976, 19, 135–142.

Baltes, P. Life span developmental psychology. *Annual Review of Psychology*, 1980, 31, 65–110.

Bankoff, E. A. *Support from family and friends: What helps the widow?* Paper presented at the annual meeting of the Gerontology Society, San Diego, CA, 1980, November.

Bowlby, J. *Maternal care and mental health*. Geneva: World Health Organization, 1951.

Bornstein, B. On latency. *Psychoanalytic Study of the Child*, 1950, 6, 276–285.

Brown, B. B. A life-span approach to friendship. In H. Lopata & D. Maines (Eds.), *Research on the interweave of social roles.* Greenwich, CT: JAI Press, 1981.

Cumming, E., & Henry, W. E. *Growing old: The process of disengagement.* New York: Basic Books, 1961.

Davis, A., & Havighurst, R. J. Social class and color differences in child-rearing. *American Sociological Review,* 1946, *11,* 698–710.

Elder, G. H., Jr. Historical experience in the later years. In T. K. Hareven (Ed.), *Patterns of aging.* New York: Guilford Press, 1981.

Elder, G. H., Jr., & Liker, J. K. *Hard times in women's lives: Historical influences across 40 years.* Unpublished manuscript, Cornell University, Sociology Department, Ithaca, NY, 1980.

Erikson, E. H. *Childhood and society.* New York: Norton, 1950.

Fiske, M. *The interplay of social and personal change in adulthood: Theoretical considerations.* Paper presented at the annual meeting of the Gerontology Society, San Diego, CA, 1980, November.

Gesell, A., & Amatruda, C. S. *Developmental diagnosis: Normal and abnormal child development.* New York: Hoeber, 1947.

Havighurst, R. J. Social and psychological needs of aging. *Annals of the American Academy of Political and Social Science,* 1952, *279,* 11–17. (a)

Havighurst, R. J. Roles and status of older people. In A. I. Lansing (Ed.), *Cowdry's problems of aging* (3rd ed.) Baltimore: Williams & Wilkins, 1952. (b)

Havighurst, R. J., with Albrecht, R. *Older people.* New York: Longmans, Green, 1953.

Horowitz, I. L. (Ed.). *Sociological self-images: A collective portrait.* Beverly Hills, CA: Sage Publications, 1969.

Hultsch, D. F., & Deutsch, F. *Adult development and aging: A life-span perspective.* New York: McGraw-Hill, 1981.

Isaacs, S. *Social development in young children: A study in beginnings.* New York: Harcourt, Brace, 1937.

Jenkins, S., & Norman, E. *Filial deprivation and foster care.* New York: Columbia University Press, 1972.

Kagan, J. Perspectives on continuity. In O. G. Brim, Jr. & J. Kagan (Eds.), *Constancy and change in human development.* Cambridge, MA: Harvard University Press, 1980.

Kahn, R. L., & Antonucci, T. C. Convoys over the life course: Attachment, roles and social support. In P. Baltes & O. G. Brim, Jr. (Eds.), *Life span development and behavior* (Vol. 3). New York: Academic Press, 1980.

Lopata, H. Friendships among widows. In L. Troll, J. Israel, & K. Israel (Eds.), *The older woman.* Englewood Cliffs, NJ: Prentice-Hall, 1977.

Maas, H. S. Personal and group factors in leaders' social perception. *Journal of Abnormal and Social Psychology,* 1950, *45,* 54–63.

Maas, H. S. Some social class differences in the family systems and group relations of pre- and early adolescents. *Child Development,* 1951, *22,* 145–152.

Maas, H. S. The role of member in clubs of lower-class and middle-class adolescents. *Child Development,* 1954, *25,* 241–251.

Maas, H. S. Long-term effects of early childhood separation and group care. *Vita Humana: International Journal of Human Development,* 1963, *6,* 34–56. (a)

Maas, H. S. The young adult adjustment of twenty wartime residential nursery children. *Child Welfare,* 1963, *42,* 57–72. (b)

Maas, H. S. Preadolescent peer relations and adult intimacy. *Psychiatry: Journal for the Study of Interpersonal Processes,* 1968, *31,* 161–172.

Maas, H. S. *People and contexts: Social development from birth to old age.* Englewood Cliffs, NJ: Prentice-Hall, 1984.

Maas, H. S., & Engler, R. E., Jr. *Children in need of parents.* New York: Columbia University Press, 1959.

Maas, H. S., & Kuypers, J. A. *From thirty to seventy: A forty-year longitudinal study of adult life styles and personality.* San Francisco: Jossey-Bass, 1974.

Moss, H. A., & Susman, E. J. Longitudinal study of personality development. In O. G. Brim, Jr. & J. Kagan (Eds.), *Constancy and change in human development.* Cambridge, MA: Harvard University Press, 1980.

Neugarten, B. L. Social class and friendship among school children. *American Journal of Sociology,* 1946, *51,* 305–313.

Neugarten, B. L., & Peterson, W. A study of the American age-grade system. *Proceedings of the Fourth Congress of the International Association of Gerontology,* 1957, *3,* 144.

Nielsen, R. F. *Le développement de la sociabilité chez l'enfant: Etude expérimentale.* Neuchâtel, Switzerland: Delachaux & Niestlé, 1951.

Peterson, J. A. Research on the socioeconomic life cycle. *Items,* 1978, *32,* 27–31.

Social Science Research Council. The humanities and the social sciences: A symposium. *Items,* 1980, *34,* 54. (a)

Social Science Research Council. Biosocial perspectives on parenting. *Items,* 1980, *34,* 62. (b)

Sullivan, H. S. *The interpersonal theory of psychiatry.* New York: Norton, 1953.

Warner, W. L. *Structure of American life.* Edinburgh: University of Edinburgh Press, 1952.

Warner, W. L., Meeker, M., & Eels, K. *Social class in America.* Chicago: Science Research Associates, 1949.

Weiss, C. H. with Bucuvalas, M. J. *Social science research and decision-making.* New York: Columbia University Press, 1980.

9

THE INTERWEAVING OF SOCIETAL
AND PERSONAL CHANGE
IN ADULTHOOD*

Marjorie Fiske and David A. Chiriboga

The purpose of this chapter is to trace change in intra- and interpersonal qualities of individuals as they live through the changing circumstances of the life-course and of the broader society in which they live. A flexible stress-adaptation paradigm (Lowenthal & Chiriboga, 1973), which is part of a more comprehensive model of change (Fiske, 1980, 1982), provides the principal framework. Within the paradigm, sociocultural change may be perceived and responded to by persons as, alternatively, positive or negative stress—or as inconsequential. The first section of the chapter reviews selected theory and data on the interweaving of societal and individual change; the second assesses normative and nonnormative events and circumstances, both personal and societal, in relation to adaptive modes and outcomes. The data for this second section are drawn from two longitudinal studies: one evaluating people passing through normative life transitions; the other evaluating persons undergoing the nonnormative transition of divorce. Both studies focus on process, and we have searched for evidence of consistency and change and for the antecedents of both. The final section is devoted to the implications, problems, and challenges of these and other longitudinal investigations.

*This research was supported by Grants MH-32305 and MH-33713 awarded by the National Institute of Mental Health, USA, and by BRSG grant S07-RR05755 awarded by the Biomedical Research Support Grant Program, Division of Research Resources, National Institutes of Health.

SOCIETAL CHANGE AND CHANGE
IN INDIVIDUALS

Agreeing with Koch (1981) that the social/behavioral sciences should maintain their deep roots in the humanities, especially philosophy and history, we have searched for and found a number of hypotheses and theories relating to the personal sociohistorical change equation. This is not the occasion for exhaustive review, but it seems appropriate to mention a few that relate particularly to aging and old age in our time. Among several humanists addressing such issues, there is agreement that there are notable and accelerating changes in both societal and personal spheres, moderate consensus about some particular changes, and less consensus about the dynamics of the person–society relationship.[1] The latter, of course, is still an unsolved problem in social science research, longitudinal and otherwise.

In speaking of societal change, Kenneth Burke, updating his earlier study of consequences of the Great Depression, notes that such change results in an "unsettling" of the individual because it requires thinking in unaccustomed ways (Burke, 1977, p. xlvii). Erik Erikson, writing from in-depth psychological as well as philosophical and historical perspectives, similarly finds that "historical crisis . . . aggravate personal crises" (Erikson, 1975, p. 22). Both writers are quite explicit about particular social changes and the accompanying sense of loss of a sense of integrity and meaning in one's own life and the world one lives in. The philosopher David Norton, in his analysis of the transformations in meanings of life as the individual moves through adulthood and old age, focuses on the individual and very explicitly does not implicate social change in the personal process (1976). There are, however, omens of societal change in his observation that awareness of aging begins with the realization that one no longer has a future. Timing of this realization may be affected by the options and potentials that are made available to older persons in a particular society. In light of the insights of Erikson on how sociohistorical crises exacerbate identity crises, and Burke's discussion

---

[1] These writers are rarely specific about the particular segments of society they address. Further, the depth and breadth of their knowledge of human history varies enormously, and this is reflected in the nature of the societal and individual changes they discuss. In much of the work we mention, however, the historical sweep of the writer is easier to trace than his purview of people. Many share a common vocabulary, using words such as world crisis, cataclysm, depletion, destruction, and annihilation in reference to social change, and disintegration, anxiety, narcissism, identity loss, and "persons in pieces" (Bersani, 1976) in regard to personal changes. This commonality, however, does not necessarily reflect similar images of man or society, and more importantly, these disparate images may not mirror those of the majority of people in the societies discussed.

of the "unsettling" process created in the individual by drastic social change (see also Marris, 1974, and Antonovsky, 1979, for discussions of related concepts), one is tempted to go a step further and conclude that in our time many people of all ages are aware of a widening gap between generations. This gap creates serious problems for older people, because it threatens to deprive them of a sense of generativity.

Recent works of Sociological Historian Richard Sennett (1977) and Social Historian Christopher Lasch (1978) address the interface of personal/societal change more directly. They share a strong interest in the concept of narcissism. Sennett's thesis is that a reaction to the restrictive Victorian era, in conjunction with the rapid growth of industrialization, has led to a retreat from public life and acts, and that an increased focus on private life has created an obsessive interest in "personalities." Sennett views society as the victim of personal change, the turning inward having been followed by a more recent obsession with self-realization at all life-stages, and goes on to note that the accompanying search for "therapeutic solutions" has now acquired high market value.

Lasch, in contrast, believes that our narcissistic culture is a straightforward consequence of social change, and he discusses a new form of narcissism, one quite different from the more traditional psychoanalytic interpretations of Sennett. Lasch, too, cites an "ideology of personal growth," but attributes it to a sense of emptiness, isolation, and lack of faith in generational continuity. While occasionally optimistic, he sees the growing obsession with self-realization as "the faith of those without faith" in people who can no longer foresee a human future.

Juxtaposing the ideas of Sennett and Lasch, we might conclude that preoccupation with the growth of the self is a conscious or unconscious symbolic substitution: the image of a continuing self replacing that of a continuing society. Lasch is of special interest because of his insights about how the "new" narcissism affects attitudes toward the aging process and the elderly themselves in our time. While mankind has traditionally dreaded old age, Lasch detects a recent increase in the intensity of the struggle against it. From a historical perspective, he sees this struggle now developing in much earlier periods of life than it formerly did, because today's young and young middle-aged adults sense that they have fewer resources than did earlier generations. With little religious faith, and an awareness of the fraying of intergenerational bonds, they have little interest in posterity:

> When men find themselves incapable of taking an interest in earthly life after their own death, they wish for eternal youth, for the same reason they no longer care to reproduce themselves. When the prospect of being superseded becomes intolerable, parenthood itself, which guarantees that it will happen, appears almost as a form of self-destruction. (Lasch, 1978, p. 211)

Both Lasch and Sennett refer to psychoanalyst Heinz Kohut's recent (1977) work, *The Restoration of the Self.* Though highly controversial in some parts, it presents an implicit challenge for longitudinal research. Kohut analyzes clinical and other evidence, and offers convincing support for the thesis that there is indeed a rapid growth of a new form of narcissism in our culture, one which he foresees as the soon-to-be dominant character type of Western society. Somewhat incidental to Kohut's principal thesis is his epilogue on social change and how it interrelates with this new variant of a long-recognized personality disorder. While firm and specific links between dominant aspects of a culture and the particular mental or character disorders prevailing within them have often been described by social scientists of various disciplines, few psychoanalysts have so explicitly linked specific societal changes within a culture to the emergence and spread of a specific personality disorder.

As a good psychoanalyst should, Kohut draws evidence from his clinical analysis of how the social environment of children has changed since the 1930s. Until recently, in Western culture, the child's need for "pleasure/gain" and its accompanying conflicts, reinforced by parental proximity and prohibitions, resulted in oedipal rivalries (Kohut, 1977). Over the past three or four decades, due to parental distancing, both physical and emotional, this classical oedipal model has become obsolete. To counter their sense of isolation with the nuclear family, many children have sought to fill the erotic void with other children, frequently a forerunner of the frenetic sexual activities of the depressed adolescent. It is thus the loss of adequate role models and the idealizable self-object (parent or parents) that has produced disturbance in the self and in personal relationships as the child reaches adulthood.

Noting that the psychological dangers that put the survival of Western man in greatest jeopardy are now of a different order, Kohut adds that the psychoanalyst cannot alone undertake to analyze and compare the changing social circumstances "that are correlated to the changing psychological disorders encountered by various generations of depth psychologists" (1977, p. 270). He goes on to challenge sociologists, in particular, to cooperate in finding answers to such crucial questions as the length of time it takes for certain "psychotropic" factors such as the increasing employment of women or the absence of fathers (in work or leisure) and war to change personality patterns and the psychological disturbances they produce. In the meantime he has no doubt that social change has brought about a decrease in "structural" (e.g., oedipal) disorders and an increase in "disorders of the self" (1977, p. 277).

"I am suggesting, then, that each change in man's social surroundings confronts him with new adaptational tasks, and that the demands made on him by *changes of such magnitude that one can speak of the dawn of a new civilization* [italics supplied] are, of course, especially great." (1977, p. 279)

Of special interest to Kohut, and a theme on which he elaborates briefly through examples of the insights of great artists, is the "tragic breakdown of the self in old age," which becomes more prevalent in times of great change.

Psychoanalyst Robert Jay Lifton also remarks a new intensity in the struggle to integrate a fragmented self, and he, too, attributes it to socioenvironmental changes. While he cites many of the changes that the preceding authors find important, Lifton focuses on the "bomb," because he believes that to cope with it requires a "quantum leap" in human consciousness. Like Kohut, he detects an upsurge of a new form of narcissism, and, quite independently of Lasch, believes that what looks like self-love is really nonlove. Nonlove is, therefore, a consequence of the isolation and immobilization of selves that have become numbed by an image of total biological destruction. Lifton believes that a deep hunger for counter-images (images lost with the onset of the thermonuclear age) prevails in order to reaffirm the sense of collective immortality and belief that life will go on after us (Lifton, 1979, p. 283).

Lifton also notes a new and sharp gap between generations, suggesting a shift in the movement–stasis balance within each. Those who were born into the nuclear world grew up with it as an almost taken-for-granted part of the human condition. There is a difference in kind between the generations, because younger people have not experienced the shock of a transition that requires the quantum cognitive leap and carries with it, for adults, the necessity of creating new modes of adaptation.

This new chasm between generations does not call into question the fact that imagery of death and destruction may pervade the consciousness (and the unconsciousness) of younger adults, for reflected among these adults is the numbing that brings with it an indifference to life (their own and others). In the way of evidence, we might note the two culturally regressive modes of coping among the young of all classes that are increasing in frequency: (1) escape into drugs and (2) the acting out of blind rage through physical violence, including to oneself, that is thus reshaping the age curve of suicide rates in Western societies. One wonders whether today's younger adults can even imagine "the special quality of life-power available only to those seasoned by struggles of . . . decades" (1979, p. 88) that Lifton envisages. Such a power comes from "extensive cultivation of images and forms having to do with loving and caring" (p. 88) and is rooted in a lifetime of commitment to parenthood and generativity, as well as to work and mastery. The aging and very old of today seem to maintain the imagery of connection, self-completion, and human continuity; but among their offspring, such symbols are faded or nonexistent. One hypothesis, then, is that among prebomb generations living today, the stabilizing and integrating trends researchers have found to characterize many people at midlife and beyond (see Chiriboga, 1981, for a review) may persist; but as the post-bomb generations age, we can expect to find altogether different kinds of change, more variations within them, and therefore less cultural consolidation and personal sense of generativity and continuity.

Within the generation now approaching middle age, researchers find empirical evidence of a new stage encompassing a "life construction" crisis. Foss and Larkin (1979), for example, see it as one involving a crisis both more acute and different in kind from the familiar adolescent conflicts of identity. These authors link this new critical period directly to recent historical events, whereas the classical adolescent conflict has its roots in the (declining) paternalistic family. From a historical perspective, this new transition is a nonnormative one, and, assuming it comes to acquire some degree of universality in Western culture, raises many questions about the future. One intriguing task, as our longitudinal groups grow older, will be to trace the nature of the future stages that this cohort encounters and how its members deal with them. Another task for upcoming life-span researchers to assess will be the extent to which the life construction (or perhaps a better word is "reconstruction") phase or crisis in succeeding cohorts may have become normative—and if so, will the earlier family-rooted, adolescent "identity" crisis have altered because of continuing changes in the family, as noted by Kohut and Lasch.

Some Evidence for the Interweaving of Societal and Personal Change

In both our ongoing longitudinal studies we detect evidence of a widening chasm between our older and younger respondents. Since its beginnings in the late 1960s, the longitudinal study of transitions in particular has paid attention to people's social horizons, their awareness of and interest in societal events and circumstances, and which of these concern them most. Here we review some findings that bear upon on the theories and hypotheses just discussed.

Our initial interviews took place with respondents facing normative transitions: high school seniors ($N = 52$) confronting departure from the family home, newlyweds ($N = 50$) anticipating parenthood, middle-aged parents ($N = 54$) facing the departure of their youngest child, and older men and women ($N = 60$) who were soon to retire. The interviews were in-depth, including, among other things, very detailed life histories, and they generally required three or more sessions. The respondents represented, for the most part, what has been called the American "silent majority": the conservative, mainly Caucasian, blue- and white-collar elements of a large metropolitan area located on the West Coast of the United States. Even at the time of our initial contact in 1969, we found indications of "unsettling" among them. Some further conclusions based on the "social horizons" section of this first encounter are as follows.

1.   The interviews took place during a time of heightened sociopolitical unrest in the United States: the escalation of antiwar protest and civil rights movements, the intensification of racial conflict, and the peaking of youth's counterculture. Voiced often was a sense of unprecedented sociohistorical change and the belief that an era had ended.

2.   Parents facing the empty nest were most likely to express distress over the changing values and behaviors of the younger generation. The two older groups shared concern for increasing violence in the streets: Middle-aged parents were primarily anxious about the security of their children, while those facing retirement were concerned about crime on the streets and the possibility of violence.

3.   High school girls and middle-aged women tended to point to the need for personal change: People should change their attitudes and values, become kinder, better, and more responsible.

4.   The middle-aged men were most likely to state that solution of social problems required action on the federal level, with the men being especially concerned about law and order.

5.   Perspectives on social conditions, as assessed by the number of ways the individual felt his life was affected by social conditions, were most complex among middle-aged parents of both sexes. High school girls and newlywed women paid the least heed to the wider world around them.

6.   Middle-aged women were most concerned about social problems, and this concern was directly associated with the number of family roles and social activities in general.

In the late 1960s, then, we found that middle-aged parents whose youngest child was a senior in high school were concerned about societal changes and, comparing the young with their own generation as it reached adulthood, found them off-schedule, though as yet not necessarily off-track. Looking at the "empty nest" and preretirement groups together, however, we found striking differences between men and women: Women far outranked men in their concern with social issues. In contrast, men in the two younger groups ranked considerably higher than both the younger women and the oldest men in social horizons complexity. There were also striking sex differences in the nature of solutions proposed for coping with the social changes in one's surroundings: Women placed the responsibility squarely on individuals (they should become more responsible) and on informal community cooperation (they should act). Women accepted some of the changes, but those that they opposed were to be changed by improvement in, and action by, "the people." Older men, when concerned at all, rather clearly wanted to restore the status quo ante and emphasized strengthening governmental restraints, particularly those bearing on "law and order."

At the fifth-year follow-up (in 1974), over half of the sample reported more concern about societal issues, and again the oldest women far outranked the oldest men in their heightened concern. While the majority of people in the two younger groups also reported more concern, the formerly newlywed men reported no change—a few even reported less concern than 5 years earlier. Interestingly, the originally empty-nest men who, at the baseline, were involved in societal issues (but less so than their female counterparts), reported by far the most increase in involvement. For the fourth interview round (in 1977) we developed a list of specific past and present socioenvironmental changes and asked our respondents about their concern with each one. This was readministered, with some additions, in the fifth and most recent contact (in 1980). Some of the changes in preoccupation that took place in the interval are notable: In the oldest group, a strong majority had become more preoccupied with war, recalling the stresses of World War II, and, among the oldest women, there was a near doubling of preoccupation with the effects of Vietnam. On the average, the two older groups combined were more concerned about war than the two younger, who, having for the most part assumed responsibilities for families of their own, had become more worried about the state of the economy.

New items added to the social change list in 1980 included nuclear danger. While obviously not yet enabling us to trace change in the preoccupation of our subjects with that threat, our interviews did provide us with strong support for the sex differences noted among the two oldest groups at the baseline, especially in regard to those issues bearing on human values and continuities: It is the older women who are by far the most concerned about the nuclear dangers of the world we live in, not only far more so than older men, but also more so than members of either sex in the two younger groups, both of which had been born into the nuclear world. Older men were less worried about nuclear problems than younger men and women. In terms of our hypothesis, then, we might conclude that we detect support for a pre/post-bomb generational dysfunction among older women in comparison with the young, but far less so than among older men. While there is other evidence supportive of this thesis, this provides a convenient transition to a discussion of some additional theories of life-course development and change for which our studies have thus far found support—or lack of support.

TRANSITIONS AND STRESS: A PARADIGM FOR CHANGE

As we have noted, humanists reviewed here draw, with some rearrangement and due acknowledgement, on Erikson's theoretical stages of development in their discussions of personal change in the context of societal change. As in Erikson's theory, there are two important implications in their work, one being that each stage leads, in more or less orderly progression, to the next one (which is "higher" than the preceding). The other implication is that the evolution of each stage centers on its own internal "crisis." There are also underlying assumptions of universality to this kind of development, at least in Western societies. This assumption is made explicit in recent work of psychologists Daniel Levinson and his colleagues, who state, for example, that a particular form of male midlife crisis, taking place within a specified age range, is "universal" (Levinson, D., Darrow, Klein, Levinson, M., & McKee, 1978). The observations of Lifton and Kohut, in particular, suggest that, to the extent that a developmental stage paradigm is appropriate, it is now of importance for longitudinal researchers to begin to explore the possibility that societal upheavals and responses to them in the "generation of the 60s" may have disrupted such normative or presumed stage sequences, and that as this generation grows older, may well continue to do so.

In our research on normative transitions such as the departure of the youngest child, or retirement, we have begun to find evidence that living through them has a variety of consequences for the individual. One analysis has indicated that the self-concept of men and women is shaped at least in part by the timing of their transitional passage (Chiriboga & Pierce, 1977), but, at the same time, is causally implicated in this timing. For example, the newlywed men who became parents early in the study were much more likely in the second- and fifth-year follow-ups to see themselves as hostile people, while those who became parents late or who did not become parents at all declined steadily in hostility. Complementing this finding was another: The more assertive newlywed men were likely to delay becoming a parent longer than less assertive men. Whether it was the less assertive—and perhaps less willing—men who became more hostile is a question we will be pursuing in future research. It may, for example, be not entirely coincidental that the primary goal of our newlywed women was to become mothers!

The reasons underlying the contribution of transitions to adult change are clearly multiple. As we have suggested in the first section of this essay, the timing and significance of normative and nonnormative transitions may be heavily influenced by societal change. As a case in point, one interpretation of the above findings concerning parenthood is that the desirability of being a father is far more open to question in today's society than it has been in the past—just as the desirability of entering old age may have declined. The impact of transitions is also influenced by the context in which they occur, including in particular the life events that may accompany them. The concept of transition is, in fact, intimately linked with that of life events. According to some formulations of a transitions model, the initial phase of a transition is heralded by what is called a "marker" event, such as the birth of a child or departure from the world of work (Chiriboga, 1979a; Marris, 1974; Parkes, 1971). Less often considered, but theoretically of importance, are the subsequent events triggered by the marker. In the nonnormative transition of divorce, for example, it was found that the marker event of marital separation is embedded in a context of growing stress in multiple role areas, spreading to nearly all such areas within 1 or 2 months following that marker event (Chiriboga, 1979c). Some transitions, then, may be considered periods of compounded stress.

Not only transitions, but psychosocial stressors of all sizes and shapes, are coming to be recognized by life-span researchers as playing a major role in how we live out our lives (see, e.g., Hultsch & Plemons, 1979; Lowenthal & Chiriboga, 1973; Lowenthal, Thurnher, Chiriboga et al., 1975; Thomae, 1979). This recognition has in effect led to a paradigm shift. Formerly, a central concern in life-span studies was the extent of stability and change in adulthood, with most of the theories thereby focusing on steady states or a sequence of stages. In studying stressors, however, the focus shifts from steady states to precursors of change. A dialectic between stability and change becomes possible, and in fact several theorists propose that stability may be a relatively rare condition. For example, in decrying the Western preoccupation with ideas of stability and homeostasis, Riegel poses the interesting paradox that "Stability appears as a transitory condition in the stream of ceaseless changes" (1976, p. 690). While we take exception to Riegel's opinion that only the "vulgar mechanists and pretentious mentalists" (1976, p. 697) contemplate the nature of stability, it certainly appears that we can learn much about both stability and change from the study of social stressors.

THE COMPLEX NATURE OF SOCIAL STRESSORS

Much of the evidence about the nature and role of stressors is conflicting (see Fiske, 1982; Chiriboga, 1982a; Lowenthal & Chiriboga, 1973), and it is now clear that both the positive and negative consequences of seemingly disruptive conditions should be considered. As both Riegel (1975) and May (1980) note, stressors create an increased potential for change: They disrupt the status quo. Where the individual goes, given this disruption, depends on a host of issues such as inner and outer resources, coping skills, and experience of similar stressors. In a longitudinal study of divorce conducted by one of the authors, for example, results suggested that divorce in midlife may on occasion free individuals who find themselves trapped in a way of life more suited to their younger years than to the present (Chiriboga, 1982c). Another aspect of stress that is of growing interest to students of the adult life-cycle is the significance of expected or normative, as opposed to unpredicted or nonnormative and stressful, experiences.

That there are certain expectable changes in the adult life-course is not a new concept. The Book of Ecclesiastes tells us that there is a time to sow and a time to reap, a time to live and a time to die. The possibility that normative periods of change exist throughout life appears heuristic to any dynamic approach to adult development. In one of the early theoretical contributions to this idea, Neugarten, Moore, and Lowe, (1965) refer to the ordering of major markers in life as a "prescriptive timetable," and Roth (1963) also refers to the idea of normative periods of change. More recently, Dohrenwend and Dohrenwend (1970), Baltes (1979) and Pearlin and Lieberman (1979) have discussed normative or developmental life events that are part of the normal and to-be-expected life-course in our culture. Going to college, getting married, having children, and going through the empty nest and retirement are some of the events that have been classified as normative; many of them have also been studied under the heading of "transitions."

Contrary to the normative are what Pearlin and Lieberman call "the relatively unexpected and occasionally eruptive exigencies of life" (1979, p. 224). Such unexpected, or nonnormative events have only recently appeared in developmental literature as possible major sources of change. For Baltes (1979), the nonnormative experiences constitute one of three general sources of change in adulthood. The other two are normative: age-graded events such as those stemming from socialization and biological maturation, and changing societal conditions such as war, marked shifts in the economic cycle, or others discussed in the first section of this essay.

Although the distinction between normative and nonnormative experiences was posited as helpful in furthering our understanding of the adult life-course, empirical studies on the two have been rather limited. Apparently Pearlin and Lieberman (1979) are the only investigators who have assessed the comparative impact of these experiences in a longitudinal investigation. Their results suggest that nonnormative, unexpected events have a greater relevance to adult change than do the more expectable. As is true for any new concept when first operationalized, problems still beset the empirical approach. These authors suggest, for example, that the loss-related component of many nonnormative events is the most critical factor. Later work by the same research team (see Pearlin & Radabaugh, 1981) substantiates this hypothesis.

The analyses we present next were based on our two ongoing longitudinal studies. We were interested in both the impact of so-called life-events and in the complex experiences represented, respectively, in normative and nonnormative transitions. One group of respondents included those from the longitudinal study of transitions described in the previous section. The second group included participants in a 3-year longitudinal investigation of men and women undergoing the nonnormative transition of divorce.

The Two Studies: An Introduction

The studies were part of the research component of the Human Development and Aging Program of the University of California in San Francisco. The same staff members were responsible for the instrument development, interviewing, and analytic phases of both studies. The samples overlapped not only in age distribution, but in occupational prestige levels as well. While comparisons indicated that men did not differ from each other in income, the current family income of the newly separated women in the divorce study was significantly lower than that for the mostly married women in the transitions study—as might be expected.

All respondents were interviewed at the time and place of their convenience. The data analyzed in this chapter were drawn from baseline interviews conducted in 1969 through 1970, as well as from second-and fifth-year follow-up contacts. This 5-year period encompassed the main portion of the normative transitions that formed the sampling base for the study: departure from the parental home, parenthood, departure of the youngest child from the parental home, and retirement. The sample N during this time was relatively stable; it dropped from 216 to 189, an attrition rate of only 12.5%, over the 5-year period.[2]

The divorce study included 125 men (average age 36.3) and 185 women (average age 34.4) whose names were drawn at random from the county clerk offices in San Francisco and Alameda counties, California, in the United States. To participate respondents had to have been separated from their spouses for 8 months or less, and to be involved in some stage of the legal process that usually culminates in the dissolution of marriage. Those with marriages of less that one year's duration and who were under 20 years of age were excluded. Only one of each divorcing couple was included in the sample.

The age range among the divorce respondents was 20–79, with slightly more than a quarter age 40 or over. For three-quarters of both the men and women, this had been their first marriage; nearly half had been married for between 5 and 19 years at the time of separation, and nearly half had been separated for between 4 and 6 months at the time of the first interview. Approximately 3.5 years after this initial contact, 283 of the divorced respondents were seen again. The attrition during this time was approximately 10%, a rate that approximates that obtained in the transitions study.

INSTRUMENTS USED IN THE ANALYSES

The interview schedules for both studies shared many of the same questions and instruments. Those used in the present set of analyses are presented next.

Life Events

A measure of stress was derived from the Life Events Questionnaire, a 138-item inventory similar to that of Holmes and Rahe (1967), but modified to conform to the experiences faced by people across a wide age range (see Horowitz, Schaefer, Hiroto, Wilner, & Levin, 1977; Chiriboga, 1977). Respondents checked off each event experienced during

---

[2]A more detailed presentation of the transitions study can be found in Lowenthal et al. (1975). Information on the divorce study can be found in Chiriboga (1982c).

the past year, whether they felt good or bad about the event when it happened, and how much they thought about it. Positive and negative stress scores, weighted by preoccupation, were developed. Only the negative stress measure is used in this report. It covers stressors for the year prior to the fifth-year contact for transitions respondents and for the year prior to the 3.5 year follow-up for divorce respondents.

Transition Status

A measure of the timing of normative transitions was available for transitions respondents. At the fifth-year contact, it assessed distance from onset of the anticipated normative transition: Had the transition commenced between the baseline and second-year contact (score = 3), between the second- and fifth-year contacts (score = 2), or was it still pending at the fifth-year contact (score = 1)?

Morale

Several measures were derived from the Bradburn and Caplovitz (1965) morale scales. These included a nonspecific question on happiness, "In general, how happy are you these days?" (very happy = 3; pretty happy = 2; not too happy = 1). Another one measured the *Positive Affect Total*; it was a summary score of how often during the past week the respondents reported feeling on top of the world, particularly excited or interested in something, or pleased and proud. A *Negative Total* consisted of a summary score for how often respondents felt lonely, bored, depressed, and restless. A *Tension Total* summated scores assessing how often the respondent felt angry, unable to get going, that he had more to do than was possible, and was vaguely uneasy without knowing why. *An Affect Balance Scale* consisted of the ratio of positive to negative affects (higher scores indicated a greater proportion of positive affects). Finally, in some of the analyses, the single Bradburn depression item was used, scoring how often during the past week the respondent had felt depressed (never = 0; once = 1; several times = 2; often = 3).

Symptoms

A measure of psychiatric symptoms was obtained from the California Symptoms Checklist (Lowenthal et al., 1975). The 42 items were primarily psychological in nature (i.e., "Have you ever contemplated suicide?" "Do frightening things keep coming back into your head?" "Is it always hard for you to make up you mind?"), although somatic complaints were also included (i.e., "Do you have tightness or numbness in any part of your body?''). The symptoms measure consisted of a count of positive responses.

Self-Criticism

The measure of self-criticism was based on the total number of self-ascribed items on a 70 item Adjective Checklist that had been circled as undesired by the respondent.

Life Evaluations

On a Life Evaluation Chart, respondents were asked to rate each year of their past and anticipated future life on a 9-point scale (''rock bottom'' = 1; ''absolute tops'' = 9). In the analyses of divorcing respondents, ratings for the present year of life and a count of the number of years projected into the future were included.

Health Status

In the analyses of divorcing respondents, the percentage of persons who reported a health problem that interfered with their life and their number of doctor's visits during the past year were included.

ANALYTIC PROCEDURES

Analytic procedures included a repeated measurement analysis of variance, computed separately for men and women. For both studies, one main effect was stress, dichotomized into high and low (different cut-off points were used in the two studies, since divorce respondents ranked much higher in the negative stress reported). Age was another main effect, and it was dichotomized for the transitions study analyses due to sample size (the original high school seniors and newlyweds vs. the originally middle-aged parents and preretirement respondents). A more detailed age breakdown was used for the divorce study: Age cuts were the 20s, 30s, 40s, and 50-plus. For the transitions study, a third variable was whether (and when) respondents had experienced the marker event that signals the onset of a transition: between the baseline and second-year follow-up (early transition), between second- and fifth-year follow-ups (''on-time'' transition), or had not yet experienced the marker event (late transition).

The ANOVAs were run separately for each sample. By way of introduction, it is clear from the results that we have not identified all major sources of variance, but such was not our intent or expectation. Our objective was to compare the effects of normative and nonnormative stressors, and we found both to be important. We also found the inter-action of these antecedents to be important; in the interest of simplicity, we here focus only on results for the Bradburn and Caplovitz (1965) measure of overall happiness. Results for the other criteria are presented in tabular form and are mentioned in passing.

THE EFFECTS OF NORMATIVE TRANSITIONS AND STRESS

Turning first to the men in the study of transitions, we find that nei-ther life-stage nor transition status bore any relationship to self-assess-ments of happiness (Table 9.1). Men did, however, tend to become happier in subsequent contracts than they had been at baseline despite the many interaction effects that indicate this was not true for all men. For example, those who had not at least begun the anticipated transition during the 5 years of study became less happy over the years, while those who underwent an early transition (between baseline and second-year follow-up) became happier. Those who underwent what might be called an "on-time" transition (i.e., between the second- and fifth-year follow-ups), in contrast, stayed relatively stable in their happiness across all assessment periods.

If we add the ingredient of stress, the dynamics of change become even more complex. While it is true that those who did not undergo the expected transition generally became unhappier as time went on, they did turn out to be the happiest at all contact points if, at the same time, they were exposed to relatively few negative events. On the other hand, men with less stress ended up by being less happy than their high stressed counterparts, in both the early and on-time transition groups. These findings demonstrate that stress does not necessarily result in less enjoyment of life. In fact, they suggest that a certain modicum of stress actually facilitates successful adaptation. It may be, for example, that without such stress, the individual is never forced to directly confront the challenge presented to most people during periods of transition.

Transition status also interacted with life-stage across time. This in-teraction only approaches statistical significance ($p = .10$), but it does help us to unravel the threads of happiness still further. In Figure 9.1 we see that those who did not undergo the expected transition were likely to decline in happiness between the second- and fifth-year con-tacts, regardless of whether they were younger or older. In contrast, those who underwent the transition early became happier, as we have already reported, but only if they were also in the younger stages of life. The sharpest age gap in happiness was among men whose transition

TABLE 9.1

MEAN SCORES AND ASSOCIATED ANALYSIS OF VARIANCE PROBABILITIES FOR SELECTED CRITERIA OF ADJUSTMENT, TRANSITIONS STUDY SAMPLE[a]

	Men				Women			
	Self-criticism	Psychiatric symptoms	Happiness	Depression	Self-criticism	Psychiatric symptoms	Happiness	Depression
Age Younger		8.09[a]		1.73[c]				1.83[a]
Older		6.60		1.22				1.79
Transition status								
Late		9.32[c]	1.86[a]	1.49[c]				
On-time		6.55	1.63	1.67				
Early		6.23	1.71	1.29				
Stress								
Low					6.82[c]	7.78[c]	1.59[b]	
High					10.89	11.29	1.76	
Time baseline	5.16[c]				6.98	11.25[c]		
T2	11.41				10.66	9.09		
T3	4.73				9.21	8.21		1.44
Age/time								
Younger/BL						10.93[a]	1.65[c]	1.93[a]
Older/BL						11.46	1.82	1.72
Younger/T2						10.09	1.59	1.74
Older/T2						8.06	1.77	1.84
Younger/T3						8.64	1.78	1.63
Older/T3						7.59	1.45	1.23
Transition/time								
BL/BL			1.64[c]				1.58[b]	
F2/BL			1.71				1.84	

(Continued)

TABLE 9.1 (*Continued*)

	Men				Women			
	Self-criticism	Psychiatric symptoms	Happiness	Depression	Self-criticism	Psychiatric symptoms	Happiness	Depression
F1/BL			2.21				1.60	
BL/T2			1.57				1.09	
F2/T2			1.68				1.59	
F1/T2			1.64				1.70	
BL/T3			1.86				1.58	
F2/T3			1.71				1.67	
F1/T3			1.57				1.55	
Stress/time								
Low/BL							1.77	1.81
High/BL							1.70[a]	1.65[b]
Low/T2							1.61	1.74
High/T2							1.74	1.83
Low/T3							1.39	1.09
High/T3							1.85	1.76
Transition/stress								
Late/low			1.56[b]					
On-time/low			1.71					
Early/low			1.83					
Late/high			1.75					
On-time/high			1.69					
Early/high			1.75					
Transition/stress/time								
Late/low/BL			1.55[c]		4.12[c]			
On-time/low/BL			1.64		6.58			
Early/low/BL			2.35		5.27			
Late/high/BL			1.68		11.20			

194

On-time/high/BL	1.78	8.26
Early/high/BL	1.88	4.40
Late/low/T-2	1.44	2.38
On-time/low/T-2	1.64	5.71
Early/low/T-2	1.55	21.36
Late/high/T-2	1.63	7.90
On-time/high/T-2	1.71	15.67
Early/high/T-2	1.88	6.60
Late/low/T-3	1.67	3.12
On-time/low/T-3	1.86	6.96
Early/low/T-3	1.60	4.36
Late/high/T-3	1.95	8.70
On-time/high/T-3	1.57	12.18
Early/high/T-3	1.50	17.30
Age/transition/time		
Younger/late/BL	1.61^a	
Older/late/BL	1.70	
Younger/on-time/BL	1.57	
Older/on-time/BL	1.86	
Younger/early/BL	2.82	
Older/early/BL	1.82	
Younger/late/T-2	1.56	
Older/late/T-2	1.60	
Younger/on-time/T-2	1.57	
Older/on-time/T-2	1.78	
Younger/early/T-2	1.82	
Older/early/T-2	1.53	
Younger/late/T-3	1.78	
Older/late/T-3	2.00	
Younger/on-time/T-3	1.71	
Older/on-time/T-3	1.71	

(Continued)

TABLE 9.1 (*Continued*)

	Men				Women			
	Self-criticism	Psychiatric symptoms	Happiness	Depression	Self-criticism	Psychiatric symptoms	Happiness	Depression
Younger/early/T-2			1.54					
Older/early/T-2			1.59					
Age/stress/time								
Young/low/BL			2.58[c]					
Old/low/BL			1.71					
Young/high/BL			1.64					
Old/high/BL			2.10					
Young/low/T-2			1.50					
Old/low/T-2			1.58					
Young/high/T-2			1.68					
Old/high/T-2			1.80					
Young/low/T-3			1.67					
Old/low/T-3			1.71					
Young/high/T-3			1.71					
Old/high/T-3			1.80					

[a]For convenience, only means for significant (or trend) effects and interactions are included.
[b]ANOVA $p \leq .10$.
[c]ANOVA $p \leq .05$.

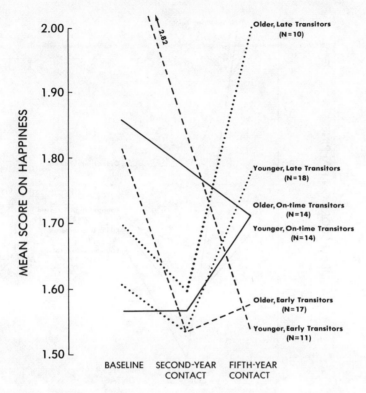

FIGURE 9.1 The interaction of transition status and life-stage across time, showing mean scores on happiness (men only).

was normatively "on-time." The older of these men became steadily happier over time, while the younger just as steadily declined. The implications of a normative transition therefore seem to vary greatly by stage of life.

Age also demonstrated a highly significant interaction with stress and time. As is shown in both Table 9.1 and Figure 9.2, perhaps the most dramatic element in this interaction was that older men in a high stress context end up being the unhappiest of any possible subgroup derived from the Stage × Stress × Time combinations. That these older men were more vulnerable to the impact of stress than were men in the earlier stages of adulthood may well be due to an impoverishment of social and inner resources such as those provided in the work arena they have either left or were in the process of leaving. On the other hand, those older men who were lightly stressed were relatively happy; their reports

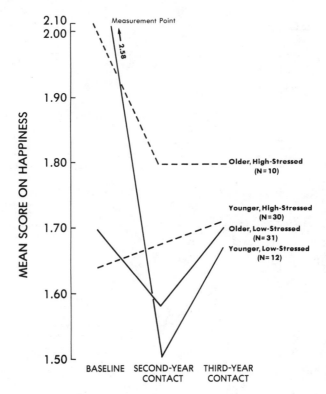

FIGURE 9.2   The interaction of life-stage and stress across time, showing mean scores for happiness (men only): transitions sample.

on happiness changed little over the years. A similar, but less pronounced pattern was found among younger men: Those who reported fewer negative stressors were initially the least happy, but they ended up happier than did those who had experienced more stress.

There was, finally, a nonsignificant ($p = .06$) but intriguing interaction of transition status, life-stage, stress, and time that is not presented in tabular form due not only to space considerations but to the fact that the cell sizes were quite small. To illustrate the complexity of this four-way interaction, let us consider only one group: men who did not undergo the normative transition. The results suggest that stress context made a difference only for the younger men. If the respondents were both young and under low stress, they improved in happiness sufficiently to become the happiest group of men at the end of the 5 years.

If they were young and highly stressed, they declined sharply in happiness between the second- and fifth-year follow-ups. In contrast, regardless of whether they were in a high or low stress context, those in the two later stages ended up tied for the rather dubious honor of being the second most unhappy group of men.

Among the women in the transitions study, the findings are somewhat less complex. Those who reported fewer negative stressors were happier than the high stress women at all assessments. The implication of this finding is that happiness and stress share in certain of their antecedents. Analysis of these same data sets have in fact indicated that there are antecedent personal and social conditions that predict both happiness and subsequent levels of stress (see Chiriboga, 1982b, 1984). On the other hand, the present results demonstrate that factors such as transitional status and stress do affect personal functioning: In longitudinal research one soon finds that what was once a cause easily becomes a consequence, and vice versa. For example, there was a suggestion ($p = .10$) that the interrelationship between stress and time of measurement was of some importance. Those low in stress had become happier between the second and fifth year contacts; those reporting more negative stress became less happy. (A similar, and significant, pattern of change was found for the Bradburn and Caplovitz [1965] measure of depression.)

Stage of life was not directly related to variations in happiness, but women in the older and younger groups followed different pathways through time. In fact, changes in happiness levels of these women substantiate the speculations of both Lasch (1978) and Kohut (1977) about the impact of the present historical period. At the baseline in 1969, the younger women were somewhat happier than the older, but their happiness decreased in subsequent years. In contrast, the older women became steadily happier and, by the last contact, were happier than the younger women. In short, there were signs that the younger generations of women are becoming more unsettled, while those who represent pre-bomb generations may be somewhat protected from the uncertainties of modern life.

Finally, as was the case for men, timing of the transition had a considerable bearing on the happiness of these women. Those who negotiated the transition more or less on time were the least happy in the beginning, and 5 years later they were still unhappy. While both the early and nontransition groups were, at the first follow-up, less happy, they had apparently resolved whatever problems these off-time conditions had generated by the last assessment.

THE NONNORMATIVE TRANSITION COMPARED TO THE NORMATIVE

Before moving to a consideration of changes in happiness for those in the divorce study, we first note differences between respondents in both studies. A series of *t*-tests were run to explore these differences, and the results are shown in Table 9.2. For purposes of these analyses, all transitions respondents who had been or were in the process of divorcing were removed from the computations. Comparisons were made between divorce respondents at their initial contact and transitions respondents at the second contact (when most were involved in some way with their appropriate transition). In general, divorcing men and women showed signs of greater psychosocial disruption at the point of comparison. Among men, those in the 50-plus age range were the most disrupted, followed by men in their 20s. Among the women, on the other hand, it was the youngest of the divorcing women who were (comparatively) the most affected, though women in their 50s were significantly less happy than were the older women in the transitions sample. These findings provide some support for the argument that nonnormative, negative transitions exert a greater impact on individuals than do the more normative.

DIVORCE AND STRESS

All participants in the divorce study were going through a nonnormative, and loss-related, transition. Inasmuch as they had all filed for divorce and had been separated from their spouses for up to 8 months at the baseline contact, they were roughly matched for point of separation, and so the timing of this marker event was not considered in the analyses. The repeated measurement ANOVA for men indicated that they had become significantly happier 3 years after the initial contact (Table 9.3). However, those who experienced greater stress between the two contacts were less happy than the low-stressed men at both contacts. This consequence of stress, also found in the transitions study, reinforces the suggestion that there are factors that relate causally to both happiness and stress. Age, in the context of time of measurement, also proved important: Men in their 40s improved most—from being quite unhappy at baseline to being the happiest group 3 years later. The two younger groups of men, those in their 20s and 30s, improved least, and while those of 50 and older did become somewhat happier at follow-up, they were still the least happy.

Divorcing women resembled the men in the general patterning of results. Like men, they had become happier by the follow-up, but this

50+/BL	8.33	11.67	2.56	2.11	6.38	14.00	2.38	2.50
20/T-2	6.47	7.94	1.80	1.64	7.89	9.35	1.67	1.85
30/T-2	6.86	7.32	1.73	1.65	6.52	9.61	1.82	1.80
40/T-2	3.56	5.67	1.53	1.59	3.32	10.36	1.70	1.87
50+/T-2	6.33	8.56	2.00	2.11	7.00	11.25	1.88	2.00
Stress/time								
Low/BL	5.40	8.25	2.02	1.69	6.19	10.44[c]	1.88[a]	2.00
High/BL	7.36	10.16	2.14	2.19	8.36	11.65	2.00	2.22
Low/T-2	5.03	6.19	1.59	1.45	5.23	7.79	1.54	1.59
High/T-2	7.86	9.35	2.00	2.05	7.70	11.06	1.88	2.01
Age/stress/time								
20 Low BL	5.81	9.59	1.69	1.76	7.21	10.05	1.79	1.84
30 Low BL	4.77	6.96	1.96	1.58	6.89	10.70	1.79	1.96
40 Low BL	4.93	7.80	2.31	1.75	3.50	8.40	2.00	2.20
50+ Low BL	8.80	11.80	2.40	1.80	4.43	13.28	2.28	2.28
20 High BL	6.39	10.26	2.05	2.42	8.36	11.47	1.89	2.08
30 High BL	8.54	10.09	2.09	1.82	9.50	11.64	2.00	2.10
40 High BL	8.33	8.00	2.00	1.67	4.50	11.75	2.31	2.85
50+ High BL	7.75	11.50	2.75	2.50	20.00	19.00	3.00	4.00
20 Low T-2	5.12	6.18	1.56	1.24	6.32	6.21	1.47	1.42
30 Low T-2	6.19	6.54	1.62	1.58	5.25	8.23	1.55	1.64
40 Low T-2	2.40	5.33	1.50	1.44	3.20	7.20	1.50	1.60
50+ Low T-2	6.60	7.00	1.80	1.60	5.14	11.00	1.71	1.86
20 High T-2	7.67	9.53	2.00	2.00	8.53	10.62	1.74	2.02
30 High T-2	8.45	9.18	2.00	1.82	7.70	10.94	2.06	1.94
40 High T-2	9.33	7.33	1.67	2.33	3.42	13.00	1.85	2.08
50+ High T-2	6.00	10.50	2.25	2.75	20.00	13.00	3.00	3.00

[a]Measurements taken at baseline (BL) and follow-up (T-2).
[b]p ≤ .10.
[c]p ≤ .05.

improvement was of course not equally distributed. For example, while even those in the high-stress context showed some improvement, they did not improve as much as did the low-stress women. Similarly, women of all ages were generally happier by follow-up, but women in their 40s and over were happier than those in their 20s and 30s. Here we do find a difference from the men, since the oldest men in the divorce study ended up being the least happy group. Like the men, however, those women who experienced the greatest stress between baseline and follow-up were less happy at both contacts. Once again we have evidence that stress is not only causally related to levels of happiness, but is itself predicted by characteristics of the people and situation.

SOCIETAL AND PERSONAL CHANGE REVISITED

Our admittedly very selective review of the literature and of findings from the transitions and divorce studies has highlighted the importance of change on both a societal and personal level and of how both older and younger people live out their lives. We live in a *Tofflerian world*: one in which the future is now and the present is nearly past. The consequences, especially with regard to the sense of generational continuity and personal worth, are of paramount importance to students of later life.

On the more immediate level of personal change, we addressed the role of social stressors, defined here in terms of both life events and transitions. Such a focus, of course, excluded the many other possible sources of change that were discussed earlier, but was warranted to the extent that it underscored the importance of a topic that has only recently come to the attention of life-span social scientists.

One overall impression to be gleaned from the analyses that have been presented is that change, where evident, was often not a simple function of the passage of time. Men and women demonstrated different trajectories of change, and these trajectories were differentially affected by life events and the timing of normative transitions. For example, there was only a suggestion of an increase in happiness over time for men and not even a hint of change in the happiness of women. On the other hand, the addition of effects due to life events and transition status significantly increased our understanding of the complex dynamics that underlie both stability and change among our respondents.

When comparisons were drawn between respondents in the two studies, the results suggested that nonnormative transitions, as exemplified by divorce, may have a greater impact on the well-being of men and women than do the more normative, and therefore more expectable, transitions such as parenthood or retirement. This interpretation, of course, bears the possibility of being confounded by the fact that nonnormative transitions are frequently of a less desirable nature than the normative. Amputation, bereavement, involuntary relocation, and divorce are among the most commonly studied nonnormative transitions (see, e.g., Marris, 1974; Parkes, 1971; Pearlin & Lieberman, 1979). A similar caution was raised by Pearlin and Lieberman (1979). In the present study however, both role gains and role losses were included among the normative transitions under study. Although desirability of the transition does not depend entirely on the gains and losses involved (Lowenthal et al., 1975), there is some overlap. In any case, we can at least conclude that the greater disruption evident among the divorcing persons reinforces the need for more study of unexpected transitions.

Of particular interest was the ambiguity often faced by respondents during unexpected transitions. For example, more than three-fourths of the men aged 50 and over in the divorce study were unable to project even 1 year into the future of a Life Evaluation Chart (see Table 9.2), as compared with only about one-tenth of the older men in the transitions study. Spontaneous comments of the divorcing men and women elaborated on their uncertainty about not only the future but the present, and suggest a continuing turmoil resembling what Turner (1970) has referred to as the transitional status of being ''betwixt and between.'' Such findings underscore the growing recognition in the literature (see Chiriboga & Cutler, 1980; Lazarus, 1980) that so-called life events are but one form of stress. The continuing strains of life represented in conditions of divorce, and probably in many normative and nonnormative transitions not yet investigated, deserve further study.

The results of the analyses presented in the second section of this chapter offer some support for the concepts and hypotheses advanced in the first section. In the study of divorce, for example, the older respondents of both sexes had been found to be significantly more distressed at baseline than the younger—suggesting that traditional sanctions against divorce remained in effect for them (Chiriboga, 1979a, 1982c). On the other hand, it was the older respondents (with one exception) who demonstrated the greater resiliency over time. Men in their 40s and women aged 40 and over improved considerably more than did their younger counterparts. These older respondents may have suffered more in the beginning not only because of social sanctions against divorce, but also because of a long and sustained interpersonal commitment; the release from long-endured chronic stress proved to be a balancing factor in the succeeding years. In contrast, the younger repondents, mislead by recent statistics and the popular press, may have thought that divorce is relatively routine and uneventful for their "with it" generation. They ended up finding they had lost something they never even knew they had.

While offering some provocative glimpses into the role of societal and personal change, the structured measures of social stressors considered here explained only small, albeit significant, portions of the variance in well-being among our samples. One reason may be that such structured approaches to measurement do not encompass the issues of most significance in the lives of respondents. From the beginning of our now 11-year study of people in different periods of life, we therefore asked them, using an adaptation of the original Rogerian "initial interview" (Merton, Fiske, & Kendall, 1955), about important changes that had taken place in themselves, their personal circumstances, and the broader world since we last talked with them. Although to systemize and to quantify this kind of material is time consuming and expensive, we have thus far found it well worth doing. An analysis recently completed by our colleague Dr. Majda Thurnher focused on turning points perceived by the transitions study respondents. It assessed these perceptions, preoccupations with turning points, and impacts, and compared them with normative and nonnormative transitions as defined in the preceding section of this essay (Thurnher, 1983). Among other differences and nuances, Thurnher's findings suggest that certain turning points resemble what Norton refers to as the intuition or recognition of a new stage. Instead of experiencing a sometimes-protracted period of transition, some individuals immediately begin to live a new way. The contexts of such apparently sudden insights range from oceanic or religious inner "events" to those triggered by external circumstances such as accidents, illnesses (mental and physical), or deaths. While such life-changing turning points have been well documented in biographical and auto-biographical works, a few sociological studies of religion, and even in national surveys, we have little knowledge about the behavioral consequences of this self-defined sudden awareness of a new way of being or of living.

A second way in which we have made use of our respondents' own percepts and assessments, also related to issues already discussed, has to do with *stress paradigms*. In our first interview, in 1969, we not only questioned respondents about the life events they had experienced but, in interviewing them about the ups and downs projected in life evaluation charts, asked them to describe in detail events and circumstances occurring around the high and low periods. In analyzing this open-ended material, we found three major domains: (1) nature or content of stressors, (2) person directly affected by the stressor (self or other), and

(3) the direction of impact, as assessed by positive or negative change, in how the individual rated the years surrounding the event (Lowenthal et al., 1975). Among other findings that influenced our subsequent research were marked differences between the sexes: Stresses experienced by others close to them were important sources of stress for women, whereas men rarely mentioned them. A second finding of considerable importance to our subsequent work, was that "nonevents" or "absence of stress" were stressful. A third is that the frame of reference utilized by older persons in their appraisals of stress were much broader than that of younger ones. Having experienced more stresses, and frequently more severe ones, than most younger people, they became less likely to be preoccupied with relatively minor ones.

In conclusion, the central concern of this essay was with those societal and personal conditions of change that cannot be handled in any routine way and that challenge the very fabric of the individual's existence. That such personal and societal changes deserve study is generally agreed, but the topic is far from simple and requires an interdisciplinary perspective. Our findings have suggested the importance of exploring in detail not only the conditions of stress, but also social and psychological resources and coping behaviors, and how these influence the way an individual handles stress, as well as their exposure and preoccupation with it. It is encouraging to note that researchers in the field of stress are acquiring more sophisticated perspectives on life-course change. Differentiation of the effects of normative and nonnormative stress conditions, both societal and personal, is but one manifestation of such a sophistication. Perhaps of greater significance is the fact that students of later life are beginning to go beyond the controversy as to whether stability or change is the norm in adulthood, to a search for the dynamic bases for both.

REFERENCES

Antonovsky, A. *Health, stress, and coping.* San Francisco: Jossey-Bass, 1979.

Baltes, P. B. Life-span developmental psychology: Some converging observations on history and theory. In P. B. Baltes & O. G. Brim, Jr. (Eds.), *Life-span development and behavior* (Vol. 2, pp. 256–279). New York: Academic Press, 1979.

Bersani, L. *A future for Astyanax: Character and desire in literature.* Boston: Little Brown, 1976.

Bradburn, N. M., & Caplovitz, D. *Reports on happiness: A pilot study of behavior related to mental health.* Chicago: Aldine, 1965.

Burke, K. *Permanence and change: An anatomy of purpose.* Indianapolis: Bobbs-Merrill, 1977.

Chiriboga, D. A. Life event weighting systems: A comparative analysis. *Journal of Psychosomatic Research*, 1977, 21, 415–422.

Chiriboga, D. A. Conceptualizing adult transitions: A new look at an old subject. In Issue on Life Transitions, D. A. Chiriboga, guest editor, *Generations,* Western Gerontological Society, Summer 1979, 4(1):4–6. (a)

Chiriboga, D. A. *Divorce in late life.* Paper presented at the 25th Annual Meeting of the Western Gerontological Society, San Francisco, CA, 1979, April. (b)

Chiriboga, D. A. Marital separation and stress: A life course perspective. *Alternative Life-styles,* 1979, 2(4), pp. 461–470. (c)

Chiriboga, D. A. Social stressors as antecedents of change. *Journal of Gerontology,* 1984, 39(4), 468–477.

Chiriboga, D. A. The developmental psychology of middle age. In J. G. Howells (Ed.), *Modern perspectives in the psychiatry of middle age* (pp. 3–25). New York: Brunner/Mazel, 1981.

Chiriboga, D. A. Consistency in adult functioning: The influence of social stress. *Ageing and Society,* 1982, 2, 7–29. (a)

Chiriboga, D. A. An examination of life events as possible antecedents of change. *Journal of Gerontology,* 1982, 37, 595–601. (b)

Chiriboga, D. A. Adaptation to marital separation in later and earlier life. *Journal of Gerontology,* 1982, 37, 109–114. (c)

Chiriboga, D. A., & Cutler, L. Stress and adaptation: A life span study. In L. Poon (Ed.), *Aging in the 1980s: Selected contemporary issues in the psychology of aging,* (pp. 343–345). Washington, D.C.: American Psychological Association, 1980.

Chiriboga, D. A., & Pierce, R. C. *The self in transition: A study in change.* Paper presented at the 30th Annual Scientific Meeting of the Gerontological Society, San Francisco, CA, 1977.

Dohrenwend, B. S., & Dohrenwend, B. P. Class and race as status-related sources of stress. In S. Levine & N. A. Scotch (Eds.), *Social stress* (pp. 111–140). Chicago: Aldine, 1970.

Erikson, E. H. *Life history and the historical moment.* New York: Norton, 1975.

Fiske, M. Changing hierarchies of commitment in adulthood. In N. J. Smelser & E. H. Erikson (Eds.), *Themes of work and love in adulthood* (pp. 238–264). Cambridge: Harvard University Press, 1980.

Fiske, M. Challenge and defeat: Stability and change in adulthood. In L. Goldberger & S. Breznitz (Eds.), *Handbook of stress.* New York: The Free Press, 1982.

Foss, D. A., & Larkin, R. W. The roar of the lemming: Youth, postmovement groups, and the life construction crisis. In H. M. Johnson (Ed.), *Religious change and continuity: Sociological perspectives* (pp. 264–285). San Francisco: Jossey-Bass, 1979.

Holmes, T. H., & Rahe, R. H. The social readjustment rating scale. *Journal of Psychosomatic Research,* 1967, 11, 213–218.

Horowitz, M. J., Schaefer, C., Hiroto, D., Wilner, N., & Levin, B. Life event question-naires for measuring presumptive stress. *Psychosomatic Medicine,* 1977, 39, 413–431.

Hultsch, D. F., & Plemons, J. K. Life events and life-span development. In P. B. Baltes & O. G. Brim, Jr. (Eds.), *Life-span development and behavior* (Vol. 2, pp. 1–36). New York: Academic Press, 1979.

Koch, S. The nature and limits of psychological knowledge: Lessons of a century qua "science." *American Psychologist,* 1981, 36(3), 257–269.

Kohut, H. *The restoration of the self.* New York: International Universities Press, 1977.

Lasch, C. *The culture of narcissism: American life in an age of diminishing expectations.* New York: Norton, 1978.

Lazarus, R. S. The stress and coping paradigm. In C. Eisdorfer, D. Cohen, A. Kleinman, & P. Maxim (Eds.), *Conceptual models for psychopathology,* New York: Spectrum, 1980.

Levinson, D. J., Darrow, C. N., Klein, E. B., Levinson, M. H., & McKee, B. *The seasons of a man's life.* New York: Knopf, 1978.

Lifton, R. J. *The broken connection.* New York: Harcourt Brace Jovanovich, 1979.

Lowenthal, M. F., & Chiriboga, D. Social stress and adaptation: Toward a life course perspective. In C. Eisdorfer & M. P. Lawton (Eds.), *The psychology of adult development and aging* (pp. 281–310). Washington, D.C.: American Psychological Association, 1973.

Lowenthal, M. F., Thurnher, M., Chiriboga, D., & Associates. *Four stages of life.* San Francisco: Jossey-Bass, 1975.

Lurie, E. Role scope and social participation. Staff memorandum #HD 10A.11, Human Development and Aging Program, University of California, San Francisco, 1972, June.

Marris, P. *Loss and change.* London: Routledge & Kegan, 1974.

May, R. Value conflicts and anxiety. In I. L. Kutash, L. B. Schlesinger, & Associates, *Handbook on stress and anxiety* (pp. 241–248). San Francisco: Jossey-Bass, 1980.

Merton, R. K., Fiske, M., & Kendall, P. *The focused interview.* Glencoe, IL: The Free Press, [1948] 1955.

Neugarten, B. L., Moore, J. W., & Lowe, J. C. Age norms, age constraints, and adult socialization. *American Journal of Sociology,* 1965, *70,* 710–717.

Norton, D. L. *Personal destinies: A philosophy of ethical individualism.* Princeton: Princeton University Press, 1976.

Parkes, C. M. Psycho-social transitions: A field for study. *Social Science and Medicine,* 1971, *5,* 101–115.

Pearlin, L. I., & Lieberman, M. A. Social sources of emotional distress. *Research in Community and Mental Health,* 1979, *1,* 217–249.

Pearlin, L. I., & Radabaugh, C. Age and stress: Perspectives and problems. In H. I. McCubbin (Ed.), *Family stress, coping, and social supports.* New York: Springer, 1981.

Riegel, K. F. Adult life crises: A dialectic interpretation of development. In N. Datan & L. H. Ginsberg (Eds.), *Life-span developmental psychology: Normative life crises* (pp. 99–129). New York: Academic Press, 1975.

Riegel, K. F. The dialectics of human development. *American Psychologist,* 1976, *31*(10), 689–700.

Roth, J. A. *Timetables: Structuring the passage of time in hospital treatment and other careers.* New York: Bobbs-Merrill, 1963.

Sennett, R. *The fall of public man.* New York: Knopf, 1977.

Thomae, H. The concept of development and life-span developmental psychology. In P. B. Baltes & O. G. Brim, Jr. (Eds.), *Life-span development and behavior.* (Vol. 2, pp. 281–312). New York: Academic Press, 1979.

Thurnher, M. Turning points and developmental change: Subjective and "objective" assessments. *American Journal of Orthopsychiatry,* 1983, *53,* 52–60.

Turner, V. Betwixt and between: The liminal period in rites of passage. In E. Hammel & W. Simmons (Eds.), *Man makes sense.* Boston: Little Brown, 1970.

ELDERS AND THE EXTENDED FAMILY SYSTEM: HEALTH, FAMILY, SALIENCE, AND AFFECT

Lillian E. Troll and Janice Stapley*

INTRODUCTION

If we look at one moment of time, can we estimate the effect of change in one part of a system—in this case, the extended or "modified extended" family—on other parts of that system? This is what this essay is attempting. Specifically, we are asking what the effect of deteriorated health of the oldest generation is upon the feelings and thoughts of members of three adult generations: the ailing grandparent himself or herself, his or her child, and his or her grandchild. The fact that we are looking at different generations complicates our task even further, because this means we are looking at a system that, in itself, incorporates change; each generation brings in different influences resulting from its location at different points of historic time (Mannheim, 1952).

Within the theme of this volume, we are following an episodic–interactionist conception, since we are focusing on the interplay between the poor health of the grandparent and several presumed personality processes of members of the family. These demonstrations of personality, furthermore, are both manifest and latent. The data we are using are within the domain of projective information rather than survey or direct self-report responses. That is, they are responses of a general sort to open-ended, "stem" questions designed to encourage "conversation" rather than "answers."

From another perspective, we are looking at the effect of something emergent (deterioration in health) upon something presumed to be preexistent (relationships among people). We are also looking at something that probably covaries with the health change—the affect of the family members (their happiness or distress). Is poor health in the oldest generation associated with negative affect—with distress—and, if so, is it more clearly associated in families whose members are more salient to each other than in those where they are less salient?

FAMILY COMMUNICATION
AND HELPING PATTERNS

We know, from an abundant body of survey data, that, in spite of almost daily announcements and predictions to the contrary, members of extended families usually maintain contact and help each other. This is seen particularly up and down the generational line, from parent to child to grandchild. Myths of alienation and abandonment of aging family members prove to be just that—myths (Shanas, 1979).

Almost all surveys of family connectedness over the past few decades show residential propinquity, frequent communication, and mutual aid (Troll, Miller, & Atchley, 1979). Parents and children of all ages keep in close touch even if they don't agree with each other on many issues and probably even if they don't think much of each other (Troll & Bengtson, 1979). Older people, in particular, are embedded in families and get most of their care, when they need it, from kin. "Disengagement" at the end of life is *into*, not *from*, the family (Troll, 1971). Even sibling and grandparental relations, while not as close as parent–child relations, are important (Troll, 1982). Generally, therefore, it is the absence of family communication or the loss of contact that needs to be explained, not its persistence.

The abused old parent is probably as rare as the abused young child. In both cases, the enormity of the situation calls it to public attention. Furthermore, social agencies and institutions still provide only a small part of the care for aging Americans. When parents become ill and disabled, it is their adult children who provide 80–90% of the health care and services they need (United States Comptroller General, 1977).

There are marked sex differences, however; older men are likely to receive much of their care from their wives. Older women are victims of unequal age/sex survival and age-disparate marriage patterns. That is, the practice of marrying men older than they, compounded by men's shorter life expectancy, means that old widows and divorcees find few older men available for replacement of a dead or divorced husband in contrast to the abundant options for replacement available to older widowers or divorced men. Old widows turn to their children—usually to a daughter, and usually to the daughter who has fewest other obligations (Brody, 1981).

Studies of attitudes about help-receiving and help-giving show that they are consistent with the behavior observed. The giving of help to older family members is seen as the way it should be (e.g., Brody, Johnson, Fulcomer, & Lang, 1983; Shanas, 1980; Sussman, 1965; Tobin & Kulys, 1979). Women believe they should take care of ailing parents and grandparents, a belief that is part of the wider prevailing belief that women should be the world's caretakers.

AFFECT

While we know that needy old people are cared for by family members, usually daughters, and that these daughters believe they are doing the right thing, we know little about their feelings. On the daughter's part, self-sacrifice does not appear to be an important value in our dominant society at the present time. In fact, the empirical literature suggests that prolonged attention to the needs of others combined with the prolonged restriction of social activities that is bound to accompany such attention leads to lower morale (cf. Arling, 1976; Troll, Miller, & Atchley, 1979). If we add the factors of love, concern, and empathy for declining parents to the restricted life associated with care, the weight upon the middle generation is heavy (see Aizenberg & Harris, 1982; Brody et al., 1983).

Depression and low self-esteem are more prevalent among women who are restricted to home and children (or parents or spouse) than to women employed outside the home (Baruch & Barnett, 1983). At the other end of the age spectrum, old people who spend most of their time with their children and grandchildren have lower morale than those who have wider social activities (Troll, 1983).

While there have been studies of communication, care, and consensus, investigations of feelings and interrelationships among older family members are recent and still sketchy. Because of their relative rarity, these data are more intriguing than normative. In general, parents and children report positive feelings and "closeness" to each other at all times of life, although there is some suggestion that the feelings may change to duty and obligation when the parents need a lot of help at the end of their lives (Troll et al., 1979).

Relationships between age and morale or other "state of being" measures have interested gerontologists for many years. In general, research points to health and money as causes of feeling states or changes in feeling states rather than age per se. Older people in good functional health and comfortable financial circumstances have higher morale and greater life satisfaction than those whose daily functioning is markedly restricted by either poor health or poverty.

It is possible that affect is altogether more intense in youth than in later life (see Lowenthal, Thurnher, & Chiriboga, 1975), although Malatesta (1981) points out that in part such conclusions come from looking at the overt expression of emotion rather than the feelings themselves.

HEALTH AND HAPPINESS

Whether bodily illness causes psychological distress or depression, or whether these are concomitants of the same process, their association has been demonstrated repeatedly, particularly in older people. The first Duke longitudinal study, for example, (Palmore & Luikert, 1974) found a clear association between health and life satisfaction of older people in North Carolina. Factor analyses of the University of Michigan Quality of Life data based on national probability samples also found that satisfaction with life is related to satisfaction with health (Cutler, 1979, Veroff, Douvan, & Kulka, 1981). When older Cleveland residents reported poor health, they were likely to score high on a Depression scale (Dunkle, 1983). Dunkle found a correlation of $-.30$ between health and depression.

Several studies suggest that there are not only age differences, but also sex differences in this connection (Cutler, 1979; Lowenthal et al., 1975); older women are more likely than older men to report health as a stressor, or producer of unhappiness, reflecting the common tendency of women to either feel worse than men or feel freer to say they feel worse—or both.

A distinction needs to be made between measures using perceptions of poor health and measures of specific health crises, as suggested by the second Duke longitudinal study (Palmore, Cleveland, Nowlin, Ramm, & Seigler, 1979). Hospitalizations did not seem to affect well-being (measured by the Cantril Ladder), feeling tone (measured by the Bradburn Affect Balance Scale), or psychosomatic symptoms. Only when crises accumulated did well-being decline. One episode of hospitalization rarely upset the long-range feelings of people with good "resources," either psychological or social, but several did.

The contribution of Bradburn (1969; Bradburn & Caplowitz, 1965), who developed a bipolar measure of affect that assessed positive and negative feelings separately, has enriched this line of research. In his analysis of the San Francisco data, Chiriboga (1979) was able to point out the independence of "happiness" and "unhappiness." Both positive and negative feelings were high among the high school seniors; both were low among the middle-aged subjects.

So far, most of the research on health and quality of life has not looked at family interactions, just as most research on family interactions has not looked at health, particularly in connection with affect. Yet, as noted above, extraordinary family service can bring distress and discomfort. When parents rally around to help teenage daughters who have become mothers or children who have divorced, they are involved in less desired grandparental activities than others they might perform, like fun-seeking or participation in family rituals (Hagestad, 1982b; Neugarten & Weinstein, 1964; Troll, 1983).

From the perspective of a younger generation, taking care of a sick older person is not the most desirable filial activity. For example, when Johnson (1983) interviewed San Francisco residents who were tending to posthospitalized elders 80% said the experience was stressful, and one-half saw it as a "serious problem." Mindel and Wright (1982), who studied families in less acute circumstances, found that adult children whose elderly parents lived with them had the lowest life satisfaction when living arrangements were inconvenient ($r = .42$), or the parent was inactive ($r = .30$). If the caretaker—usually a daughter or daughter-in-law—was not married, she was also likely to be low in life satisfaction (.30). A study of 148 adult children whose mothers were over 60 (Cicirelli, 1983) similarly reports that the adult children had fewer negative feelings about their mother if they had a higher score on "filial obligation" ($r = .17$), if they felt close and perceived themselves similar to their mother (.34), and if their mother was less dependent upon them ($r = .27$). Adult daughters in a Boston study (Baruch & Barnett, 1983) said they had better feelings about their mother if their mother's health was better. That at least part of these negative feelings are in response to the parent's poor health is suggested by two studies of families in which parents lived with their children (Dunkle, 1983; Lee & Ellithorpe, 1982). In both cases, the household contribution of the old parent had no significant effect on the feelings of their children. It is not the extra work, apparently, so much as the fact of parental deterioration and its emotional implications of mortality, coupled with life restrictions, that produce this effect.

FAMILY CONNECTEDNESS

Living near one another, visiting, and helping are all overt and easily quantifiable indices of closeness among family members. There are also more subtle, covert aspects. Ideally, one should be able to observe the actual behavior when family members are together. Who sits next to whom? Who faces whom? Who is responsive to whom? Unfortunately, verbal material like that used in the study reported here lends itself to more limited interpretation, such as who speaks of whom, and what kinds of references are made. For example, an early analysis of the present data showed that when men and women are asked to describe a person, the majority of them—of all ages—choose to describe a family member (Troll, 1972).

One area of interest to developmentalists across the life-span is that of attachment between family members (see Antonucci, 1976). Most of this research has been confined to the first 2 years of life, but recently several studies have focused upon the ''mother–daughter attachment'' in adulthood (e.g., Walker & Thompson, 1983). Weishaus (1978) was able to review mother–daughter relationships in a longitudinal study, using the Berkeley panel. Unfortunately, she only had sufficient data to look at 47 dyads. Overall, relationships were better between mothers and daughters whose life circumstances were better. When the daughters were 40 years old, those who were more educated and had higher marital satisfaction were more likely to feel positive about their mothers, particularly if their mothers had better mental health and higher social class. Daughters who felt they were raising their children much the same way that their mothers had raised them and that their mothers approved of both them and their children were also more positive about their mothers. On the average, the daughters' feelings about their mothers worsened somewhat over the three data collection points: the age of 17, the age of 30, and the age of 40. Women who had felt friendly toward their mothers in childhood, however, tended to maintain these feelings to the age of 30. Weishaus noted two points of discontinuity in the general theme of continuity. One was the finding that those daughters whose satisfaction with their mothers was highest at the age of 8 or 9 were the least satisfied with them at the age of 40. This discontinuity was interpreted as over-dependency in childhood that led to hostility in adulthood. The other discontinuity was a general one between the ages of 30 and 40. Since the mothers would have been changing from about the ages of 50 or 60 to 60 or 70 during that decade, it is conceivable that some of them were experiencing ill health or widowhood or other changes in circumstances that made them more needy and thus less congenial to their daughters.

GENERATIONS

The term *generations* has been used in many different ways (see Bengtson, 1970; Troll, 1970). In the present discussion, the meanings most relevant apply to individual development, family lineage, and cohorts in society. These processes are, of course, intertwined. In individual development, there is a transition from irresponsible nonadulthood to responsible membership in society (including the family) that is contingent partly upon parenthood and thus care-giving to spouse and children. At the opposite end of the age scale is the transition from independence or self-care to care-needing, which is contingent upon poor health. While chronological age may have some relevance for the early adulthood transition, it has little relevance for the late one. In the family, people become grandparents between 30 and 120, just as they can become ill and in need of help at any age.

Similarity in values can be an index of family connectedness. Empirical studies of generational similarities in the family, often labeled *transmission*, generally agree in finding statistically significant, albeit moderate, correlations between parents and their children on a variety of values and personality characteristics (cf. Troll & Bengtson, 1979; 1982). Variations by type of characteristics are notable. General religious and political affiliations, for example, seem to be shared or transmitted more than specific religious practices or political strategies. It is also possible that general ideas of filial obligation can be shared or transmitted, although specific ideas about the way in which those obligations should be carried out may change from immediate personal care-giving and nursing to visiting, monitoring, and procuring others for immediate care-giving.

Troll and Bengtson (1979) proposed that each new birth cohort, upon coming of age, adopts a distinctive theme—a *generational keynote theme*—that encompasses values, behavior patterns, and tastes. These distinguishing styles serve to differentiate new cohorts from preceding generations. The two older family generations in the present study (the grandparents and their children) might thus be more alike in their attitudes about care-giving for ailing family members than the middle generation and their young-adult children. Specific care-giving or child-rearing values, it is suggested here, have changed.

Cognitive characteristics such as Objectivity versus Egocentrism may show much less historical or keynote-connected generational change than would humanitarian values, although there may be sex by generational interactions in cognitive characteristics associated with increased opportunities for women's education and employment during the last two decades. Consistent with the contingent nature of grandparental relations (Troll, 1980), which needs bridging by the middle generation to permit them to flourish, correlations between grandparents and grandchildren are not usually as high as those between the two parent–child dyads: grandparent–parent and parent–grandchild.

While similarity in values can be an index of extended family connectedness, it has been found to be related to neither the frequency of communication among family members nor to expressed regard (Adams, 1968; Troll et al., 1979; Troll & Bengtson, 1982). Further, most generational-similarity studies have found no differences among the four possible parent-child dyads: mother–son, mother–daughter, father–son, and father–daughter (Troll & Bengtson, 1982; Troll, Neugarten, & Kraines, 1969). That is, neither sex of parent nor sex of adult child seems to contribute to their similarity. Recently, however, Hagestad (1978) reported noticeable sex-lineage effects in patterns of influence between three-generation female and male lineages. A grandmother–mother–granddaughter line shows stronger reciprocal influence than does a grandmother–daughter–grandson or grandmother–son–granddaughter line. Grandfathers interact more influencially with their sons and son's sons than with other combinations of descendants. The areas of influence also differentiate by sex lineage, with men up and down the generational line tending to influence each other in instrumental topics such as financial and career behaviors, and women in expressive and relational behaviors.

FOCUS OF PRESENT STUDY

In the present essay, we are interested not only in members of the oldest family generation, but in the family context within which they, their children, and grandchildren are embedded. We are interested in the connection among generations as it may vary with presumed shifts in behavior associated with health.

The following specific questions are addressed:

1. Is poor health in a grandfather or grandmother correlated with his or her own happiness or distress?
2. Is the poor health of a grandfather or grandmother correlated with the happiness or distress of his or her child or grandchild?
3. Is similarity in values correlated with the salience of family members for each other or their happiness or distress?
4. Are there generational and sex differences in correlations between grandparents' health and the salience of family members for each other?
5. Are family patterns in the salience of family members for each other related to the members' affect?

SUBJECTS

Members of 156 same-sexed three-generation lines were interviewed. These included 47 male lines (141 individuals) and 110 female lines (330 individuals). The age range was from 12 to 92. The sample for the present study was selected from a larger data set on the basis of completeness of protocol. It represents a mixture of ethnic heritage, including those from Eastern European, Mediterranean, and Western European countries as well as blacks. Many of the first, or oldest, generation members were immigrants to this country from Europe or to urban Northern cities from the South. Most families lived in Detroit, Chicago, and other cities or suburbs, although some were in Appallachian and middle western rural areas. Not all three generations resided in the same community, either, though in a few families two generations lived in the same household. There were no three-generational households.

Education, occupation, and interests reflect the upward mobility of the past century in the United States. Only a few of the subjects from the oldest generation had any college education. One-quarter of the second generation had some college, and one-half of the third generation either were attending college, were college graduates, or intended to go to college. Because of this upward mobility in the sample, reflecting the upward mobility of the American population, it is difficult to categorize these families according to social class.

INTERVIEW PROTOCOLS

The data for the present study were obtained from responses to a semi-projective instrument, consisting of 12 open-ended stem questions designed to elicit a "slice of style." These responses were rated in a semi-clinical fashion, as is described in the section on coding below. The 12 questions are:

1. Tell me something about yourself. If you like, you could start in your childhood and say anything you wish about your life in general.
2. What are some of the kinds of things you like to do?
3. What are some things you do that you would just as soon not have to be doing?
4. What kinds of people do you admire?
5. What kinds of people don't you like?
6. Now think of some man you have known well, and tell me what he is (or was) like.
   If Respondent is male add:

    a) In what ways are you like him?

    b) In what ways are you different from him?

7. Now think of a woman whom you have known well and describe her.

    If Respondent is female add:

    a) In what ways are you like her?

    b) In what ways are you different from her?

8. In what ways do you think you have stayed pretty much the same over your life?

9. In what ways do you feel you have changed the most?

10. If money were no object, where and how would you like to live?

11. What do you think we in this country could do about the problem of law and order?

12. What is your opinion of our educational system?

The interviews were gathered over 10 years by students in classes on Adult Development and Aging and Life-Span Family Psychology, as part of their course work. Most of the interviews were conducted for each individual separately, person-to-person, although a few were over the telephone and several done through forms filled out by the respondents themselves. When the interviewers asked the questions, they recorded responses verbatim. The time spent with individual family members was about 1 hour.

The main advantage of this method of data collection is that the possible effects of interviewer bias are diminished by having a different interviewer for each family. In some cases, students interviewed members of their own families. This probably resulted in data of comparable quality to that obtained when the student was not interviewing family members, since the advantages and disadvantages tend to balance out: Although responses may have been richer due to the interviewer's rapport with the subjects, some parents or grandparents may have been hesitant to be as candid with a child or grandchild as they might have been with an impartial interviewer.

CODING

The responses to these open-ended stem questions were coded by the authors and graduate psychology students. Scales for the different variables were devised by deductive processes from a priori definitions of the constructs selected. Thus, for example, the definition of *humanitarianism* decided upon was the "belief that it is important to help other people, in a generic sense." This basic definition was operationalized for each of the 12 questions in terms of the kind of response a humanitarian person would be likely to make to that particular question. To illustrate, the question, "What kinds of people do you admire?" should elicit a response from a humanitarian person indicating that he or she admires people who help other people. A nonhumanitarian would admire some other virtue, such as "people who are able to stand up for themselves," but show no indication of a helping-others orientation. The first kind of response, "people who help others," would be a score of 3 on Humanitarianism; the second kind of response would be a score of 1; and an ambiguous response, such as "people who want to make the world better," would be a score of 2. Examples of different types of answers and their scores constituted the codebook.

Further information concerning each of the variables follows.

AFFECT

Originally, an "affect" or a "happiness versus unhappiness" score was derived for each of the 12 stem questions using a 5-point scale in which a score of 1 was "sad and despondent" and a score of 5 "happy." A score of 3 indicated either neutral affect or ambiguity of response. This final affect score was the average of the scores assigned for each of the 12 stem quesions. Thus, the possible range of scores was from 1 to 5. Examples of responses coded 5 for Question 1 are "My parents were very good to me"; "My children have turned out very well"; and "I moved up through the company, and now I have gotten to be foreman." Examples of responses coded 1 for Questions 2 are "I can't do anything now" and "I just want to be alone."

This original bipolar/average score was subsequently revised to address two empirical problems and, more important, a theoretical issue. The two empirical problems were low variability in scores and low interrater reliability. This average score, as should have been anticipated, defeated the original purpose of examining both positive and negative affect that was to follow the earlier substantive work on affect suggesting two orthogonal dimensions: positive (happiness) and negative (distress) (Bradburn, 1969). We therefore factor analyzed the 12 single-item affect scores and did, in fact, find two orthogonal factors that could readily be interpreted as negative affect and positive affect, thus offering face validity for these constructs. Interview questions 1, 7, and 8 did not load on either factor and thus were not used in calculating the final two affect scores. When we eliminated these three items, our interrater reliability improved to 74% perfect agreement. Questions 2, 4, 5, 9, and 11 tapped happiness and Questions 3, 6, 10, and 12 tapped distress. We also found

more variability in these two affect scores than in the original unidi-
mensional score. The happiness score was the sum of the codes for 2,
4, 9, and 11, minus the code for 5 (which contributed negatively). The
distress score was the sum of the codes for 3, 6, 10, and 12. The range
of scores for happiness were 6–18 for women and 7–18 for men. The
ranges for distress were 5–20 for women and 6–19 for men. This method
of coding allowed us to examine independently the relationship of both
positive and negative affect to the other variables of interest.

Health

All first-generation subjects (the grandparents) were coded 1 point for
each spontaneous mention of poor health in the interview. Thus, higher
scores represent poorer inferred health. Interestingly, the range of scores
was only 0–2, even among this older sample (50–92 years of age).

Individual Family Salience

The number of times respondents spontaneously mentioned other
family members, whether older, younger, or of their own generation,
constitutes their individual family-salience score. Higher scores represent greater salience of the family for that individual. If relatives were
referred to specifically (e.g., "my son") a score of 1 was assigned. An
aggregate reference (e.g., "I have seven children" or "my parents")
was also scored 1. The range of scores is 0–9 for each of the four indices:
family in general, older family member, younger family member, and
same-generation family member.

Triad Family Salience

The sum of the three individual family salience scores is the triad family score. It ranges from 0 to 36 on each of the four indices: general,
older, younger, and same generation.

Unity of Family Theme

This measure reflects the degree to which members of a lineage are
alike in the three values scores: *objectivity, aestheticism,* and *humanitarianism* (each defined below). It was derived by summing the absolute
values of the differences between individual scores for the three family
dyads on the three values scores. Thus, lower scores represent greater
unity of a family theme or greater congruence among the three family
members on these characteristics. The range of scores is 8–76.

Objectivity Versus Egocentrism

According to the general definition of this construct, objective people look at themselves, other people, ideas, or events independently of how they themselves are affected. They can thus describe or discuss themselves and others and see others' points of view. The scale is conceived as bipolar: A rating of 3 on each response indicates clear objectivity; a rating of 1 indicates its opposite, egocentricity; and a rating of 2 is ambivalent or in-between. An example of an objective response for Question 3 is, "I have to accept neighbors who are minding their own social contacts. This is disagreeable in a way. . . . I want a Christian type, considering my age and the type of world in which I'm living." An example of an egocentric response for Question 4 is, "I admire my neighbors; they're very friendly, they like me, they do things for me." The range of scores is 0–23.

Humanitarianism

This variable was described earlier. The possible range of scores is 0–8.

Aestheticism

A response is rated 3 on this value if it indicates that the person appreciates or has a feeling for beauty or shows a concern with emotions deriving from the perception and experience of beauty or from creativity in artistic or expressive ways. The range of scores if 0–13.

Between-rater reliability coefficients for these value scores ranged from .69 to .90.

DATA ANALYSIS

All statistics including correlations, multiple regressions, and the varimax factor analysis of the affect scores were carried out through the use of Statistical Analysis System (SAS), a commonly used computer software package for statistical analysis.

FINDINGS

HEALTH AND AFFECT

Our first interest is in the association between the health and the affect of the grandparents. Tables 10.1 through 10.4 present ANOVAs and Table 10.5 correlations for both happiness and distress. Consistent with

TABLE 10.1

GENERATION 1, WOMEN, TWO-WAY ANOVA ON HAPPINESS

Sources of variance	df	SS	F	p
Health	1	40.82	10.18	0.00
Family connectedness	1	5.07	1.26	0.26
Error	106	424.97		

TABLE 10.2

GENERATION 1, WOMEN, TWO-WAY ANOVA ON DISTRESS

Sources of variance	df	SS	F	p
Health	1	2.04	0.39	0.53
Family connectedness	1	5.35	1.03	0.31
Error	105			

TABLE 10.3

GENERATION 1, MEN, TWO-WAY ANOVA ON HAPPINESS

Sources of variance	df	SS	F	p
Health	1	65.68	16.11	0.00
Family connectedness	1	0.20	0.05	0.82
Error	42			

TABLE 10.4

GENERATION 1, MEN, TWO-WAY ANOVA ON DISTRESS

Sources of variance	df	SS	F	p
Health	1	1.30	0.17	0.68
Family connectedness	1	15.15	1.97	0.17
Error	42			

TABLE 10.5

THREE GENERATIONS, MEN AND WOMEN, CORRELATIONS
BETWEEN HEALTH OF G-1 AND AFFECT

	Happiness		Distress	
	r	p	r	p
G-1 Women	−.28	.00	.09	.35
G-1 Men	−.53	.00	−.05	.77
G-2 Women	.01	.92	.19	.05
G-2 Men	.10	.52	−.11	.46
G-3 Women	−.09	.37	.09	.35
G-3 Men	−.25	.10	.01	.96

much of the literature cited earlier, poor health, as indexed by spontaneous mention of physical problems, is significantly related to lowered
happiness ($r = .28$ for women and .53 for men; an F of 10.18 for women
and 16.11 for men). What is curious, though, is the lack of relationship
between health and negative affect. Apparently, while people who state
that they have health problems are not as happy as those who do not
mention poor health, they do not display heightened distress.

HEALTH AND GENERATIONAL SPREAD OF AFFECT

As shown in Tables 10.5 through 10.13, poor health of a grandparent
in this sample does not have a profound effect upon the affect of the
child and grandchild. There is a statistically significant but somewhat
marginal association ($r = .19$) between the distress scores of the middle-
generation women and their mothers' poor health, but no association
between either happiness or distress scores of the youngest generation.
No relationships appear in the male line. Perhaps if we had restricted
the middle-generation sample of women to caretakers, the association

TABLE 10.6

GENERATION 2, WOMEN, TWO-WAY ANOVA ON HAPPINESS

Sources of variance	df	SS	F	p
Health of G-1	1	0.24	0.06	0.81
Family connectedness	1	2.43	0.58	0.44
Error	105			

TABLE 10.7

GENERATION 2, WOMEN, TWO-WAY ANOVA ON DISTRESS

Sources of variance	df	SS	F	p
Health of G-1	1	15.18	2.10	0.15
Family connectedness	1	8.57	1.18	0.27
Error	106			

TABLE 10.8

GENERATION 3, WOMEN, TWO-WAY ANOVA ON HAPPINESS

Sources of variance	df	SS	F	p
Health of G-1	1	4.09	0.89	0.35
Family connectedness	1	2.98	0.65	0.42
Error	106			

TABLE 10.9

GENERATION 3, WOMEN, TWO-WAY ANOVA ON DISTRESS

Sources of variance	df	SS	F	p
Health of G-1	1	1.31	0.20	0.66
Family connectedness	1	15.89	2.39	0.12
Error	106			

TABLE 10.10

GENERATION 2, MEN, TWO-WAY ANOVA ON HAPPINESS

Sources of variance	df	SS	F	p
Health of G-1	1	1.29	0.37	0.55
Family connectedness	1	8.20	2.33	0.13
Error	40			

TABLE 10.11

GENERATION 2, MEN, TWO-WAY ANOVA ON DISTRESS

Sources of variance	df	SS	F	p
Health of G-1	1	4.87	0.64	0.43
Family connectedness	1	6.50	0.85	0.36
Error	43			

TABLE 10.12

GENERATION 3, MEN, TWO-WAY ANOVA ON HAPPINESS

Sources of variance	df	SS	F	p
Health of G-1	1	10.73	3.07	0.09
Family connectedness	1	5.35	1.53	0.22
Error	43			

might have been stronger. Also, perhaps if we had interviewed the wives of the grandfathers who were ill—again presumably their caretakers—we would have found a significant correlation. The fact that it is only daughters who show any effect is consistent with earlier findings in the literature, however. A look at Table 10.14 shows that while there is no wide variation in affect scores by sex and generation, the oldest generation is lowest in happiness and highest in distress. On the other hand, the youngest generation differs from the Chiriboga findings in that they are not the highest on either positive or negative affect. It is the middle generation that is happiest and the youngest that is least distressed. The fact that the sampling here is by generation, not age, could easily account for the difference between these findings and the San Francisco high school seniors. The youngest generation here ranges in age between 10 and 50.

SIMILARITY OF VALUES AND FAMILY SALIENCE

Figure 10.1 shows, first, that all three generations of men share (within families) in Objectivity versus Egocentricity, although only the two older generations of women do. Shifts in employment opportunities and thus life styles for women in recent years may have increased the generational distance between young women and their mothers and grandmothers. The male lines do not, however, share values of either Aestheticism or Humanitarianism. Here the female lines are somewhat

TABLE 10.13

GENERATION 3, MEN, TWO-WAY ANOVA ON DISTRESS

Sources of variance	df	SS	F	p
Health of G-1	1	0.03	−0.00	0.94
Family connectedness	1	27.13	4.25	0.04
Error	43			

TABLE 10.14

MEANS AND STANDARD DEVIATIONS OF HAPPINESS AND DISTRESS
BY SEX AND GENERATION[a]

	Happiness				Distress			
	Women		Men		Women		Men	
	M	SD	M	SD	M	SD	M	SD
G1	10.6	2.1	11.0	2.3	13.2	2.3	12.9	2.8
G2	14.2	2.0	14.5	1.9	12.0	2.7	11.4	2.7
G3	13.6	2.1	14.1	1.9	11.1	2.6	11.5	2.6

[a]M = mean; SD = standard deviation.

closer. Grandmothers and granddaughters tend to be alike in Aestheticism and middle-generation women and their young-adult daughters
in Humanitarianism. Unity of Family Theme, which is based upon
dyadic similarity in these value scores, shows no relation to any of the
other variables—neither the health of the oldest generation, the affect
of any of the three generations, nor the salience of family members for
each other. As earlier writers have noted, family closeness is not related
to family similarities.

Family salience does seem to "run in families," however, as can be
seen in Tables 10.15 and 10.16. Both intraindividual and intrafamily consistencies appear. Thus, if an individual has many mentions of family
in general, he or she is also likely to mention older, younger, or same-

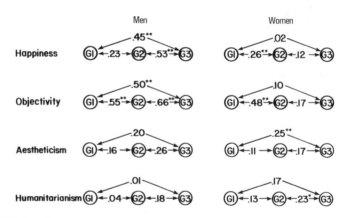

FIGURE 10.1 Intergenerational correlations on happiness and personality characteristics for male and female lineages. * Significant at .05 level. ** Significant at .01 level or
below.

TABLE 10.15

INTERCORRELATIONS AMONG FAMILY SALIENCE SCORES, WOMEN

	$F_1{}^a$	F_2	F_3	$O_1{}^b$	O_2	O_3	$Y_1{}^c$	Y_2	Y_3	$S_1{}^d$	S_2
$F_2{}^a$	.16										
F_3	.04	.04									
$O_1{}^b$	.18*	.02	−.04								
O_2	.01	.33*	.10	.29*							
O_3	.08	.25*	.27*	.09	.17						
$Y_1{}^c$	.04	.07	−.08	.17	.22*	.11					
Y_2	.12	.07	.03	.04	.24*	.27*	.26*				
Y_3	.12	.23*	.06	.03	.10	.17	.03	.09			
$S_1{}^d$	.13	.05	−.03	.26*	.24*	.15	.43*	.28*	−.08		
S_2	.00	.25*	−.02	.13	.26*	.25*	.24*	.30*	.03	.47*	
S_3	.03	.20*	.16	.11	.11	.38*	.17	.24*	.31*	.17	.20*

*Significant at .05 level or better.
$^a F_1$, F_2, and F_3 refer to mention of "family in general" by Generation 1, 2, and 3, respectively.
$^b O_1$, O_2, and O_3 refer to mention of older family member by Generation 1, 2, and 3, respectively.
$^c Y_1$, Y_2, and Y_3 refer to mention of younger family member by Generation 1, 2, and 3, respectively.
$^d S_1$, S_2, and S_3 refer to mention of same-generation family member by Generation 1, 2, and 3, respectively.

TABLE 10.16

INTERCORRELATIONS AMONG FAMILY SALIENCE SCORES, MEN

	$F_1{}^a$	F_2	F_3	$O_1{}^b$	O_2	O_3	$Y_1{}^c$	Y_2	Y_3	$S_1{}^d$	S_2
F_2	.25										
F_3	.04	.03									
O_1	.07	.30*	.26*								
O_2	.09	.45*	−.13	.47*							
O_3	−.07	−.03	.16	.45*	.08						
Y_1	.38*	.22	.11	.41*	.16	.38*					
Y_2	.08	.69*	−.12	.23	.58*	.07	.17				
Y_3	−.00	.10	.31*	.35*	−.01	.09	.22	−.11			
S_1	.34*	.33*	.10	.45*	.36*	.30*	.54*	.19	.36*		
S_2	.09	.38*	−.06	.27	.41*	.23	.38*	.38*	.29*	.32*	
S_3	−.12	.32*	.23	.23	.24	.12	.05	.40*	.11	.07	.25

*Significant at $p = .05$ level or better.
$^a F_1$, F_2, and F_3 refer to mention of "family in general" by Generation 1, 2, and 3, respectively.
$^b O_1$, O_2, and O_3 refer to mention of older family member by Generation 1, 2, and 3, respectively.
$^c Y_1$, Y_2, and Y_3 refer to mention of younger family member by Generation 1, 2, and 3, respectively.
$^d S_1$, S_2, and S_3 refer to mention of same-generation family member by Generation 1, 2, and 3, respectively.

generation relatives and to belong to a family in which other members also mention relatives spontaneously.

GRANDPARENTS' HEALTH AND FAMILY SALIENCE

While poor health of a grandmother or grandfather does not have a direct or overall effect upon family salience, a few interesting particular relationships may be observed, as seen in Table 10.17. Thus, older women whose health is troubling them are somewhat more likely than other older women to talk about their family in a global way ($r = .19$),

TABLE 10.17

CORRELATIONS BETWEEN HEALTH OF GRANDPARENT
AND FAMILY (TRIADIC) SALIENCE SCORES OF THREE GENERATIONS,
BY SEX OF RESPONDENT

Generation	salience score	r	p
Women			
1	Triadic score	.18	.06
	Family in general	.19	.05
	Older relatives	.09	.33
	Younger relatives	.15	.12
	Same-generation relatives	.07	.47
2	Family in general	−.04	.70
	Older relatives	.15	.13
	Younger relatives	.26	.01
	Same-generation relatives	.07	.47
3	Family in general	.13	.18
	Older relatives	.17	.07
	Younger relatives	.03	.73
	Same-generation relatives	.09	.37
Men			
1	Triadic score	.09	.53
	Family in general	.13	.37
	Older relatives	.01	.93
	Younger relatives	.05	.76
	Same-generation relatives	.09	.53
2	Family in general	.30	.04
	Older relatives	.11	.46
	Younger relatives	.20	.18
	Same-generation relatives	−.07	.66
3	Family in general	.12	.44
	Older relatives	−.29	.04
	Younger relatives	.11	.46
	Same-generation relatives	−.10	.51

that is, to mention "my family" rather than specific relatives. Their daughters, for their part, are more likely to talk about younger family members ($r = .26$) than about the family in general, older family members (not even their ailing mothers), or same-generation relatives. The granddaughters, though, do not seem to be influenced in their family connectedness by the health of their grandmother.

The men show a different pattern from the women. Older men who mention their poor health are not more likely to mention family members (including their wives), either generally or specifically. On the other hand, if their fathers are ill, the middle-generation son seems to be more likely to talk about his family in a general way, like the sick grandmother ($r = .30$). What seems most intriguing is the relation between the grandfather's poor health and his grandson's tendency to move away from spontaneous mention of older family members. That is, grandsons are only likely to talk about older family members if their grandfathers are in good health. They seem to be drawing away from both their father and their grandfather at the same time that their father is turning to generalized thoughts of family.

FAMILY SALIENCE AND AFFECT

Table 10.18 shows the relation between spontaneous mention of other family members and respondent's happiness or distress. Clearly, the few correlations that are significant are about what we might expect by chance. Their pattern is intriguing, however, and coupled with the fact that the ANOVA for the youngest generation of men is also significant (see Table 10.13) tempts us to look at this pattern. Thus, when grandmothers are happy, they are likely to refer to younger family members, or perhaps it's the other way around, that is, when grandmothers refer to younger family members, they are more likely to sound happy. Grandfathers, on the other hand, show no relation between family mentions and affect. Middle-generation women—but not middle-generation men—show more distress when they talk about their families in general, although not when they refer to specific people. Again, we are struck by the pattern of the youngest generation of men. Talking about older family members is associated with happiness, while talking about same-generation family members is associated with distress.

It might be instructive to examine the means and standard deviations of the family salience scores (Table 10.19). In general, the grandmothers speak of younger and same-generation family members, and grandfathers speak mostly of same-generation ones, often their wives. Middle-generation women talk about younger relatives; middle-generation men,

TABLE 10.18

FAMILY SALIENCE AND AFFECT OF WOMEN AND MEN IN THREE GENERATIONS

Generation	Sex	Affect	Correlation with triadic salience score	Significant correlations with individual salience scores
1	Women	Happiness	.09	Younger relatives .19[a]
		Distress	.02	
	Men	Happiness	−.10	
		Distress	.09	
2	Women	Happiness	.04	
		Distress	.26	
	Men	Happiness	−.20	
		Distress	−.00	
3	Women	Happiness	.02	
		Distress	.12	
	Men	Happiness	−.11	Older relatives .32[a]
		Distress	.04	Same-generation relatives .41[a]

[a]Significant at .05 level or better.

like their fathers, talk more about people of their own generation. Young-adult women and men both mostly refer to older family members. Since a good many of these young adults are themselves parents, we might conclude that the nature of the interview questions turned their thoughts to other adults rather than to small children.

TABLE 10.19

FAMILY SALIENCE SCORES BY SEX AND GENERATION[a]

Who is mentioned	G-1		G-2		G-3	
	M	SD	M	SD	M	SD
Women						
Family in general	1.1	1.3	0.9	1.5	0.5	0.9
Older family member	1.7	2.3	1.9	2.3	2.5	2.5
Younger family member	2.9	2.7	2.1	2.3	0.4	1.1
Same-generation family member	2.3	2.2	1.9	2.1	1.0	1.7
Men						
Family in general	1.2	1.8	0.8	1.3	0.3	0.7
Older family member	1.9	2.3	1.5	2.0	2.3	2.7
Younger family member	1.4	2.1	1.5	1.9	0.1	0.5
Same-generation family member	2.1	2.4	2.1	2.3	0.5	1.0

[a]M = mean; SD = standard deviation.

DISCUSSION

We opened this essay with a question about family system dynamics, wondering whether we would be able to catch glimpses of changes in interactions and feelings on the part of members of extended families that were presumably experiencing change. At least, we wanted to assess the relationships between family salience and affect of men and women in different generational positions. The change we looked at is the deterioration in health of the oldest member of a three-generation lineage (the grandmother or grandfather). We did, in fact, observe certain point-in-time relationships that we can guess might be the effects of the change in question.

First, it is probably safe to say that there is a relationship between whether one reports health problems and how happy or unhappy one seems in later life. But this result is limited: Happiness is reduced, but distress or negative feelings are not increased. Can we extrapolate and suggest that, at least for functioning older people, poor health casts its shadow over much of life, affecting responses to questions about everyday issues but not causing acute stress or distress? Such an extrapolation would be consistent with the Duke findings reported by Palmore et al. (1979).

Second, it appears from these data that similarity among family members is extraneous to their thoughts and feelings. Neither sharing the same values nor differing markedly on these values enhances or reduces family ties.

Third, there are interesting sex and generation interactions associated with grandparents' ill health. Since we did not choose our respondents on the basis of their participation in caretaking, we are able to assess possible effects of the burdens of caretaking only for women; it is probably many of the middle-generation women who have assumed this role if their mother is ill. Not all of the middle-generation women are caretakers, however, so whatever effect caretaking would have is undoubtedly vitiated here. Nevertheless, we see that daughters of sick old women are more distressed than daughters of those who are not sick and, further, that these daughters turn their thoughts to younger family members, perhaps in a compensatory or balancing fashion. It is easier to talk about the positive attributes of the young at a time when your heart aches about the old. Or perhaps we should say that thoughts of one's own future morbidity and mortality seek assuagement in thoughts about the perpetuity provided by coming generations. While illness in fathers may lead middle-aged men to think about their family in general, their affect is not related to such thoughts. The fact that the highest mean of family mentions for these men is to the same generation suggests that they may turn to their wives for solace as the women of their cohort turn to their children.

As noted in the previous section, it is the youngest generation observed that is most intriguing. The women seem curiously unrelated to either the woes or anything else about their mother and grandmother. Table 10.19 shows that they are not oblivious to family in general, because their mean reference to younger family members is the highest in the table, and they also refer often to same-generation relatives. It is suggested that some of them are preoccupied with getting a husband, with their relations with their future or present husband, and with their children, so that there is little familial concern left over. Perhaps more importantly, the existence of their parents' generation acts as a buffer against the concerns of mortality that may distress the middle generation because of its being on the verge of becoming the oldest generation and thus vulnerable, in the natural course of events, to extinction.

The youngest generation of men respond to family trouble by turning away from thoughts of older family members. On the other hand, their references to other family members are associated with much affect, both positive and negative. If they refer to older family members they are likely to be happy; if they refer to same-generation family members they are likely to be distressed. Without a qualitative analysis of the responses themselves, it would be presumptuous to try to interpret these results. Perhaps the generational buffer effect is more powerful for women. Perhaps, also, the wide spread of ages at this time of life is a more serious contaminating factor than it is for either the youngest generation of women or the two older generations. Females mature earlier than males, and an 11-year-old boy is still turning to thoughts of parents and sports (see Family 200 below) while a girl his age is starting to think of stereotypically women concerns.

Although no qualitative analysis is attempted here, several excerpts are presented for both male and female lineages, one in which the oldest-generation member is ill and one in which he or she does not mention health problems. Excerpts are from responses to Question 2 (like to do), Question 6 (describe a man), and Question 7 (describe a woman).

FAMILY 131: ILLNESS IN GRANDMOTHER

Grandmother, aged 89 ''can't do much any more.''
    I like to sit in my rocking chair and look out the window at the people. . . . girls with their legs hanging out there at 11 o'clock at night. Well, I guess I knew my husband best. He was a good man, worked hard all his life, went to church. I guess Aunt Dolly. . . . She died about five years ago. . . . She baked all her own bread, wouldn't buy anything from the store. She's friendly and happy.

Daughter, aged 45

I like to sew and go to my bridge club meetings. I like just sitting and watching television. Oh, my husband. . . . He's good looking, tall, blue eyes. He's an executive and works pretty hard. He's more decisive than I am. I suppose I know my mother best. She's a strong, strict, very religious woman. She's tiny but solid rock.

Granddaughter, aged 21

I like writing. . . . I love talking to people, dancing, skiing, tennis, bowling. I like parties and reading. I know C. well. He's like a whole lot of things that I respect and admire and like and love. . . . He's a dreamer, but an idealistic one. She's my roommate. . . . She has so much in the now. . . . so alive.

FAMILY 015: NO ILLNESS IN GRANDMOTHER

Grandmother, aged 65

Working out of doors, gardening and getting the place in shape. I like to crochet rugs, and I enjoy reading and crossword puzzles. My oldest brother. He's quiet, soft-spoken, intelligent. But, well, I guess if you make him mad you think you've tangled with a buzzsaw. My sister. I guess she was everything I would want to be and wasn't. She could do many things, and she was a good mixer.

Daughter, aged 40

I like to travel, paint. . . . sometimes I like to be alone and do things like painting, writing. He's intelligent and converses well. Has a good sense of humor and is able to appreciate and enjoy many things. A person who is admired for her leadership and capabilities as a nurse. She's very quickly able to see the many sides of a complicated situation.

Granddaughter, aged 17

Dance and sing. . . . art work . . . something, anything unusual. Very spiritual—not in a religious way, not apathetic. Cares what's going on, cares what other people are doing. A teacher. She's kind of insecure. She's a wrong type of person dealing with the type of job she's in.

FAMILY 200: ILLNESS IN GRANDFATHER

Grandfather, aged 73

I enjoy gardening and working with flowers. I'm limited by a heart condition so I spend a lot of time in the house working on puzzles. This would be an old school friend from Italy. Everything we did we did together, played, stole fruit. . . . we were the same age and dated girls together. An old childhood girlfriend that I knew till I left Italy. She was dark haired . . .

Son, aged 37

I enjoy sports both as a spectator and participant. A friend of mine for 15 years. He is hard working, honest, and an interesting person to talk to. He is well read and educated, although he never attended college. Physically she is tall, brown haired, and thin. She is kind, gentle, and a lover of music and literature.

Grandson, aged 11

I like playing baseball and watching football. I like all kinds of sports, because I like being active and watching active things. My father. He fights with me a lot (playing around). He takes me places. He is a fair sport. He is kind and generous and helpful. My mother. She is helpful and kind and sympathetic.

FAMILY 199: NO ILLNESS IN GRANDFATHER

Grandfather, aged 91

I like to make money more than anything. It gives me great stimulation. I guess for me it becomes an end in itself. My grandfather, who was a hardworking, hustling man. He was a gambler who used his skills and knowledge to make a fortune. My mother, a warm wonderful person. She always had a great concern for others.

Son, aged 64

This might seem strange, but I like to drink, make love, and work math problems. I guess I just get a great deal of pleasure from them. He was a thinker, a brilliant man with true intellectual abilities. My wife, a tall well-built excellent warm individual.

Grandson, aged 35

I enjoy the sensual things in life. I like them because I find them to be the only reality that one encounters in life. An unassuming witty, elegant male. The woman I should have married, beautiful, big-busted, tall, milky skin, a happy outdoors type person.

SUMMARY

Events in one part of an extended family do seem to affect the feelings and directions of family concern of members of three generations. Patterns of affect are different for men and women, which is consistent with their different roles vis-à-vis caretaking and kin-keeping. The focus of this research on generations highlights the generational processes and family positions related to generations, perhaps more so in women than in men. These findings do suggest that an analysis of developmental state—indexed, if nothing else, by chronological age—would clarify some of the puzzling findings for the youngest generation. The buffer effect of an older living generation for the middle generation may balance the emotional impact of deterioration in that oldest generation, so that the full impact of moving up to "front line" may not be felt in full until the death of that parent.

ACKNOWLEDGMENT

Louis Burdman assisted in the early work on this project.

REFERENCES

Adams, B. *Kinship in an urban setting.* Chicago: Markham, 1968.

Aizenberg, R., & Harris, R. Family demographic changes: The middle generation squeeze. *Generations,* 1982, 7(2), 6–8.

Antonucci, T. Attachment through the life span. *Human Development,* 1976, 19(3), 1.

Arling, G. The elderly widow and her family, neighbors, and friends. *Journal of Marriage and the Family,* 1976, 38(3), 757–68.

Baruch, G., & Barnett, R. C. Adult daughters relationships with their mothers. *Journal of Marriage and the Family,* 1983, 45(3), 601–606.

Bengtson, V. The generation gap: A review and typology of social-psychological perspectives. *Youth and Society,* 1970, 2(1), 7–32.

Bradburn, N. *The structure of psychological well-being,* Chicago: Aldine, 1969.

Bradburn, N., & Caplovitz, D. Reports on happiness: A pilot study of behavior related to mental health. Chicago: Aldine, 1965.

Brody, E. M. "Women in the middle" and family help to older people. *The Gerontologist,* 1981, 21(5), 471–480.

Brody, E., Johnson, P. T., Fulcomer, M. C., & Lang, A. N. Women's changing roles and help to elderly parents: Attitudes of three generations of women. *Journal of Gerontology,* 1983, 38(5), 597–607.

Chiriboga, D. A. Conceptualizing adult transitions: A new look at an old subject. *Generations,* 1979, 4, 4–6.

Cicirelli, V. G. Adult children's attachment and helping behavior to elderly parents: A path model. *Journal of Marriage and the Family,* 1983, 45(4), 815–825.

Cutler, N. Age variations and life satisfaction. *Journal of Gerontology,* 1979, 34(4), 573–578.

Dunkle, R. E. The effect of elders' household contributions on their depression. *Journal of Gerontology,* 1983, 38(6), 732–737.

Hagestad, G. O. *Patterns of communication and influence between grandparents and grandchildren in a changing society.* Paper presented at the World Congress of Sociology, Uppsala, Sweden, 1978, August.

Hagestad, G. O. Divorce: The family ripple effect. *Generations,* 1982, Winter, 24–25. (a)

Hagestad, G. O. Parent and child. In T. Field, A Huston, H. C. Quay, L. Troll & G. Finley (Eds.), *Human development.* New York: John Wiley, 1982. (b)

Johnson, C. L. Dyadic family relations and social support. *The Gerontologist,* 1983, 23(4), 377–383.

Lee, G. R., & Ellithorpe, E. Intergenerational exchange and subjective well-being among the elderly. *Journal of Marriage and the Family,* 1982, 44(1), 217–224.

Lowenthal, M. F., Thurnher, M. T., & Chiriboga, D. *Four stages of life.* San Francisco: Jossey-Bass, 1975.

Malatesta, C. Affective development over the life span: Involution or growth. *Merrill-Palmer Quarterly,* 1981, 27, 145–173.

Mannheim, K. The problem of generations. In Karl Mannheim, *Essays in the sociology of knowledge* (pp. 276–320). London: Routledge & Kegan Paul, 1952.

Mindel, C. H., & Wright, R. Satisfaction in multigenerational households. *Journal of Gerontology,* 1982, 37(4), 483–489.

Neugarten, B. L., & Weinstein, K. K. The changing American grandparent. *Journal of Marriage and the Family,* 1964, 26, 199–204.

Palmore, E., Cleveland, W. P., Nowlin, J. B., Ramm, D., & Siegler, I. Stress and adaptation in later life. *Journal of Gerontology,* 1979, 34(6), 841–851.

Palmore, E., & Luikert, C. Health and social factors related to life satisfaction. In Erdman Palmore (Ed.), *Normal aging II.* Durham, N.C: Duke University Press, 1974.

Shanas, E. The family as a social support system in old age. *The Gerontologist,* 1979, *19,* 169–174.

Shanas, E. Older people and their families: The new pioneers. *Journal of Marriage and the Family,* 1980, *42*(1), 9–15.

Sussman, M. Relationships of adult children with their parents in the United States. In E. Shanas & G. F. Streib (Eds.), *Social structure and the family: Generational relations.* Englewood Cliffs, NJ: Prentice Hall, 1965.

Tobin, S., & Kulys, R. The family and services. In C. Eisdorfer (Ed.), *Annual review of gerontology and geriatrics.* NY: Springer, 1979.

Troll, L. E. Issues in the study of generations. *Aging and Human Development,* 1970, *1,* 199–218.

Troll, L. E. The family of later life: A decade review. *Journal of Marriage and the Family,* 1971, *33,* 263–90.

Troll, L. E. *The salience of members of 3-generation families for each other.* Paper presented at the meeting of the American Psychological Association, Honolulu, 1972, September.

Troll, L. E. Grandparenting. In L. Poon (Ed.), *Aging in the 1980's.* Washington, D.C.: American Psychological Association, 1980.

Troll, L. E. *Continuations: Adult development and aging.* Monterey, CA: Brooks/Cole, 1982.

Troll, L. E. Grandparents: The family watchdogs. In Timothy Brubaker (Ed.), *Family relationships in later life.* Beverly Hills, CA: Sage, 1983.

Troll, L. E., & Bengtson, V. Generations in the family. In W. Burr, R. Hill, I. Nye, & I. Reiss (Eds.), *Contemporary theories about the family.* NY: The Free Press, 1979.

Troll, L. E., & Bengtson, V. B. Intergenerational relations through the life span. In B. B. Wolman (Ed.), *Handbook of developmental psychology.* Englewood Cliffs, NJ: Prentice Hall, 1982.

Troll, L. E., Miller, S., & Atchley, R. *Families of later life.* Belmont, CA: Wadsworth, 1979.

Troll, L. E., Neugarten, B., & Kraines, R. Similarities in values and other personality characteristics in college students and their parents. *Merrill-Palmer Quarterly,* 1969, *15,* 323–337.

United States Comptroller General. *The well-being of older people in Cleveland, Ohio.* Washington, D.C.: U.S. General Accounting Office, April 19, 1977.

Veroff, J., Douvan, E., & Kulka, R. A. *The inner American: A self-portrait from 1957 to 1976.* New York: Basic Books, 1981.

Walker, A., & Thompson, L. Intimacy and intergenerational aid and contact among mothers and daughters. *Journal of Marriage and the Family,* 1983, *45*(4), 1–9.

Weishaus, S. S. *Determinants of affect of middle-aged women towards their aging mothers.* Unpublished doctoral dissertation, University of Southern California, 1978.

11

THE STUDY OF PSYCHOSOCIAL CHANGE IN LATE LIFE: SOME CONCEPTUAL AND METHODOLOGICAL ISSUES

Peter G. Coleman and Andrew W. McCulloch

THE NATURE OF CHANGE IN LATE LIFE

One of the major trends in the social sciences over recent years has been a new interest in human ageing. Perhaps the most exciting aspect of this development is the desire to see old age in the context of the whole life-span. Seen in this context, old age becomes as interesting in its own way as childhood and adolescence, for both ends of the life-cycle are associated with biological and social transitions that often result in rapid changes in thoughts, feelings, and behaviour.

In many countries the steadily increasing numbers of very old people in the population has lent urgency to the study of issues surrounding the assessment, prediction, and prevention of breakdown in functioning in old age. In any analysis of such a breakdown, social and physical factors play an important role. The individual's maintenance of an independent but isolated existence in his own home, for example, may be the result of a delicate balance between the decremental influences of ageing, disease, and loss of social contact and stimulation on the one side, and compensating factors such as support by family and neighbours and the health and social services on the other. All factors in this equation may need attention at one time or another. But psychological characteristics of the individual elderly person also deserve consideration. It needs to be remembered that, although many elderly people succumb to loss, many cope remarkably well, and we therefore need to take account of such factors as the individual's previous experience of coping with loss and the meaning he attributes to continued survival. Therapy must also focus on the coping strengths that individuals possess and the capacity to find or rediscover meaning to life.

It is now well recognised that clinical depression has a very high incidence in the elderly population. But it is less well realised that depression is only part of a much larger phenomenon of maladjustment in late life. According to a recent review, if the rates of clinically significant depression are in the region of 10 to 15% of the general elderly population, "the rates of 'demoralization' are probably at least double this figure" (Gurland & Toner, 1982). Demoralisation, although less dramatic in appearance than clinical depression, is a more diffuse condition and more difficult to change because of its associated characteristics of loss of motivation, apathy, and neglect of potentialities. People may be well aware of their problems but unable to cope effectively with trying to find a new role, a new spouse, or a purpose in life. Depression and demoralization both influence, and are influenced by, decline in physical and social functioning. Studies in England indicate that depression is a major factor leading to the decision to apply for residential care (Challis, 1978).

The particular fragility of late life is well expressed by Taylor and Ford in a recent article on life style and ageing, wherein they speak of "the possibility of viewing later life as a constant struggle to maintain cherished life-styles against the threatening impact of both external events and internal changes" (Taylor & Ford, 1981). The meaning an individual gives to his life is expressed in his particular life style. Taylor and Ford quote the much neglected study of Williams and Wirths, *Lives through the Years*, published in 1965 and based on in-depth interviews and observation of elderly people over a 10 year period, which provides much insight into the problems of adjusting to life events faced by individuals with different life styles. It indicates the value of a longitudinal and holistic approach to understanding change in old age and to the importance of life-span data for discovering the origin of life style, whether it be focussed on work, particular interpersonal relationships, the broader family, and so on.

Although the negative changes of late life are obviously of great concern, it would be misleading to introduce the concept of change in old age solely in a negative way, that is, as the loss of a desired stability. Adaptability remains an important quality of the human organism right into late life. Wisdom is a word we particularly apply to competent old people who have come to know themselves as well as their culture. Competence also implies being able to respond to new demands. Certainly we must not underestimate the ageing individual's capacity to make adjustments, learn new skills, and start afresh on certain tasks.

Perhaps the most attractive image of old age in the scientific literature is the one briefly depicted by psychotherapist Erik Erikson in his book, *Childhood and Society* (Erikson, 1963), in which he proposes the achievements of "generativity" and "integrity" as the final developmental tasks of life. Although what he writes about them is brief, *generativity*, which arises in middle age and represents the individual's need to gain a sense of having contributed to the future, and the different components of *integrity*, which is an acceptance of one's own past life without regrets, a loss of fear of death, and an advance to an "eternal" perspective on human life, provide appealing answers to the problems of ageing and death. Even if unrealistic as goals for all, these concepts provide standards against which to judge the contemporary experience of elderly people.

Some advances have been made in giving more substance to such developmental theories of ageing as, for example, the delineating of the nature of ego transcendence in old age (Peck, 1968; Sherman, 1981); the describing of attitudes to the finitude of human life (Munnichs, 1966); and the analysing of the role of grandparenthood experience in psychosocial development in late life (Kivnick, 1981). Also related to Erikson's theory is Butler's concept of the *life review* (Butler, 1963), in which reminiscence in old age is seen to reflect a universal process of analysing one's past life in search of an acceptable identity with which to face the end of life. But there has been, relatively speaking, little investigation of psychosocial change in old age. The different functions of reminiscence, for example, remain little understood despite their potential importance (Merriam, 1980). Certainly old people vary considerably in the significance they attribute to reminiscence (Coleman, 1985). We thus return to the subject of attitude to past life later in the essay.

The study of change, both positive and negative, in late life raises a great number of conceptual and methodological issues, and the aim of this chapter is to highlight a few of them. The first is the issue of the interrelationship between psychological and social change in old age. It is now well understood that psychological development varies according to a particular society's norms and values. The study of old age in a changing society, however, raises more profound issues, because the old people studied may have, in the course of their own lives, experienced major changes in their society's norms and values. Adjustment to old age is, in part, adjustment to such changes.

The second issue discussed is the very notion of change in adult life. It can be argued that "development" is an inappropriate word because of its biological connotations of predetermined stages of growth. But if biology does not provide appropriate models, are there other models available from different disciplines that might be found more useful in describing change in adult life?

Thirdly the issue of quantitative versus qualitative research is addressed. Given the complexity of individual change in adult life, it may be doubted whether large sample quantitative research is likely to be fruitful in delineating the nature of this change. Large numbers both of subjects and variables have to be included to produce generalisable results, which may in the end have little explanatory power. A case is made for more qualitative research on individual cases, although it is acknowledged that such an approach has problems of its own.

Finally the issue of life-span data is addressed. This book's theme is the importance of a life-span perspective for studying change in individual lives. In the study of elderly people this often means an analysis of retrospective data. Such data can, at one and the same time, be both invalid as a historical record and valuable as a source of evidence about the individual's self-concept. We therefore need to be clear about the status we give to data acquired from reminiscence.

THE INTERRELATIONSHIP OF PSYCHOLOGICAL AND SOCIAL CHANGE IN OLD AGE

A first step in making progress toward understanding change in old age, both positive and negative, is to achieve greater clarity in conceptualising the nature of the phenomenon we are interested in. However since Erikson formulated his particular theory of human development, we have become more conscious of the fact that the idea of a life-span psychology focussing on psychological variables alone is something of an illusion. All life-span study by definition has to be sociological as well, that is, concerning itself with development and change in people's lives in a given society and over a given time period.

Moreover, it is suggested that the rate of change in society has quickened. As Fiske and Chiriboga remark in their chapter (Chapter 9), "societal upheavals and responses to them in the generation of the 1960s may have disrupted such normative or presumed stage sequences." They point to generational differences in reaction to divorce. Taking an extreme view it is possible to imagine that the pace of change could be so rapid that longitudinal studies would only be of historical interest, and the idea of drawing preventative policies from longitudinal research, which Maas in his chapter (Chapter 8) puts stress on, could not be realised. The situation to which one applied these policies would always be different. For preventative work we therefore need to concentrate on research topics with short term payoffs.

Our own studies have highlighted the particular problems of old people in adapting to British society of the post 1960s. Both of us interviewed elderly people living in special housing for the elderly: one in a longitudinal study that commenced in the early 1970s and continued for 10 years, focussing on the function of reminiscence in adjustment to old age and including material on attitudes to contemporary society (Coleman, 1972, 1985); and the other in a study focussed on adjustment to old age in a changing society (McCulloch, 1981, 1985). It was clear in both studies that the majority of elderly people interviewed expressed a distinctly negative attitude to modern society when comparing past and present. We would agree with Fiske and Chiriboga who write in their contribution that a generational gap such as the one that has now come to exist "creates serious problems for old people because it threatens to deprive them of a sense of generativity."

Of particular interest is our finding that whereas both a positive attitude to one's own past life and a positive attitude to modern society are correlated positively with high morale, they are independent of one another. It is thus possible to argue that the past and the present tend to form different routes to adjustment to old age, either taking the form of acceptance of modern values or a successful retreat from them. In the latter case the individual seems to need not only to take a positive attitude to his own past life, but also to be very sure of himself (i.e., have a strong self-concept). In other words a negative attitude to present society is compatible with high morale so long as the individual has a self-assured view of himself, his own values, and his past life. Such an alienation or lack of feeling at home in modern society could be considered to be distinctly at odds with the Eriksonian concept of "integrity." But it must be admitted that a number of elderly people appear to gain strength from a rejection of the present and from a sense that they have seen the best (Coleman, 1985).

In his study of elderly people's attitudes, the second author of this essay carried out detailed analysis of data collected from 46 individuals in semi-structured interviews focussing on the individual's attitudes to young people, the state of modern society, religion, death, and the individual's satisfaction with his own life (McCulloch, 1985). Both qualitative and quantitative methods of analysis revealed the presence of three major clusters or groups of attitudes. The first of these was referred to as *moral siege*. Individuals in a state of moral siege tended to have a high moral estimation of old people and a low estimation of the young. Differences rather than similarities between generations were emphasised, and such individuals tended to actively compare past and present. Thus this group of ideas seems to represent a belief that the elderly individual has made the right choice and holds the right values. The second group of attitudes was referred to as *questioning*. This group seems to embody a perception that society is falling apart, and this was linked specifically to an inability to maintain religious beliefs and make sense of the way society is moving. The third and final cluster of attitudes identified was referred to as *negative view of present*. This represents various attitudes of condemnation towards modern society. In a follow-up study focussing on the elderly individual's perception of change in society, a similar but better defined cluster of attitudes designated "accepts/rejects change" was identified.

There was some evidence in the study for both age-related change and the existence of a relationship between morale and attitudes to modern society. The questioning construct was significantly negatively related with morale and age, and very significantly associated with women rather than men. Possibly a state of questioning could be a transitional state to other patterns of thought, or it could be associated with a particular cohort. The negative view of present construct was also significantly and negatively related to morale. Moral siege, however, showed no relationship with morale, perhaps because this very pervasive pattern of thought could show at least two outcomes: It could lead to a detachment from society in the sense of alienation or to a valuing of one's past life, leading to high self-esteem.

The likelihood of alienation from modern society is of course crucially related to social change and may well have increased in the 1960s and 1970s in the way Fiske and Chiriboga suggest. This phenomenon of increasing alienation with time is well illustrated by one old man, the first author interviewed in 1971, who, though very negative about what had happened to Britain in the previous two decades said emotionally that Britain had been, and still was, a country worth fighting for. In 1981 he denied this to be so, and when confronted with this difference stressed that his current feelings reflected a changed attitude over the years. In other ways he was well adjusted and had indeed become more accepting of his past life. But he was less at home in Britain. Things had changed too much, and most importantly so, the values—those fundamental ideas that were perceived to be important in the society in which he lived. (Coleman, 1985).

A graphic description of one type of "wise old man" in contemporary society seems to us to be contained in Saul Bellow's novel, *Mr Sammler's Planet* (Bellow, 1969). This portrayal is of a dignified and kindly old man who has survived a lot, but who has now ceased to be at home in his own society—he sees it, as it were, from outside—and who is constantly made conscious of his own impotence in that society. This is made brutally clear to him when he is asked to give a lecture to a group of students and is jeered off the rostrum, his contribution being too "out of date."

Perhaps gerontologists have paid insufficient attention to the crucial issue of values. People are brought up with certain standards for evaluating behaviour, and it is very difficult for them to accommodate great changes in their own lifetime that overthrow these values. There is a remarkable passage in George Orwell's *Coming Up for Air* that indicates the importance of continuity:

> It's also true that people then had something that we haven't got now. What? It was simply that they didn't think of the future as something to be terrified of. It isn't that life was softer then than now. Actually it was harsher. . . . And yet what was it that people had in those days? A feeling of security, even when they weren't secure. More exactly, it was a feeling of continuity. All of them knew they'd got to die . . . but what they didn't know was that the order of things could change . . . It's easy enough to die if the things you care about are going to survive . . . Individually they were finished but their way of life would continue. (Orwell, 1939)

There is the implication in this passage that in the past (in this context, before World War I) it was easier to achieve integrity, because the values a man was born with were likely still to be dominant when he died. It is certainly worth exploring the idea that sharing common values or goals is vital to continued integration in society and that adaptability in respect of values may be particularly difficult in old age. Kalish (1969) puts it thus:

> Old people, inevitably, have internalised the values of their society. They have lived by these values all their lives and have transmitted them to subsequent generations. Once old, of course, these values may work against them, but denying the validity of these values would be tantamount to denying the validity of their lives. (p. 87)

THE CONCEPT OF DEVELOPMENT

It might be countered that a notion such as integrity is more than just idealistic; it is in some sense a natural state of development and a damning reflection on the aberrant nature of a society that hinders its development. In such an argument we have to be very careful of the enticement of the word *development*. As a term applied to change that we value positively, it obviously has a very wide use. But in the context of the study of psychology the idea is often an epigenetic one, derived from embryology, wherein development proceeds along a certain path towards a specific end point, and the pattern is universal in the species. There is a passage in Erikson's *Childhood and Society* that indicates his thinking was indeed epigenetic: "society, in principle, tends to be constituted as to meet and invite the succession of potentialities for interaction and attempts to safeguard and to encourage the proper rate and proper sequence of their unfolding" (Erikson, 1963). It is clear from this passage that Erikson was viewing human development as determined by an inner logic and that the role of the environment is only to facilitate this development.

Such a framework is seen as untenable today. We do not now see the social environment either as stable or passive in regard to its effects on human behaviour. Indeed if stages in human development do exist in a particular society it may well be because they reflect social requirements. For example, one way of interpreting the developmental changes in a longitudinal study, such as the one Haan analyzes in this collection, is to show how people come to conform to certain standards (in her case, to the ideal of "mother" and "father" in post war American society, becoming more nurturant and so on). But these social requirements vary to a greater or lesser degree across societies and over cultural periods.

It is also in the sociocultural context that one can perceive more clearly that the essential problem for elderly people in modern western societies is precisely the lack of clear societal expectations as to the roles they should adopt. Erikson's remark that "society . . . tends to be constituted as to meet and invite the succession of potentialities" has a hollow ring for most elderly people in modern societies.

Aside from the notion of predetermined growth, however, there is one idea contained in epigenetic models of development that may be more applicable to the study of adulthood and ageing: the concept of emergence of new properties. The second author of this chapter has detailed this in a recent article in which he also illustrates the application of catastrophe theory to the study of transitions in old age (McCulloch, 1981). As stressed earlier it would be of great value if we could understand more fully the often quite sudden changes that older people show, whether these changes take the form of deterioration of physical function, motivation to live independently, or retreat into an inner world. Internal and external factors are both likely to be involved, separately and in concert, triggering decisive change of direction in behaviour.

Such turning points have been well documented in biographical and autobiographical works. A telling example of a turning point of this kind in the life of an ageing person is that of Sibelius's creative "suicide." Sibelius, the great Finnish nationalist composer, lived to the age of 91, but he published no new works after the age of 61. This was surprising, for some of his greatest works were published when he was in his late fifties. These included the sixth and seventh symphonies and the tone poem "Tapiola." Why Sibelius suddenly stopped producing music has always puzzled musicologists such as Parmet (1959), who states that:

> It is difficult to believe that Sibelius' creative output, which had been so abundant up to the time of the seventh symphony . . . should suddenly have petered out. Despite the fact that he had already reached the age of sixty Sibelius still enjoyed uninterrupted . . . creative power, no sign of age, no weakening . . . in his power of expression had been noticeable in his work during the years immediately preceding the self imposed silence. (p. 145)

In his analysis Parmet postulates two major factors as precipitating Sibelius's silence. Firstly was the "revolution in the world of music", in which Sibelius played no part, following World War I. Indeed he found this revolution alienating, as his private correspondence shows: "I have acquired an inconquerable distaste for the modern tendency. And out of this grew a sense of solitude." He described his fourth symphony as a "protest against the compositions of today."

At this time Sibelius was probably referring to the impressionist movement. However, from his point of view there was worse to come in the shape of composers like Stravinsky and Schoenberg. In the 1920s, Parmet argues, all that was not radically modern was either overlooked or condemned. Therefore, "because of the hypersensitive nature of his [Sibelius's] disposition the intensity of his distaste [for modern music] was increased to such an extent that his decision not to publish any new works was final." (Parmet, 1959, p. 151)

The other major factor in Sibelius's creative suicide was, Parmet believes, his lack of self-confidence. Sibelius suffered greatly from stage fright and often did not allow works he thought inadequate to be published despite the favourable opinions of others. But, paradoxically, it was at this point in his career when Sibelius was beginning to achieve a universal reputation. Drawing all these strands together Parmet comes to the following conclusion:

> Sibelius found himself in such a position that every new work he published would meet with terrible competition from two opposite directions. From one direction he would have to withstand the competition of his own earlier compositions . . . from the other . . . he would be faced with the competition of the great modernists . . . he had no faith in himself or his position in the contemporary world. (Parmet, 1959 p. 156)

So Sibelius simply stopped working. This transition can be expressed in a catastrophe model in which the controlling variables are the development of modern music and Sibelius's low self-esteem (McCulloch, 1981). It is the combination of these two factors that leads to the sudden change in Sibelius's behaviour. Thus his life shows how an interaction between social and psychological variables can bring about psychosocial change in late life.

QUALITATIVE VERSUS QUANTITATIVE RESEARCH IN PSYCHOSOCIAL ADJUSTMENT

In building up knowledge of individual change in old age, we are painting on such a vast canvas—involving changing individuals in a changing society—that the pieces thrown up by research hardly seem to add up quickly enough to maintain a sense of progress. In such conditions there is considerable value in researchers concentrating their attention on particular topics for study.

In fact the great areas of stability in personality throughout adulthood make a focussing on actual periods of change a less daunting prospect than it might at first appear. It is at the limits of stability that we can make our most rewarding observations: for example, where the individual personality faces new challenges and is threatened with breakdown. The study of a way a person copes in abnormal conditions provides crucial evidence of his basic psychophysiological makeup and personality processes. The same point is made by Olbrich in his contribution (Chapter 7): "normative and nonnormative periods of transition, critical life-events, hassles, or crises and conflicts requiring new adaptations seem to be important situations in which to look for processes of adaptive functioning and in which to detect personal strategies or programs of functioning."

It is in old age that failures to cope are most likely to occur. The extent and unpredictable nature of breakdowns in the relation between environmental demands and a person's abilities may make the restoration of equilibrium well-nigh impossible. The person ceases to live as he wants to. A multitude of minor maladjustments may occur or even a major mental breakdown. How the individual copes with life's difficulties in old age is therefore a most crucial area for research (Munnichs, 1980).

If psychosocial adjustment and breakdown are to be the main focus of our concern in the study of individual change in old age, we are still left with major dilemmas regarding how we should set about this task. For instance, should we choose to study a few individuals in depth or as many as we can relying on more easily obtainable information? This is the fundamental dilemma of qualitative versus quantitative research. The nomothetic tradition has been dominant in the social sciences, especially psychology, for a long period. However, there is now a great deal of disillusionment with the results of mass surveys and the grave restrictions they put on a researcher who has to conceptualise and categorise his data even before he has collected it; so many opportunities to explore and develop ideas while still in contact with the individual being studied are missed. On the other hand, the traditional arguments against ideographic approaches, such as lack of control and generalisability, have not lost their force.

One of the most vigorous recent exponents of the case-study approach has been Bromley (1977, 1978), and he has applied his arguments most particularly to the study of ageing. He believes that psychological case study is the method of choice for studying adjustment to old age for a number of reasons. It allows the investigator to focus on the "person in a situation" rather than ignoring environmental influences. It also allows the investigator to use his imagination, explore the individual perceptions, and follow up lines of enquiry relevant to the particular individual in his unique situation. By looking at a lot of variables at once, certain relationships can be teased out, which could never be possible in a large-scale study. Indeed, even if one was able to cover a large number of variables in a survey study, one would need a correspondingly enlarged number of subjects to carry out the relevant statistical procedures to test for significant relationships.

Though this approach clearly produces a problem of generalisability, Bromley believes that this can be overcome by the accumulation of a sufficient body of research such that "one could develop a systematic body of 'case law'—based on comparisons and contrasts between individual cases—which would constitute the empirical generalisations and rational principles required for an objective . . . science of personality study" (Bromley, 1978, p. 38).

The first author of this essay has tried the aforesaid approach in an exploratory longitudinal study into the functions of reminiscence, with results arguably more satisfactory than in the standard types of study (Coleman, 1985). The problems with such an approach seem largely practical: Subjects need to be highly motivated to take part in a study involving a case approach. If the study were "academic," there would ostensibly be little the investigator could offer the subject in exchange for his cooperation. If the study were restricted to applied settings, the subjects would presumably already be defined as "problems," therefore making it difficult to formulate theories of adjustment that had general relevance. More importantly it is not clear that different investigations would produce data comparable in such a way as to lead to a general theory; the "case law" would not be uniquely valid, but restricted by the idiosyncracies and interests of the investigators. Moreover, as we have already implied, a body of case law might not emerge fast enough to keep pace with sociocultural change. It is doubtful whether we have the time to build up knowledge of psychosocial adjustment in old age by the detailed examination of individual cases before the case law becomes obsolete.

There are grounds for thinking, however, that in an applied setting all this might be less of a problem. In an applied setting observations are likely to be less sporadic, and there are other trained professionals involved who can act as observers. Indeed in certain specialised fields, such as psychogeriatrics, case law is already emerging, informal and unsystematic as it may be. Psychiatrists have begun to develop theories on the prior personality styles of people both especially vulnerable and especially resistant to developing depression in old age. They also have theories on the physical and social stress most likely to lead to depressive reactions, as well as on the importance of heriditary factors and life-history events. These theories are of course based on detailed acquaintance with a substantial number of individual cases (Bergmann, 1978).

Psychologists have every reason to feel ashamed that they are isolated from this process of establishing case law. A large number of studies have taken place in social gerontology on adjustment to change in old age, but it seems a great pity that little or no attempt has been made to link them to studies of functional psychiatric disorders. We know that these disorders are associated with the same factors as poor adjustment in old age, namely bad physical health, isolation, and poverty, and it seems false to draw such a sharp distinction between concepts of maladjustment, unhappiness, and mental illness. Depression in old age, for instance, is not an exceptional condition. It is so common in our society as to be regarded as one of the "normal" conditions of old age.

Our response to depression and the other functional disorders in old age needs to be based on an understanding of adjustment to ageing as it emerges in the social sciences, as well as in clinical medicine. At the same time social scientists should be working hand in hand with psychiatrists in elucidating a greater understanding of the whole range of maladjustments in the elderly. Here the case-study approach is undoubtedly of great value. As Bromley himself indicates, most examples of maladjustment are amenable to common-sense analysis, using ordinary language (Bromley, 1978).

THE IMPORTANCE OF LIFE HISTORY TO AN UNDERSTANDING OF LATER LIFE ADJUSTMENT

One further point worth making concerns the importance to be given to life-history information. There is a significant distinction to be made between retrospective material, which is being used as evidence to construct an objective history, and that which is being used to show how an individual perceives himself and his past history. In her contribution Haan concludes, quite correctly in our opinion, that "self reports . . . probably do not provide a reliable base for building a general developmental theory." Each person can probably tell from his own experience how very difficult it is to reconstruct previous states of mind and processes of thought we have undergone. The changed perspectives we have gained in the meantime tend to make the previous viewpoint unobtainable: The new viewpoints get in the way. This is not to say that past memories are worthless records. There is some evidence that in certain situations they can be very accurate (Field & Honzik, 1981). They can also be very useful in suggesting ideas for longitudinal studies.

The remembered past is also of great importance in itself. We try to maintain our life story in good order, as a coherent account (Johnson, 1976). We change it subtly but purposefully as we grow older. It reflects a great deal about how we have learned to live with ourselves. We are not indifferent to its implications for our self-esteem, and it is therefore often selective. However our life story is not wholly biased; sometimes certain unpleasant features cannot be excluded. Regrets and guilt feelings remain associated with particular episodes, and their resolution forms the basis of Butler's theory of the life review. In the study already referred to, it was shown that dissatisfaction with past life can be associated with demoralization and depression even in the presence of such otherwise positive factors as a strongly expressed sense of self and a positive view towards contemporary society (Coleman, 1985).

Remembering is of course an area of human psychology that is important at all stages of life. Children need someone who has shared all or part of their life history with them, someone whom they can ask "do you remember?" How pitiful is the plight of a child in an institution, with high turnover of staff, who is left with no one around to whom these words can be said! At the same time even private memories, and in particular memories of childhood, can be a great source of comfort and strength in adult life, as witnessed by a number of writers, and most perceptively by Salaman (1982).

In old age there are grounds for arguing that reminiscence becomes of especial importance. Studies have been carried out which indicate that life reviewing is adaptive at least for those who feel dissatisfied with their pasts (Coleman, 1974). A number of observations suggest that those who put a high value on their memories of past life cope well with old age (McMahon & Rhudick, 1967; Coleman, 1985). Indeed the one major developmental process during ageing that has been observed in a wide variety of settings is an increase in *interiority*, a change in orientation from outer world to inner world, including, importantly, one's memories (Neugarten, 1964, 1979).

It is easy to see how one's inner thoughts and feelings can assume greater importance as one is cut off from the outer world through factors common to old age, such as loss of occupation, physical disability, sensory deprivation/attentional difficulties, bereavement, isolation, and the changed norms and values around one. Truly an old person can come to live in a world of his own. The individual's past may remain the one sure possession he has left if he knows how to use it. In institutional settings this is often, tragically, not the case, as individuals have often both been uprooted and deprived of links with their past lives, such as photographs and other simple reminders, among their possessions.

However, as in the whole field of study of adjustment to old age, we have no easy answers. Past memories for some may be a help in coping with loss in old age, and for others they may not be. The very contrast between past and present situations may be too much to bear. Adjustment to the present may more easily be obtained by resisting the "call" of memory as far as is possible and turning to whatever activity still lies to hand (Coleman, 1985). Only by acquainting ourselves deeply with the circumstances of each individual's life can we hope to understand their various attitudes toward ageing.

SUMMARY AND CONCLUSIONS

The study of psychosocial change in late life poses a great challenge to contemporary social sciences. The rising number of very old people in the population and the consequent pressure on health and social services have at last brought into prominence issues to do with deterioration and breakdown in functioning in old age. The social sciences, in conjunction with the medical and biological sciences, have a very important role to play in studying the onset and possible prevention of deteriorative change in old people—minimising the period of "predeath" in individuals' lives. At the same time there is a danger in emphasising the negative aspects of ageing to the neglect of positive aspects. Wisdom and integrity are also important themes in the study of late life.

It has however been argued in the present essay that such positive developments, and in particular, the achievement of integrity, may be more difficult to achieve in a society with fast-changing values. Rejection of the values by which one has lived is hard to endure, and as many elderly people disapprove strongly of modern values, successful adjustment to old age can often only be achieved by emphasising the superiority of the past. Integrity, if it is understood to include an accepting attitude to both past and present, is as a result difficult to realise. The issue of the relativity (i.e., culture-specific nature) of the study of psychosocial development has then a particular twist when it comes to the study of ageing, for the process of ageing involves adjustment to changes in the culture to varying degrees. In modern societies it is particularly marked.

We can no longer assume a harmony between the nature of society and individual needs as earlier authors on human development such as Erikson seem to have done. Modern society indeed may be inimical to the potentials of elderly people. Rather than applying a uniform developmental model of change in later life, it may therefore be more fruitful to study in detail the problems of individuals adapting to changing circumstances in changing societies. The solutions particular individuals find are interesting and worth recording in their own right, and may serve as models for others.

For such reasons it is very important to develop a proper methodology of qualitative research involving case studies. The social sciences and in particular psychology have neglected the potentials of case studies in the wake of enthusiasm for the new possibilities opened up by technological advances in the analysis of large number data. But in the field of ageing, in particular, we need much more illuminative research, which case studies provide. The case study attempts to assemble sufficient evidence—and here we can learn from the practice of the legal profession—on a single case. This way one is able to answer with confidence the question set, for example, on adjustment to change. It provides paradigms whose limiting conditions can be tested by further case studies. That such a programme of research seems so daunting is a sad comment on the overemphasis statistical survey research has received. However such inductive activity as the building up of theory from individual cases does take place, necessarily, in many practical fields of work concerned with change in later life (i.e., in the psychiatry of old age). All concerned would benefit from a closer link between social gerontological research and applied activities such as medicine and social work, which have never lost their respect for the significance of the study of the individual case.

In all research on ageing, whether case study or not, it is important to preserve the links with earlier periods of life. It cannot too often be stressed that old people are people who have grown older. The links with earlier life and even, and maybe in particular, childhood could be much closer than we imagine. Developmental models such as Erikson's, which stress the interconnectedness of the individual's tasks at all stages of life, have great value, although we should treat with caution inferences on rigid progression of stages. However as opportunities for truly longitudinal research on the life-span are rare, we must often rely on retrospective information about the past, and here we must be clear about the status of the information we gain. Memory has as one of its functions to serve the present, and indeed it needs to be studied in old age for this very reason as well. But we must also try to build up as accurate picture as we can of the real past. Perhaps here too social sciences can learn from other disciplines—in particular from recent developments in the study of oral history.

REFERENCES

Bellow, S. *Mr. Sammler's planet*. New York: Weidenfeld & Nicolson, 1969.

Bergmann, K. Neurosis and personality disorder in old age. In A. D. Isaacs & F. Post (Eds.), *Studies in geriatric psychiatry* (41–75). Chichester: Wiley, 1978.

Bromley, D. B. *Personality description in ordinary language*. London: Wiley, 1977.

Bromley, D. B. Approaches to the study of personality changes in adult life and old age. In A. Isaacs & F. Post (Eds.), *Studies in geriatric psychiatry* (17–40). Chichester: Wiley, 1978.

Butler, R. N. The life review: An interpretation of reminiscence in the aged. *Psychiatry,* 1963, *26,* 65–76.

Challis, D. J. *The measurement of outcome in social care of the elderly.* Paper presented at the Department of Health and Social Security seminar on care of the elderly, University of Kent, 1978, June.

Coleman, P. G. *The role of the past in adaptation to old age.* Unpublished doctoral dissertation, University of London, 1972.

Coleman, P. G. Measuring reminiscence characteristics from conversation as adaptive features of old age. *International Journal of Aging and Human Development,* 1974, *5,* 281–294.

Coleman, P. G. *The ageing process and the role of reminiscence.* Chichester: Wiley, in press.

Erikson, E. H. *Childhood and society* (2nd ed.). New York: Norton, 1963.

Field, D., & Honzik, M. P. *Personality and accuracy of retrospective reports of aging women.* Paper presented at the International Congress of Gerontology, Hamburg, 1981, July.

Gurland, B. J., & Toner, J. A. Depression in the elderly: A review of recently published studies. In C. Eisdorfer (Ed.) *Annual review of gerontology and geriatrics* (Vol. 3, pp. 228–265). New York: Springer, 1982.

Johnson, M. That was your life: A biographical approach to later life. In J. Munnichs & W. van den Heuvel (Eds.), *Dependency or interdependency in old age* (147–161). The Hague: Martinus Nijhoff, 1976.

Kalish, R. A. The old and new as generation gap allies. *The Gerontologist*, 1969, *9*, 83–89.

Kivnick, H. Q. Grandparenthood and the mental health of grandparents. *Ageing and Society*, 1981, *1*, 365–391.

McCulloch, A. W. What do we mean by "development" in old age? *Ageing and Society*, 1981, *1*, 229–245.

McCulloch, A. W. *Adjustment to old age in a changing society.* Unpublished doctoral dissertation, University of Southampton, 1985.

McMahon, A. W., & Rhudick, P. J. Reminiscing in the aged: An adaptational response. In: S. Levin & R. Kahana (Eds.), *Psychodynamic studies on aging: Creativity, reminiscing and dying* (64–78). New York: International University Press, 1967.

Merriam, S. The concept and function of reminiscence: A review of the research. *The Gerontologist*, 1980, *20*, 604–609.

Munnichs, J. M. A. *Old age and finitude.* Basle: Karger, 1966.

Munnichs, J. M. A. Gedrag, ouder worden en levensloop (Behaviour, ageing & life span). *Gerontologie*, 1980, *11*, 84–92.

Neugarten, B. L. and Associates *Personality in Middle and Late Life.* New York: Atherton, 1964.

Neugarten, B. L. Time, age and the life cycle. *American Journal of Psychiatry*, 1979, *136*, 887–894.

Orwell, G. *Coming up for air.* London: Collancz, 1939.

Parmet, S. *The symphonies of Sibelius.* London: Cassell, 1959.

Peck, R. C. Psychological developments in the second half of life. In B. L. Neugarten (Ed.), *Middle age and aging.* Chicago: The University of Chicago Press, 1968.

Salaman, E. A collection of moments. In U. Neisser (Ed.), *Memory observed: Remembering in natural contexts.* San Francisco: Freeman, 1982.

Sherman, E. *Counseling the aging: An integrative approach.* New York: The Free Press, 1981.

Taylor, R., & Ford, G. Lifestyle and ageing: Three traditions in lifestyle research. *Ageing and Society*, 1981, *1*, 329–345.

Williams, R. H., & Wirths, C. G. *Lives through the years.* Chicago: Aldine-Atherton, 1965.

THE FAMILY SUPPORT CYCLE: PSYCHOSOCIAL ISSUES IN THE AGING FAMILY

Vern L. Bengtson and Joseph Kuypers

INTRODUCTION

Certainly one of the things older people fear most is the specter of being a burden to their families. One of the most sobering prospects for middle-aged children is the possibility of formerly independent parents becoming chronically ill and in need of long-term care.

Aging of course brings change. What may be insufficiently recognized is that the changes associated with aging present challenges to the family as well as to the individual.

Confronting the challenges of aging within its overall context is often difficult, both for the family members themselves and the professional seeking to help them. There are several reasons for this. First, the problem of sudden dependency or chronic illness facing an aging family is so often unexpected—and the prognosis so often appears to be hopeless—that the family becomes immobilized. A second reason is the lack of norms regarding filial duty. The crisis of an aging parent or grandparent often generates confusion, and with it guilt and conflict, among family members regarding responsibility for caretaking and support. A third reason is the lack of precedent in modes of dealing with the problem. In adolescence, crises are expected: Parent–child conflict is anticipated, and the negotiation of crises and conflict is carried out as a matter of normal family processes. No parallel expectations or normative guidelines are readily apparent for the negotiation of conflict situations in old age, nor are there conceptual tools and theoretical models from which the professional can chart a course of action (Bengston & Treas, 1980; Brody & Spark, 1977; Kuypers & Trute, 1978).

This essay suggests one conceptual framework for understanding some problems and processes involving family networks and aging. We employ a heuristic systems model derived from what was originally termed the *Social Breakdown Syndrome* and applied to the etiology of mental health. The focus is on social mechanisms of labeling that operate upon and within aging families under stress. We feel this perspective can assist gerontologists and family practitioners in understanding successful or unsuccessful negotiation of change, as confronted by aging individuals and their families. We focus on four psychosocial constructs important in understanding family supports and aging: (1) negotiation of change and continuity; (2) competence in individuals and families; (3) crisis and labeling; and (4) intervention and the restoration of competence.

THE NEGOTIATION OF CHANGE AND CONTINUITY

Consider the inevitable challenge that continually confronts the aging individual and his family: the negotiation of change. There are three characteristic processes that are reflected in family negotiations of continuity—not just in the older family, but in younger families as well (Bengston & Treas, 1980). These mirror issues of family life, which forever confront participants and may never achieve complete closure, are autonomy versus dependency, connectedness versus separateness, and continuity versus dislocation of the family as a functional unit.

AUTONOMY VERSUS DEPENDENCY

The tension between autonomy and dependency (or interdependency) can be seen at each stage of individual development. The family is often the most central arena for conflict in this area. Adolescents and parents struggle with demands to loosen family ties and authority, while still receiving and giving succor and support. Erikson (1950) has characterized the dilemma for the developing adolescent as reflecting first the crises of identity and role diffusion and second the crisis of intimacy versus isolation. In the parents' eyes, this strain toward autonomy may signify chaos, a challenge to family life itself, as children strive for greater freedom to determine their own fate. In the teenagers' eyes, the struggle is over personal control: the wish to define their lives as independent of parental authority.

In the transitions of old age we also can see the confrontation between autonomy and dependency: A previously independent autonomous adult encounters sudden dependency brought on by sickness, or gradual shifts in dependency prompted by retirement, widowhood, or other role losses. The older parent, facing uncertainty or crisis, may long for unsolicited signs of concern and caretaking from their children; yet the older parent may recoil from the prospect of being dependent on children. Their children, by the same token, struggle with ambivalence: between duty to parents and duty to themselves and their own children, and between doing too much for their parents and doing too little. The tension between autonomy and dependency requires negotiation as both generations struggle with the adaptations required of normal changes of aging (Smith & Bengtson, 1979).

Connectedness versus Separateness

The negotiation of autonomy involves both generations and is frequently a source of conflict. Often it has an effect on a second characteristic issue: the tension between connectedness to the family and separateness from it. Some personality theorists subsume this issue under the term *individuation*: the capacity to establish and maintain an identity and life style that is supported in, but not unduly determined by, family definition and history. Hess and Handel (1959) suggest this is the major psychosocial agenda in family socialization during adolescence.

But the issue of connectedness versus individual separateness persists throughout later life. Following a crisis such as a stroke, adult children must struggle to sort out a reasonable and balanced degree of family involvement and caretaking. A less dramatic example is when a parent appears to psychologically disown a child for reasons of unconventional lifestyle, sexual preference, or even religion. In these instances, guilt may reign supreme as all parties uneasily confront the issue of how strongly the family will strive to hold power over an individual's behavior. Fundamental to these differences of autonomy/dependency and connectedness/separateness are issues of power, authority, and control—issues that persist over the entire history of a particular family's biography.

Transitions involving new social roles (widow, retiree, "empty nest" parent) may cause changes in definitions of what is good or bad, moral or immoral. Often it is supposed that other family members will disapprove of new behaviors or involvements, and thus a shroud of secrecy may be involved that is the source of puzzlement for the family.

Continuity versus Dislocation of the Family over Time

A third recurrent issue facing the family as it ages concerns the fundamental question of whether that family and its interpersonal bonds will survive into the future. Change involves confrontation of the unknown—an anxious challenge at the best of times—and prompts concern as to what will be lost and what will remain. Often the unknown in the older family is the spectre of disintegration of family life itself (Kuypers & Trute, 1978). Hence parents may harbor a deep-seated apprehension that family life, as they have known it and nurtured it, will be lost when the children launch their more autonomous existence. Later in time, children may fear a loss of their own hard-fought autonomy if they come closer to their elderly parents in times of need.

While the form of the issue of continuity versus dislocation may change as the family ages, we maintain that the issue is constant. For the parents, the essential struggle may be to hold onto family as they know it, but for the child, the struggle is to loosen the bonds of family as they have experienced it. This is a manifestation of the "developmental stake" (Bengtson & Kuypers, 1971)—the psychosocial investment that each generation has in the parent–child dyad. Parents strive to hold on, while children strive to loosen bonds. Faced with a family transition (expectable or otherwise), the question of the family's very survival, as defined in the past, is at stake. The negotiation of family bondedness persists within families far beyond adolescence, just as developmental stake agendas persist well into later life. This is illustrated in the plot line of the Academy Award-winning film, *On Golden Pond,* wherein the 40-year-old Jane Fonda and her aging father attempt to negotiate three decades of uneasy truce regarding family dislocation.

Psychological Well-Being and Family Ties

The relationship between family life and mental health is reflected in each of these tensions. We have thus far argued that the normal course of family life involves negotiation between generations and, furthermore, that the negotiation often embodies conflict. Such conflict is often centered on the normal and inevitable—if often unanticipated—tension that surrounds recurrent issues of autonomy, connectedness, and survival.

How does family involvement in late life relate to the mental health of its members? It is often assumed that family relations influence the well-being of older family members. After all, families are, or should be, a source of assistance: most personality theories even suggest that families provide a context in which the self-concept is shaped. In the public mind, the relationship between family life and the mental health of the aged is unequivocal: Many assume that close intergenerational ties promote happiness, that a close knit family will care for its elder members, and that all parties should feel satisfied in the expression of their "filial maturity."

To be sure, there is some foundation for these assumptions if most older people derive satisfaction from interaction with their kin (Bengtson & Treas, 1980; Shanas, 1979). But there are other elderly individuals who have no families (Lopata, 1973) and others whose families are indifferent to them. In still other families, children are a source of continuing shame and discomfort to the aging parent.

Despite our cultural bias toward cordial and intimate family life, there is surprisingly little explicit evidence from surveys that older people without supportive kin networks are at a psychological disadvantage (Bengtson & Treas, 1980; Glenn, 1975). Indeed, several surveys suggest that intense interaction need not lead to greater happiness for older family members. For example, Kerckhoff's (1966) study of retired couples found that husbands and wives who lived close to their offspring had lower morale than those who lived farther away. In a large national survey of Americans aged 58–63, married men living with kin were less likely to report themselves "happy" than were those who shared housing solely with a wife (Murray, 1976). In a South Carolina survey of older widows, Arling (1976) reported no association between morale and contact with kin, especially that with children. Contact with friends and neighbors, on the other hand, did serve to reduce loneliness while increasing feelings of usefulness.

Given these data, as well as our own personal observation of the intense ambivalences encountered by all family members as they adapt to their aging family, we must caution against a simple notion that more family is necessarily better, or that closer is happier. As Hagestad (1981, 1984) has pointed out, the dynamics of aging families are complex, the issues are fundamental, and any image of what is a "good" or "happy" older family must be tempered by the immense variability displayed among families.

Contrasts Between Stages of the Family Cycle

Thus far we have implied that the older family and younger family face many similar concerns and issues; that these issues are complex; and that they involve change and renegotiation of issues such as autonomy versus dependence, connectedness versus separateness, and continuity versus dislocation.

But the older family is different, in many respects, from the younger family. These differences are crucial to explore, for they imply needed changes in family intervention theory. The contrasts help explain unique dilemmas facing participation in the aging family. The differences point the researcher to important areas of inquiry.

There are several important ways in which the family facing a crisis that involves an older person is different from the family in which the problem involves a younger member (Kuypers & Bengtson, 1983). A first contrast is our assumption of *decreasing involvement* with the family-of-orientation throughout life. It is culturally expected that "a man should leave his parents and cleave to his wife." There is the norm that problems of old age should not involve the middle aged as much as problems involving the middle-aged's children.

Second, there is the assumption of *diversification of loyalty*. Bondedness to one's parents is expected to decrease with adolescence and certainly into young adulthood. If seen in middle age, overdependency on one's parents, especially among males, is often regarded as a sign of weakness, immaturity, and a flaw of character.

A third contrast in the problem-solving style of older and younger families involves the greater use of *denial*. There may be a greater temptation to avoid facing the potential crisis, in part, because of the dismal subjective meaning attached to problems of aging. The problems of aging are often seen as irreversible, negative, and unresolvable. Moreover, they occur in the life of someone who has previously been independent and self-sustaining—unlike crises involving a child or a youth. Under such conditions, there is the temptation to deny, or to compartmentalize, the potential crisis.

A fourth difference between older and younger families dealing with crises involves the potential *negative history of the family* as a problem-solving unit. Families as they age carry with them the history of prior conflicts and problems: past issues and unresolved tensions concerning autonomy, connectedness, and innovation between the generations and among siblings. An older family has to deal with two, three, and perhaps four decades of unresolved intergenerational tension—historical baggage that may hinder the family's effective resolution of crises involving an aged parent.

In short, the three challenges involving autonomy, connectedness, and continuity can be seen in each stage of the family life-cycle. But they are particularly apparent as families attempt to negotiate the changes associated with the passage of time, and they may be particularly difficult to work through because of contrasts between older and younger families encountering crises.

Many families face crises of aging. And many deal with the difficulties of aging very adaptively. Why is it that some families negotiate these changes more easily than others? Why is it that some individuals appear to accept the consequences of aging more easily than others?

COMPETENCE AND BREAKDOWN

In charting the poorly understood dynamics of aging families, a second major construct that we find useful is that of *competence* and its opposite, *breakdown*. Competence is a useful description of the behavioral goal or ideal in negotiating the transitions of aging. Similar to definitions of mental health and to what is called adaptation, it is a practical conceptual tool for describing successful dynamics of the aging family.

THREE FACES OF COMPETENCE

Competence, as it relates to aging, can be defined in terms of three separate dimensions, as we have done in an earlier paper (Kuypers & Bengtson, 1973). The first is *adequate role performance*. Competence in a sociological sense involves doing what the social context sees as appropriate and carrying out in normatively acceptable ways the expectations of social positions one occupies. A second dimension of competence is more psychological: the *capacity to adapt*, or to cope, in response to new or unusual stimuli. Yet a third dimension of competence is social-psychological, involving *experienced mastery*, the sense that one has some degree of control or power over events or changes in one's situation. Competence must be seen in these facets: as adequate social performance, as the psychological capacity to adapt and cope, and as the phenomenological experience of mastery or efficacy over one's fate or surrounding environment.

LABELING AND PSYCHOSOCIAL INCOMPETENCE

An individual's competence may be assaulted in each of these dimensions by changes associated with aging. In an earlier essay, we examined the concept of the *Social Breakdown Cycle* to help understand how this massive assault might occur. Our model is represented in Figure 12.1. We posit a six-step cycle, a malignant spiral of breakdown and dependency and increasing incompetence, which may occur as individuals grow old in complex, industrialized societies. The steps of the cycle are indicated by numbered circles connected by negative valences (ar-

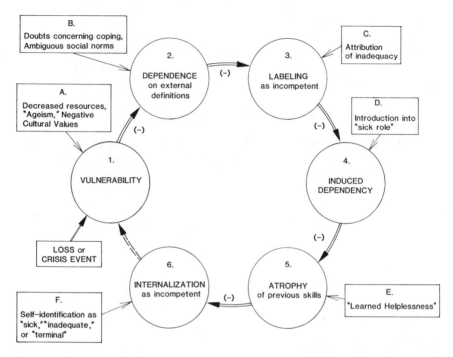

FIGURE 12.1   Social breakdown in old age; a vicious spiral of induced incompetence.

rows). The boxes represent inputs to the cycle that exacerbate the vicious spiral of incompetence. These inputs are from the social environment of the older person: some from the broader societal context and others from the immediate interpersonal environment of family, friends, or professionals.

The cycle begins (Step 1 in Figure 12.1) with *vulnerability,* wherein circumstances combine to increase the susceptibility of the older individual facing a crisis or loss. This vulnerability may arise from several inputs representing a potential change in the older person's psychological network (Input A in Figure 12.1), such as suddenly decreased resources (lack of health or economic problems following retirement); "ageism," (societal stereotyping about the aged or discrimination against them); or societal values that emphasize productivity at the expense of respect for eldership. These factors leave the older individual vulnerable; he is at risk in terms of his capacity to adequately perform roles, adapt to new stimuli, or have a sense of mastery. The vulnerability becomes acute in the presence of a crisis event, such as sudden illness, or from social losses, such as widowhood or retirement. Note that these losses can be normal, expectable changes in the aging individual's social world, and yet they are challenges to his or her continuity of psychosocial competence.

The older person is then susceptible to Step 2, *dependence on external definitions* of the situation. In new contexts with new stimuli, one frequently distrusts past patterns of behavior and orientations. The older individual, in the midst of a transition involving retirement, the empty nest, widowhood, chronic illness, or relocation, may be particularly dependent on external definitions of reality—since former experiences may be judged inadequate. Input B to this stage includes doubts expressed by others, or by the older individual, concerning the adequacy of past coping strategies and resources. A related set of inputs reflects ambiguous norms or expectations concerning behavior in this new and vulnerable situation.

This can lead, in turn, to Step 3, *social labeling of the older person as incompetent* (incapable of caring for oneself). The older individual receives the attribution of helplessness, or inadequacy, from his interpersonal environment (Input C). This leads to Step 4, *induced dependency.* Others begin to do for the older individual what he had previously done for himself. In a new environment, such as a nursing home, this step is particularly apparent. The older person becomes induced into a "sick role," by the surrounding environment (Input D) and is expected to act accordingly.

The fifth step of the cycle involves *atrophy of previous skills* for competence and independence. The external system may encourage this "learned helplessness" (Input E), which leads to the sixth stage, *internalization* of the new, dependent identity. The individual has been self-labeled as incompetent, and the Social Breakdown Syndrome can be said to have occurred. Yet this only leads to another round of the spiral, with the new identification creating yet more vulnerability (Step 1 again) and susceptibility to external labeling (Step 2), as well as labeling by self and others as incompetent (Step 3), and induced dependency (Step 4) and atrophy (Step 5). A self-fulfilling prophecy has been enacted and repeated.

This vicious spiral, originally developed to describe the creation of mental illness, is here applied to older individuals made vulnerable by fundamental developmental changes. It is a vicious cycle of incompetence, leading to a defined breakdown in terms of previous role performance, coping ability, and a sense of mastery or confidence.

Note that the key issue is vulnerability, which varies with individual circumstance. In our earlier formulation (Kuypers & Bengtson, 1973), we argued that most old people in contemporary industrial societies are vulnerable to incompetence labeling because of reduced resources, age-ism, and societal emphases on economic productivity values. But it should be pointed out that not all individuals succumb to the vicious spiral of the Social Breakdown Syndrome, even when a crisis event or significant loss occurs. Many who are vulnerable because of one role loss, such as in widowhood, are sufficiently able to continue other role performances and to use existing coping or adaptive strategies to main-tain a sense of mastery. They are effective enough to avoid dependence and labeling, the subsequent stages of the cycle. It is at this point that the family becomes crucial in the labeling of competence or incompe-tency as definitions of crisis, or of challenge.

CRISIS AND REALITY DISTORTION IN THE AGING FAMILY

The third construct necessary for a more comprehensive conceptual-ization of the aging family is *crisis*. A change becomes a crisis when the event is perceived, labeled, and responded to as a dramatic alteration in one's level of competence. According to contemporary crisis theory, as described by Kuypers and Trute (1978), there are three issues that define a crisis for a family or for an individual.

The first is a *hazardous event or problem*. The event or difficulty facing an aging family member may take various forms: illness, economic loss, death, relocation, accident. At any rate it involves change, a potential dislocation of previous patterns and accommodations.

A second component of crisis is the subjective response of witnesses who define the hazardous event as *threatening*. The meaning that actors attach to the event is crucial. As Spector and Kituse (1973) point out in discussing social problems, not all disasters are social problems; not all misfortunes are seen as requiring collective action; and not all difficulties are perceived as amenable to amelioration. Labeling the event as a crisis involves the social reconstruction of reality; the same event may not be defined as a crisis by different families.

The third feature of crisis is an *inability to respond with previous coping skills*. Prior patterns are seen as inadequate. The issue of adequate cop-ing focuses on whether the family can work as a unit through the crisis, wherein the aging individual is precariously placed, to give support and amelioration of the problem.

Our basic argument in this essay is that the older family, as it faces the recurrent issues of family life and as it faces the unique issues of its own aging members, is placed in a highly vulnerable position. This vul-nerability increases the crisis elements confronting the family and makes adaptation more difficult to deal with than when the family is younger. As depicted in Figure 12.2, there are several reasons for this particular susceptibility of aging families to the Social Breakdown spiral.

1. There is *vulnerability:* susceptibility to a shared view that the family is unable to cope with the crisis of aging dependency. Several inputs (as diagrammed in Figure 12.2) increase the vulnerability of the family to incompetent action in the face of crisis involving an older member. This crisis may be seen as more serious or less amenable to change than it may objectively be, because of the unprecedented degree or severity of the event or because problems of aging are viewed as instances of progressive, hopeless decline. This is *perceptual distortion* (Input A).

2. There may be conflicting loyalties and roles regarding generational membership (Input B) and apparent conflicts concerning how members should be involved in that crisis.

There is also (Input C), the lack of normative guidance in dealing with problems involving aged family members. In our culture we lack clear expectations concerning what one should do with a parent or parent-in-law in need.

There may be a resistance to greater intensity of involvement on the

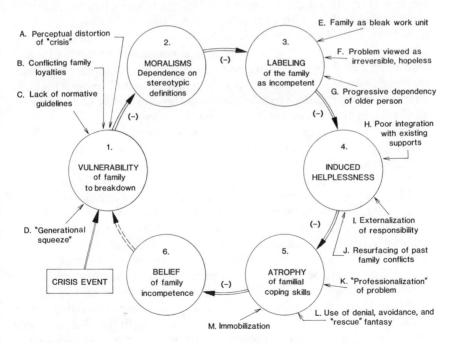

FIGURE 12.2 Family breakdown in old age: a vicious cycle of familial incompetence.

part of middle-generation children. The "generation squeeze" (Input D) is felt by many children who, with limited time, resources, and alternatives, are caught between demands of their children and demands of their aging parents.

This vulnerability of family competence created by the multiple inputs indicated above is often characteristic of many otherwise well-functioning extended families. But the presence of a stress event such as a stroke, mental incompetence suggesting senility, or even losses such as widowhood may lead (Step 2 in Figure 12.2) to a reliance on external prescriptions: *moralistic* and *stereotypic prescriptions* of what should be done, regardless of conditions leading to family vulnerability. ("I should help my mother." "We should not let her go into the nursing home." "I should be more attentive and available. After all, she did so much for me when I was young!"). These overgeneralized expectations are, obviously, difficult to fulfill, and failure is a logical consequence. Following failure comes the guilt, in large part from vague societal values regarding loyalty, filial obligation, and responsibility across generations—each of which is unclear in specifics.

3.   This may lead to Step 3, a *negative labeling of the existing competence* of the family to deal with a crisis. There is a possibility of a bleak family history (Input E), in which prior efforts to work together to solve problems were met with difficulties. In the past, many problems may have been solved only by default—the leave-taking of children, which seemed to resolve persistent conflicts. Immobilization of the family and a growing belief in its own incompetence may be prompted by family members viewing the problem as irreversible (Input F), perceiving it as an instance of progressive dependency of the older person, and fearing an overextension of the family's limited resources.

4.   The fourth step can be termed *induced helplessness*. There may be poor integration with existing social supports (Input H), and families often do not know what agencies exist, public or private, from which help might be sought. Alternatively, there may be externalization of the problem (Input 1) and the resurfacing of past family conflicts (Input J).

5.   The immobilization of the family blocks eventually leads to *atrophy of previous family coping skills* (Step 5). Often there is a frantic reliance on external support, professionalization, the use of denial, and of a rescue fantasy ("We don't have to deal with the problem; a social worker can!"). There may be sibling conflict over duty and a resurfacing of past family conflicts. This may lead to a resurgence of denial and avoidance of the problem once again, with the final stage being an internalization of the belief that the family is incapable of coping with the older person's problem. A self-fulfilling prophecy has been initiated; the vicious cycle

is begun anew with the family competence vulnerable to future break-down.

INTERVENTION AND COMPETENCE RESTORATION

The above presents a bleak heuristic picture of the aging family's vulnerability to breakdown of competence in the presence of sudden dependencies of aging. But our fourth theme concerns *intervention:* how professionals and caring individuals can break into the spiral of increasing incompetence. We do not mean to suggest, of course, that all older families break down and are in need of ameliorative intervention. The point is that the conditions for breakdown exist and must be understood.

In Figure 12.3 we suggest the means by which one can reduce the vulnerability of families and older individuals, and reverse the malignant cycle of family incompetence to deal with the expectable transitions of aging. We call this the *Family Support Cycle.*

Competence restoration involves the professional and the family working along two major axes: *clarification* of both the event and of the

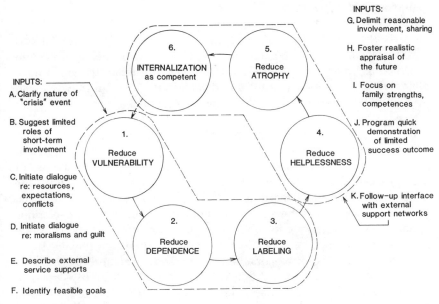

FIGURE 12.3 The family reconstruction cycle: cycle of intervention to enhance incompetence.

family's resources, and *intervention to restructure* the definition of the problem and the family's response to it. This has been imaginatively described by Zarit and his associates (Zarit, Reever, & Bach-Peterson, 1980; Zarit & Zarit, 1982) in an intervention experiment with Alzheimer's disease families.

The first step is to reduce vulnerability or decrease the susceptibility of both the individual and the family to break down in the face of an event that can be viewed as a crisis. This can be done by attending to various input factors indicated in Figure 12.3. Input A is time-consuming but crucial: For the professional to spend time clarifying a medical event with the family, for example, (discussing realistically the level of probable impairment after a stroke or the likely progression of Alzheimer's disease) is critical. Most family members operate in a relative informational vacuum as they confront a disabling event. The professional must offer clear guidelines of support as an informational means of redefining the crisis (Zarit et al., 1980).

A second input (B in Figure 12.3) by the professional involves discussion of the acceptable and limited involvement on the part of family members. The family—and the professional—should avoid overextension of family resources. The professional should recognize the personal anxieties concerning overtaxed resources of time and effort (Smith & Bengtson, 1979).

Related to this, the counselor should alert the family participants to the existence of competing intergenerational demands (Input C) and their expectability; at the same time he should avoid being lured into "correcting" historically stabilized dynamics in the family, which have their own unique history of roles and coalitions. A useful ploy to avoid over-involvement (Input E) is the clear and repeated suggestion of other external supports.

The second step in the Family Support Cycle involves reduction of dependence on external and inappropriate labels—specifically, moralisms and cliché obligations—that lead to guilt (Input D). The helper or therapist can also assist (Input E) by fostering open dialogue with the family and individual regarding expectations, resources, and conflicts. Frequently family members are fearful of confronting such expectations openly; yet the dialogue itself releases guilt and lowers fears of unreasonable expectation. Verbal communication can then be followed (Input F) by the delimiting of reasonable interdependencies and expectations for the family. Sometimes this involves institutionalization, which in many cases appears to enhance family solidarity (Smith & Bengtson, 1979).

In the third step, the cycle requires a collective redefinition of the "hopeless" event. The professional can assist the older family in crisis by requiring a collective redefinition of the event that has been labeled thusly. He can also assist the family by identifying feasible and appropriate goals (Input G). This may mean (1) resisting efforts of those involved to exaggerate (out of fear or helplessness) the extent of the crisis and (2) helping them to recognize and grieve their real losses, which they will confront as they begin to accept the limitations of recovery. It is necessary (Input H) to foster an honest, realistic appraisal of future developments—improvement and decrement.

The fourth point in the Family Support Cycle concerns mobilization of realistic coping skills. This reduces the atrophy of skills apparent prior to the crisis and reduces dependence on external definitions. The professional should focus on strengths (Input I), emphasizing what the family *can* do as contrasted with what *might* or *should* be done. It may be useful (Input J) to program some quick demonstration of success and to affirm a positive (and delimited) experience of mastery. It is certainly necessary to follow this up by demonstrations of interface with external support networks, realistically identified (Input K). This final input is crucial. By identifying and mobilizing support (contacting concerned friends and neighbors and coordinating professional networks) the isolation and fear in older families may be countered. More importantly, perhaps, an important piece of prevention may be accomplished: The efforts, struggles, and successes of one family can be shared and advertised, so to speak, beyond the family. In going beyond the family, all involved will apply these new experiences to future crises.

SUMMARY

This essay has presented one conceptual framework for understanding both the problems and the processes involving family networks and aging. We have employed a heuristic systems model derived from what was originally termed the *Social Breakdown Syndrome*. The focus has been on social mechanisms of labeling that operate upon and within aging families under stress. We felt this perspective could assist gerontologists and family practitioners in understanding successful or unsuccessful negotiation of change, as confronted by aging individuals and their families.

We have focused on four psychosocial constructs important in understanding family supports and aging: (1) negotiation and change; (2) competence; (3) crisis; and (4) intervention and the restoration of competence.

We have suggested that change is a normal consequence of aging and that competence is the desired outcome of normal changing. We suggested that recurrent and unique issues facing the older family may reach crisis levels, because older families are more vulnerable than younger families. We explored various reasons for this vulnerability, and we described a possible negative cycle of breakdown, in which incompetence was likely. We also suggested that intervention might take place at any step of this vicious spiral.

By looking at the family as a unit, and recognizing its limitations and capacities, we see hope for intervention in what too many families experience as a relatively hopeless situation: crises and dependencies in old age. Some promising developments have already taken place in intervention strategies, as in the work of Zarit and associates (1980, 1982).

We conclude with a caution: As economics and policy shifts combine to encourage the family to assume more responsibility in assisting its elders, we must become informed as to the unique strengths and weaknesses that unfold in older families. Our caution is that we cannot uncritically borrow from a theoretical and practice literature that is young-family focused. We must borrow selectively and construct our own perspective based on a clear belief that while the older family is similar to all other families, it is also unique. In knowing its uniqueness, we will be able to acknowledge the limits of social science theory as well as to expand the limits of family intervention theory in reaching toward better service. To this end, we hope to have contributed.

REFERENCES

Arling, G. The elderly widow and her family, neighbors and friends. *Journal of Marriage and the Family,* 1976, *38,* 757–768.

Bengtson, V. L., & Kuypers, J. A. Generational differences and the developmental stake. *Aging and Human Development,* 1971, *2,* 249–260.

Bengtson, V. L., & Treas, J. The changing family context of mental health and aging. In J. E. Birren & R. B. Sloane (Eds.), *Handbook of Mental Health and Aging.* Englewood Cliffs, NJ: Prentice-Hall, 1980.

Brody, E., & Spark, C. Institutionalization of the aged: A family crisis. *Family Process,* 1977, *5,* 76–90.

Erickson, E. *Childhood and society.* New York: Norton, 1950.

Glenn, N. D. Psychological well-being in the postparental stage: Some evidence from national surveys. *Journal of Marriage and the Family,* 1975, *37,* 105–110.

Hagestad, G. Problems and promises in the social psychology of intergenerational relations. In R. Fogel, E. Hatfield, S. Kiesler, & J. March (Eds.), *Stability and change in the family.* New York: Academic Press, 1981.

Hagestad, G. The continuous bond: A dynamic perspective on parent–child relations between adults. *In* M. Perlmutter (ed.), *Minnesota symposia on child psychology,* Vol. 17. Princeton, NJ: Lawrence Erlbaum, 1984.

Hess, R. D., & Handel, G. *Family worlds*. Chicago: University of Chicago Press, 1959.

Kerckhoff, A. Family patterns and morale in retirement. In I. H. Simpson & J. C. McKinney (Eds.), *Social aspects of aging*. Durham, NC: Duke University Press, 1966.

Kuypers, J. A., & Bengtson, V. L. Social breakdown and competence. *Human Development*, 1973, *16*, 181–201.

Kuypers, J. A., & Bengtson, V. L. Toward competence in the older family. In T. H. Brubaker (Ed.), *Family life and aging*. Beverly Hills, CA: Sage Publishing, 1983.

Kuypers, J. A., & Trute, B. The older family as the locus of crisis intervention. *The Family Coordinator*, 1978, Oct., 405–411.

Lopata, H. *Widowhood in an American city*. Cambridge: Schenkman, 1973.

Murray, J. Family structure in pre-retirement years. In M. Irelan, (Eds.), *Almost 65: Baseline data from the retirement history study* (82–101). Washington, DC: Government Publishing Office, 1976.

Shanas, E. The family as a social support in old age. *The Gerontologist*, 1979, *19* (2), 169–174.

Smith, K. F., & Bengtson, V. L. Positive consequences of institutionalization: Solidarity between elderly parents and their middle-aged children. *The Gerontologist*, 1979, *19*, 438–447.

Spector, M., & Kituse, J. *Constructing social problems*. Menlo Park, CA: Cummings, 1977.

Zarit, S. H., Reever, K. E., & Bach-Peterson, J. Relatives of the impaired elderly: Correlates of feelings of burden. *The Gerontologist*, 1980, *20*, 649–655.

Zarit, S. H., & Zarit, J. M. Families under stress: Interventions for caregivers of senile dementia patients. *Psychotherapy: Theory, Research and Practice*, 1982, *19*, 461–471.

AUTHOR INDEX

SUBJECT INDEX